For the generation of children growing up in the aftermath of the Second World War, the map of the future was drawn from the two great landmarks of the Education Act and the founding of the Welfare State. The sense of possibilities that marked these beginnings was to accompany many through adolescence and the social and political movements of the 1960s and seventies. For these twelve women, growing up in the fifties, their past and their present are marked by feminism.

Truth, Dare or Promise is a vivid reminder of what it was like to grow up with that chimera of 1950s promise. Here are memories as diverse as the landscapes they recall: the loved Scottish Highlands, the Jewish world of Blackpool, London's newly established West Indian community. Schooldays are recalled of blossoming aspiration and stultifying narrowness. These are intimate, personal memoirs, ordinary and impossible stories that remind us how individual lives are shaped in infinitely complex ways.

Liz Heron was born in Glasgow in 1947. She went to school in Lanarkshire and Ayrshire before taking a degree at Glasgow University from 1964–67. She spent several years living and working abroad before returning to live in London, where she works as a freelance writer, translator and editor. She has contributed to a wide range of publications, including the *Guardian*, the *New Statesman*, the *Listener, New Society*, the *Times Educational Supplement* and *City Limits*, for which she worked part-time during its first two years.

Contributors: Alison Fell, Harriett Gilbert, Alison Hennegan, Liz Heron, Ursula Huws, Gail Lev̶ ̶ ̶Stef Pixner, Denise Riley, Sheila Rowbotham, Car̶ ̶ ̶ ̶ ̶ ̶ ̶ ̶ ̶

Truth, Dare or Promise

Girls Growing Up in the Fifties

Edited by Liz Heron

VIRAGO

Published by VIRAGO PRESS Limited 1985
41 William IV Street, London WC2N 4DB

British Library Cataloguing in Publication Data

Truth, dare, promise: girls growing up in Fifties
    Britain
  1. Women——Great Britain——Social conditions
  I. Heron, Liz
  305.4′2′0941   HQ1593

  ISBN 0-86068-596-9

Photoset in North Wales by
Derek Doyle & Associates, Mold, Clwyd
Printed in Great Britain by
Anchor Brendon Ltd of Tiptree, Essex

For my father, James Heron

Acknowledgements

I would like to thank all of the other contributors, not only for what they have written, but also for conversations in which they generously shared insights and memories.

Thanks to Ruthie Petrie for her support and thoughtful editorial advice, to Anne McKenna for rediscovered friendship after twenty-four years – which helped me think about this book, and to Maggie Millman.

Particular thanks to Malcolm Imrie and Margaret Green.

Contents

Liz Heron

Introduction

I would like to think that this book is as much about the future as it is about the past. After all, childhood is where we all begin, and for the generation from whom the contributors to this book are drawn, the idea of a particular future was fundamental to the way in which we experienced the world. The end of the Second World War marked the start of an era, of a new period whose initial character shaped the way we live now. And although the past can never be disposed of, can never be cut off from our knowledge or experience of the present, there are times in history that hold all the possibility of new beginnings. One of them was 1945.

The women writing here were all born in Britain between 1943 and 1951. We grew up in a period we all describe as 'the fifties' – a shorthand that doesn't match the exact, rounded chronology of the decade. We all have different stories to tell, stories that in their singularity and uneven reflections of that time, disturb the balanced generalities of social history. Each story belongs somewhere inside that general pattern, yet none of them quite fits; just as individual lives can never be contained or wholly explained by the social and economic realities that circumscribe them. Among the impulses that animate their progress there is also imagination, and the infinity of desires released by optimism.

The year 1945 and its immediate aftermath ignited that fever of optimism which was to accompany a large portion of our generation all through childhood, adolescence and involvement in the social and political movements of the last two decades. As well as being a conscious political philosophy, the post-war vision of prosperity and limitless possibilities deeply underlay our everyday view of how things would be. After the hardships and horrors of the war, our parents' generation had a desire to break with the past and look to the future, and until recently our own expectations of what life could offer continued to expand. We had confidence in the future – a confidence that has been severely shaken since the end of the seventies. Britain's economic recession and the ravages of a right-wing government on the foundations of the very Welfare State that nurtured us were, until then, unthinkable.

In the early years of the present women's movement it was important for women to affirm a common identity. Much of feminist thinking and consciousness-raising has dealt with the need to return to childhood experiences as a way of understanding the roots of our oppression as women, and to identify those aspects of our socialisation that we shared. But if we are to acquire genuine insights into the versions of femininity we now inhabit, we also need to look at the specific features of our childhood.

I wanted the contributors to this book to reflect some of the diverse ways in which childhood was experienced by women of the same generation. What draws us together as a generation is our share in the momentum of the post-war period, whether through our part in the changes that affected our parents' lives, or as the subjects of the post-war social policies and legislation directly affecting children. But what also matter are the values and material circumstances of our parents, the place and region where we grew up, our class and ethnic identity. They were part of what influenced our perceptions of femininity, our expectations and our fantasies, along with the pressures and possibilities we had inherited. These elements of our childhood also relate to particular communities or allegiances which may have been a source of strength or conflict in growing up.

Many of us writing here express a sense of not belonging, of feeling like outsiders, either in relation to others beyond our immediate family or community, or in a more singular sense of exclusion. This very common feature of childhood and adolescence was inevitably sharpened in a period when industrial expansion and technological development led to a substantial degree of geographical and social mobility, so that the bonds of community were loosening. Housing developments and slum clearance contributed to this process, and it must also have been heightened by the forms of education which, for some of us, demanded that we separate ourselves from our class or cultural identity.

We were also the first post-imperial generation, and if the references to an awareness of this are only incidental – with the definite exception of Gail Lewis's account of a childhood in Kilburn's West Indian community – they are still there, as casual testimony to a colonial era that was ending. It was, of course, to haunt our own future, so deep and enduring are its marks on the psyche of British culture, so connected to its class and economic structure and to the many gradations of superiority and inferiority inscribed in British social behaviour.

The momentum of our generation has its high point in 'the sixties', the time universally regarded as our true historical moment, though its mythology increasingly sours as the decade itself retreats. It was certainly the point in our lives when our choices and our sense of ourselves assumed greatest significance and could be seen as quite distinct from those of our parents as they had embarked on young adulthood.

The sixties are always contrasted with the fifties, not only because of the political events across the world that made history accelerate for a brief moment, but also, in the West, because of the enormous differences in social sensibility between the two decades: differences in the perception of class; sexual 'permissiveness' and more freely available contraception in newly developed forms, as well as legalised abortion; the pre-eminence of youth, and a chain of political and social reactions against the rigid conventions of everyday life that were to culminate in the 'politics of liberation'.

The sixties are seen as the point at which our lives became

3

different from those of our parents, and particularly, for us as girls, different from those of our mothers. Yet it's also true that the differences began in our childhood, and were influenced not only by what was to come, but also by what had been.

The war years had brought about dramatic personal upheavals and social disruption. Shifts in the way society was organised to meet wartime needs included changes in the role of women and the value placed on their work. The fifties, with the advent of a Tory government and an ideological retreat to conservatism, is seen as a decade of loss for women of what they had gained.

It is seen as the time when women, yielding their jobs to the returning male population as soon as the war was over, lost the paid employment that had given them independence; as the time when the family was recemented, when women were redomesticated, their role redefined as that of home-maker; when progress itself had a domestic incarnation, with the kitchen at the centre of the new developments in consumer technology. It is seen as the time when all the outward signs of sexual difference were re-emphasised through style and fashion, and women's femininity pronounced in the clothes of the New Look.

But this neatly encapsulated version of the period doesn't take account of the untidy contradictions in how it was experienced, nor of the residual effects of the war years or the conflicting demands of the expanding post-war economy which needed women's labour. Nor does it take account of the complexities of change.

One factor that did most certainly influence the movement of women towards the home was the post-war baby boom. It reached its peak in 1947, which was, incidentally, the year the divorce rate peaked, at 60,000, ten times the pre-war figure. It was also the year in which the Atlee government initiated a campaign for the recruitment of women to the labour force, while at the same time defining the need for women workers as a temporary, crisis measure. Women were to be the reserve army of labour that could be called on in the event of shortage then be freed to return to their primary role of wives and mothers when the emergency was over. To all ideological intents and purposes, women did not work outside the home, while in effect they did and have continued to do

4

so, in increasing numbers. This double bind is still unresolved, despite the subsequent anti-discrimination legislation of the seventies, and it is always complicated by the unmet need for adequate childcare and the actual conditions of women's work.

The family looms large in the image of post-war Britain. But just what this meant cannot simply be explained in terms of re-establishing the pre-war male/female hierarchy by displacing women from paid labour and forcing them back to the home, partly through the widespread closure of nurseries. For one thing, there were, as there often are, disparities between the public images and the private realities. While women were undermined as paid workers and elevated on to a domestic pedestal, they were not in fact evicted wholesale from the labour force, and the closure of nurseries came about unevenly and for more complex reasons.

However, giving central importance to the family was part of an effort of national reconciliation, of blurring class differences and sex antagonisms, an effort of reconciliation and consensus that was being made in many parts of Western Europe as order was imposed on the threat of chaos. It is the family, in the comforting sameness of its image, replicated a million times across the barriers of wealth and class, that can transcend and overwhelm the significance of the other structures and institutions in which ordinary lives are caught. The proliferation of official reports and commissions on the family are testimony to its crucial weight in the balance of post-war reconstruction.[1]

The Welfare State was in many ways a continuation of the state intervention in domestic life that was such a feature of the war. There is the resonance of late nineteenth-century philanthropy in the welfare rhetoric (like the need to educate the working class for parenthood – working-class girls, that is), while the extent of state intervention in children's lives was unprecedented.

In her contribution, Carolyn Steedman writes about this historical phenomenon, and about the gap between the spirit in which the good things of the Welfare State were given and our subjective experience of receiving them. Whatever the political and philosophical imperatives or the socio-economic and psychological arguments that underlay the intentions of the legislators, the reality of our childhood experience was that these good things were our birthright. We took them for granted, just as we took for granted our right to be in the world. Along with the orange juice and the cod-liver oil, the malt supplement and the free school milk, we may also have absorbed a certain sense of our own worth and the sense of a future that would get better and better, as if history were on our side. (In the light of the eighties, and a Welfare State that has become increasingly impoverished, it is also worth noting that it might have been quite different in its original structure from what that legislation created: it could have been more democratic, more accountable to its workers and users, less vulnerable to subsequent attack – the National Health Service being the notable example.)

It seems also that as little girls we had a stronger sense of our possibilities than the myths about the fifties allow. There was a general confidence in the air, and the wartime image of women's independence and competence at work lingered on well into the decade in the popular literature and the girls' comics of the day, even while these registered an ambivalence about what women *should* be doing. If the Education Act of 1944 failed to give equal pay to women teachers, it did not discriminate against girls in the matter of access to education. For the first time local education authorities were required to provide free secondary education for all pupils up to a minimum age of fifteen, which became the statutory school-leaving age.

Fees in state-maintained secondary schools were abolished in 1945. But those of us born around the end of the war were the first children truly to benefit from the Act's provisions, which had in the immediate post-war years been only barely implemented owing to shortages of accommodation, equipment and teachers. It was only in the fifties that the benefits were fully realised. The benefits were, of course, selective, since the structure of the education system still paralleled the class structure it was part of, and the odds were still heavily weighted against the majority of working-class children taking the route to higher education and better jobs than their parents could have had access to. It also contained assumptions about the kind of education suitable for girls, specifically those who were not academic achievers and for whom motherhood was seen as the only job for which it was worth preparing.

The first step on the academic route was the eleven-plus, or its Scottish equivalent, the 'Qualifying Exam', a hurdle which a substantial number of working-class children did overcome, though many did not. For a number of us writing here, that first step made a lot of difference to the future.

Like aspects of the Welfare State, the immediate post-war education policies had a basis inspired by a deep-rooted philanthropy. It was education *for* the working class, not conceived of as a continuity with the traditions of self-organisation and self-education for socialism, but as an avenue to individual self-improvement, a share in what had hitherto belonged only to the few. It was up to those of us who were privileged to enjoy its greatest benefits to make the most of them. To take what was offered and run. In the end, with the expansion of higher education, a significant proportion of us weren't content with that.

The experience of class mobility (from working class to middle class, through education or through the development of a particular kind of confidence connected with the workplace and arising out of material improvements in working-class life) was given expression during the fifties and sixties in both fictional and sociological form. But the protagonists were almost exclusively male (the working-class hero), their conflicts and dilemmas assumed as masculine by their very nature. The experience was neither examined from a woman's point of view nor looked at in terms of what it meant to women.

This is partly because class is usually not seen as having the same meaning for women as for men. Class for women is both simple and more complicated. It is marriage, traditionally, that eases a woman into another class; it is her rite of passage into another place of belonging, no matter that her husband's class is different from that of her father. Perhaps without marriage women who are uprooted from their class retain the unease and sense of not belonging that Valerie Walkerdine describes. It is certainly true that the subjective experience of class has been given scant attention by the women's movement, although this is changing as feminism becomes less

7

narrowly a middle-class outlook. Education has a lot to do with this too; the growth in adult education for women – Second Chance and Women's Studies courses – has given many women a framework for consciousness-raising and confidence-building that began in a different context for others some ten or fifteen years ago.

All of these accounts contain an implicit avowal of how we see the world: all as feminists, though perhaps speaking with the voices of different feminisms, and all informed by other commitments – to socialism, anti-racism, or to other recognitions of ways in which the world needs to be changed. Whether these are happy or unhappy childhoods recedes with the knowledge that our past held enough hope for us to know now that we are not its victims. Since memory itself is an act of construction the past is always illuminated by the present. If we were children in a time when hope existed in general abundance – though our hold on it may sometimes have been harder to measure at close quarters – that is not to say that its relative shortage is fatal for children and young women growing up today. Resilience is still their asset.

Our lives are very different from those of our mothers, and this applies to all women of our generation. For the changes of the last thirty-odd years have made a greater and deeper impression on women than on men. Through educational expansion and changes in the law, through a greater control over women's reproductive capacity and a greater sexual freedom both for heterosexual and lesbian women, for the first time in history we are not at the mercy of our biology and we have a sense that we can still move forward, even though the equality that is our goal may still seem a long way off.

But, for some of us, our mothers are difficult to deal with. They were not, perhaps, the warm, supportive, generous and loving beings that sentimentalists see at the core of all women, of all mothers. Mothers are people and motherhood is a condition not likely to bring out the best in people if it is undergone with reluctance (however unacknowledged), with material hardship or with bitterness. Women today, with more room to choose what they want, and with more room to know there is a choice, also have the possibility of being more fulfilled as mothers. But if we reproach

8

our mothers, or feel that they failed us, it is also because of what motherhood had to be – often a relationship that stifled in its enforced bonding of mother and child and was jealous of its very tyranny over both. Too much of such mothering is no compensation for the skewed balance of the family equation, in which men and women have a different given value.

Childhood is the world we have lost. The children we were are still a part of us, and also quite separate from us. The past is a partial script for the present, but to interpret our adult selves as determined by those children would be a mistake. In recognising the past the reality lies in the other direction. We are the ones who can reach back with our reminiscences and give those children meaning.

Liz Heron, London, 1984

*

1. I can suggest only some of the complexities of the period. Denise Riley, Elizabeth Wilson and the Birmingham Feminist History Group have all written about it in ways that are helpful to an understanding of what it meant for women, and I refer the reader to their work: Birmingham Feminist History Group, 'Feminism as femininity in the nineteen-fifties?', in *Feminist Review* 3, London, 1979; Riley, Denise, *War in the Nursery*, Virago, London, 1983; Wilson, Elizabeth, *Only Halfway to Paradise*, Tavistock, London, 1980.

Alison Fell

Rebel with a Cause

In 1944 mothers' milk leaves a lot to be desired: a sense of grievance starts early. I can see my mother, pretty, acned, skinny with fretting, on a packed train from Scotland to South Wales. That bawling six-week-old the troops dandle is me: always hungry, never knowing whether to spit out this thin stuff or yell for more, nearly starving before the doctor twigs.

We're off to Barry to meet my father, who has bombed Hamburg and Dresden and D Day France, and has survived. (He has also, he tells me years later, boobed so badly he's lucky to be in the RAF at all. This greenhorn, in charge of the tin-foil 'window' they use to confuse enemy radar, has dropped it too early, over the Channel, sending the whole of Coastal Command into a flat spin.) On the station platform my father, seeing his new daughter for the first time, will blurt out: 'Och, Doris, what a penny-faced wee bugger', and my mother, exhausted, will burst into tears. It was a boy they'd wanted, anyway, not this peely-wally thing, not another girl when they've got Sheila already.

By 1945 they will be feeling more optimistic. Well, they won the war, didn't they, and they're alive, more than can be said for some,

11

and now Nye Bevan's going to see the working man all right at last: we'll have the National Health, and school milk will be free, and even daughters will have the education they deserve.

Times are still tough, though, in 1949 in grey Lanarkshire, with sweetie rationing as well. We've moved, the four of us, to a two-room basement in Hamilton, a cramped, sooty, outside-lavvy type of tenement opposite the Public Baths and the steamie. I start school at Beckford Street Primary in red lacing clogs (cheaper than shoes) and spend my first day in the headmistress's office clutching a rag doll and howling for my mammy to come back. Later I behave myself and write ABCs with hard grey chalk on screaming slates and stand still once a month for the Public Health nit inspectors.

At nights there are forbidden pit byngs to slide down, allotments to raid and rival gangs of kids to stone. 'Dirty Papes' we yell from behind dustbin lids and the dark mouths of concrete closes: ignorant, tattered and ragamuffin, the lot of us. 'Proddy Dogs', they howl back and we have no idea what that means either, we only know the aggro is obligatory.

If religious differences are way above this five-year-old's head, so too is the notion of gender. She has no real idea what she is – except dirt poor, and frightened. For her these are dangerous times. Dangerous if you tear your hand-me-down coat. Dangerous if you just *cannae* get bread and butter pudding (so slimy and white) down your throat at the tea table. Dangerous if you accidentally break a rationed egg. So full of beatings and beltings. Twenty or more years later those chickens will all come home to roost, and in a therapy group I'll hear an awful young scream sirening up from that black basement place: 'It isn't fair, it isn't fair.' I've done nothing wrong: why, then, the punishment? Even now, all traps and enclosures in my life bring me back to this angry question, this banging around in a box. No wonder, then, that I put up such a fight for justice, equality, socialism and what have you: it's no mere matter of ideology or principle, but an obsession in the very flesh. It strikes me, too, that I may have been lucky, for couldn't I equally have turned into a blood-bitter working-class fascist – Miss National Front leading marches through Hoxton in Union Jack sash and peroxide hair, or a UDA girl, tartan-scarved, brazening down the

Shankhill to see the buses set alight? An exaggeration, maybe, but watching them, the question always nags.

Perhaps it's true that if she had stayed much longer in Hamilton the urban pathology would have eaten her alive. But in 1949 what saves her is finding something she can love excessively without fear of punishment. Grace appears, then, in the form of a landscape. Luckily for her, her father – a right Bolshie, that Andy Fell – gets fired from his garage job in Glasgow, and the four of them move lock stock and bread-pudding basin to Kinloch Rannoch in the Grampians. A granite village, lochs still and long or fierce from the winds coming down Glencoe. Crags burning one minute like leopards or bruised black and blue the next by running cloud: the incomparable light and shade and shifts of Scotland. A place where humans are more dwarves than kings, and the family shrinks to a safer size, no longer fills the whole horizon. And the space, the space! Never to get under anyone's feet. Space to tear off your clothes and race down Beinn A'Chuallaich with a curtain for a cloak. Space to build huts, stalk deer, eat blaeberries, lose yourself. Space for daring and visions and naming, and no one to interfere. (Except when the daring turns to stealing, but that comes later.)

Reading, or rather – writing. In 1950 in the corrugated-iron schoolhouse below the waterfall she learns magic. The letters on the blackboard, and the spoken sounds, join forces to make words. She has never felt so powerful. This, then, will be her army, under her control, to order about. She writes compositions and parades her spelling (just as well, too, for it's the tawse every morning if you fail your spelling test). 'Enough', she scribbles lustily, 'I picked *enough* flowers to make a crown', and the teacher nods her head in pleasure at this big word, this achievement. ('You were always an awful timid wee thing,' says my mother years later, 'but then you got on well at school and you seemed better, then.')

It's 1951 now, and the Hydro-Electric Schemes are sprouting all over the Highlands – dams and tunnels and flooded areas, work camps full of Poles and Irish and Ukrainians, with a travelling picture show every month and open-air latrines Sheila and she peek into, marvelling at the multi-colours of this communality of shit. Her father, once again, quarrels with his boss and leaves the Co-op

Me, the wee one on the left, Perthshire
1951

garage for a better-paid job on the Scheme, on diggers and crushers. They have to get out of the Co-op house, of course, and move from there to a corrugated-iron gamekeeper's house on Dalriach estate, six miles from the village, no running water and thirty bob a week to Shalto-Douglas, Anglo-Scottish aristocrat with an accent like nobody's business and a big black and white house where her mother goes to clean. Her father takes her fishing at the Tummel or poaching up the loch, and she learns from him who to hate. Landowners, bosses, vested interests, all fattening themselves on the sweat of the poor. English, too, as likely as not. Going past the Big House, she and her sister carol: 'Shalto in his Douglas tartan, he blows holes in it wi' fartin'.'

One day in summer a film crew arrives and turns the village upside down to make a documentary for the Tourist Board. Kilts and shawls and Cairngorm brooches are hauled out of trunks, and her mother is picked out to sweep the step of the oldest house in the square with a birch broom. In her best blue dress and with her arms powdered at the tops to hide the weatherbeaten bits, she glows for the camera in close-up, a regular red-headed Scottish beauty. Later *The Heart is Highland* goes on release down south with *Duel in the Sun*, or Lust in the Dust, as her father calls it, and her uncle, taken by surprise, leaps to his feet in the balcony and shouts, 'By Christ, that's bloody Doris!'

Shortly afterwards, the stealing begins. Och, why not just pinch a crate of lemonade meant for the Highland Games: the Co-op's got loads, hasn't it? Bet ye cannae. Dare you. Discovered, she submits to punishment fatalistically. Not so, however, when Duncan McRae the constable calls at Dalriach a month later. Someone's been stuffing sand and paper into the petrol tanks at the Co-op garage, and they're the only vandals on record. Never mind that they swear innocence, never mind that they don't know enough about fuel systems to think up a trick like this; her father simply sets to with his belt – 'I won't have lying in this house' – and it isnae fair, it isnae fair.

Up till now, boys have been nothing to write home about. There are two pupils in her class besides her, Sandy Latto and Ian Blain, and she's better than both of them, but they can call themselves her boyfriends if they don't step out of line. Femininity, as such, doesn't exist, although there are glimmerings of it. A party frock which comes on mail order from the back pages of the *Glasgow Herald* and is nothing like as full-skirted or frilled as the drawing, a terrible disappointment. A calendar pin-up in the barber's shop where her father takes her to get her hair cut – a stardust blonde with tumbling waves and wet lips. That long snaky hair. She's never seen it in real life, it's not allowed, for hair has to be nice and neat. She wants it badly. Later she will want to be Belle of the Ballet, Dan Dare, Biggles and Veronica at the Wells. Now she simply wants to grow up to be blonde.

Catastrophe strikes in 1953, Coronation Year, when a telegram arrives from the Borders. Her grandfather has died, and her grandmother is alone in the house; would Doris and Andy be prepared to move down? They would, and the two girls cry their eyes out, but it's no good complaining. (Thirty years later, the rending feeling is still raw enough to force its way into a novel-in-progress: 'And then, in an open-backed truck, swaddled in rugs, over the high moor, in the night of starry snow and startled badgers' eyes, she was carried south, torn out of paradise.')

Unlike Kinloch Rannoch, Lochmaben shrinks like old gums as the years pass. It's a largish village in dark orange sandstone and pebbledash, surrounded by lochs, reedy shores, a cemetery, bungalows: English tourists who come to fish find it pretty. But even then she was comparing it with the north, seeing a dour and narrow town with houses pressed meanly up against pavements, and the country around it Solway-damp, flat and forbidding. And she mourned.

'It's her age,' says her mother.

'Maybe she's anaemic,' says her grandmother.

'Try her on these pills,' says the doctor. 'She'll be as right as rain in a fortnight.'

She listens to the voices, and hears no part of herself spoken for.

Her mother, meanwhile, gets a part-time job in the Town Hall, taking in council rents and dues from the caravan site which has just been opened to tempt the tourists in. She also exhibits, when requested, the rare prehistoric fish which lives in the Mill Loch and which sits, pickled and brown, in a jar by her desk. Her father gets work with the County Council Roads Department in Dumfries and grumbles at the low pay and the Toryism of farming counties. If there's little money, though, there's rather more status for his daughters here, where it matters that your grandfather was tailor to the County folk and your great-grandfather was Provost. Granny queens it on the High Street, sucks genteel, pan-drops in the kirk, and tells them to remember who they are; at home, however, the mask slips and she can be as midden-mouthed as she likes, delighting them with her lapses. The girls pester her for stories and broad Ecclefechan accents: 'Yow and mie and the barndoor kie and the sow and the thrie wie pigs.' 'A lassiefellaffalarryandcutherheid.'

At school, accents are a bother. They laugh at hers, for it's not Lowland, but she sticks her nose in the air, for what does she care? She'll make her mark, just wait and see. When Sheila comes joint top of the Primary School, she prepares secretly to outstrip her.

16

Already she's finding that she can silence their titters with the written word, for when her compositions are read out in class they're all ears. 'Now that's what I call a *story*,' beams Miss McLaren. 'You were as quiet as wee mice, weren't you?'

'Yes, miss,' the class murmurs (big shite, big show off, they'll say when they get her alone later) and she blushes down at her desk, for she really only wrote about Kinloch Rannoch, and maybe even lied a bit as well, but now here's Miss McLaren swelling her head, Miss McLaren who each morning says sweet thank-yous for the posies which litter her desk, and the whole class, too, goggle-eyed and believing every word of it. It's a bit like stealing all over again, this fine trickery.

Soon she's running in gangs again, all of them on old bangers of bicycles – she and Sheila, Hazel and Rhoda, Avis Holt and Elaine, building huts around the Castle Loch, doing plays in Hazel's loft, writing to the papers about the UFOs they've absolutely definitely spotted in the sky over Eskdalemuir. A local political controversy sees them out petitioning, young militants at ten or twelve, egged on by proud dad. The land around the loch shore is common, for the use of the people, everybody kens *that*. Robert Bruce laid it out centuries ago in a Royal Charter, so that bloody Englishman with his estate and his double-barrelled name can put that in his pipe and smoke it. There are meetings in the Town Hall, packed out. (Note that there are few television sets in the village at this time, and the villagers are accustomed to organising. There's a yearly Gala, there's a Youth Club, WRI, Women's Guild, Bowling Club – my mother seemed to be in all of them.) In due course the village wins its case, and she and Sheila and Hazel get a mention in the local paper.

The weasel, her father calls her, but really it should be the beaver, for she's always busy making things, dreaming things up. Dress designs, cowboy ranches in plasticine, rag dolls with yellow wool for hair, ballet costumes, the architecture of reed huts, irrigation systems for half of India. When her mother takes over the village library on Tuesdays and Saturdays, she swallows six books a week – Westerns, Biggles, and Mills and Boon, and eventually she regurgitates them in exercise books, feverishly illustrated. It's good collateral with Elizabeth and Rhoda and Elaine, who are all better

17

off than she. Rhoda has a record player, Elaine a fitted carpet in her bedroom, and none of them get their clothes from jumble sales, so it's hard to think of how to impress them. All the same, they certainly seem to like these raven-haired bandit girls, masochistic and defiant, and these baddies bristling with knives, and these sudden transformations of rancher's wife into stagecoach robber ... Her ambitions fluctuate. She'll be an artist – a great one, although she doesn't actually know the names of any – or else a great writer. Or maybe a prize-winning scientist splitting atoms, once she gets to Junior Secondary and starts chemistry and physics.

Even dreaming, though, had better be unspoken, for the world is full of those who'd like to take her down a peg. Granny will hoot at her, and tell her she'll get mairrit like a' the rest, and Elizabeth and Elaine will pour cold water: who does she think she is, just because she's top of the school and all? Perhaps they don't actually say it, but it rings in her ears all the same. She becomes proud, truculent, poised to defend herself. Swimming at the Castle Loch jetty, some of the boys run off with her vest and knickers, and yell joyfully at the sight of the darns. She draws herself up. 'Us Fells,' she says bitingly, 'spend our money on education, not *entertainment*' – which somehow isn't the word she was searching for, but at least it's big and muscular enough to flatten these ignoramuses.

In 1957 she's thirteen, and the Sputnik passes overhead, zigzagging, with that poor wee dog inside, what a shame, but a thrill too: maybe one day it could be her up there and famous. She's at Junior Secondary in Lockerbie now, and figures are bursting out everywhere, particularly in the lower streams, or so it seems: it's as if the girls in the A class are saving themselves for better things. In the playground it's nothing but waspie belts and transparent blouses, a wiggle when you walk and a giggle when you talk, *really* vulgar, the lot of them. At home Granny casts a grim eye over her skinny flatness and snorts: 'Straight up and doon like a shit-hoose door.' Aspiring to femininity feels like imagining you could climb Mount Everest – all these film stars so impossibly hourglass and formed and grown-up, Lana Turner and Marilyn with their hips and hand-span waists and big cone-shaped breasts. (It's still years, remember, before Twiggy and flat chests, denims and the androgynisation of glamour.

Only Audrey Hepburn gives cause for hope.) Femininity is a vocation in itself, and it looks to her as if it would take a lifetime; surely Art would be easier.

While Elizabeth, Rhoda and the others congratulate themselves on their breasts and their periods, she fumes. What's so great about growing up to be a woman if it means staying at home and bleeding and having babies? And when busty Joyce pinches Ronnie Ballantyne, who was quite clever and therefore meant for *her*, it's the last straw. In a grand public demonstration of contempt for the whole business, she carves Ronnie's initials into her arm in the school playground: well, that showed them, didn't it, and no repercussions either, because she's still the cleverest in the school, after all, bound for the Dux Medal and the teachers know it.

For the Second Year Christmas Dance she gets a red dress with a junior bustline which predates the bust by six months, so she gets a junior bra to fill the gap. 'Sexy Fell' some of the boys whisper in class, which she supposes is better than 'Brainbox', but if they think this means they can beat her at lessons they've got another think coming. She's not sure whether to stare them out, as usual, or droop her lids and look mysterious. What a stew, and thoughts bob up to the top like dumplings. Heroism she can relate to ... Douglas Bader, Odette, and all the others who suffered in order to win the war ... but this thing called sex? Ethical problems begin to preoccupy her. If she were a spy like Mata Hari, and under orders, would she be able to grit her teeth and prostitute herself for her country?

In the village things carry on as normal, with the talk circling around funerals and weddings and who's fallen pregnant by whom, except that winter it's grimmer; there's foot and mouth disease everywhere, which costs Rhoda's father his herd and has half the county in quarantine. That winter a bitter gloom hangs between her and the future, for what's the good of getting full marks for your composition, what's the use of being the Dux: if you're poor, don't you just end up working in Lockerbie Cheese Factory or selling brassieres in Binns in Dumfries? It isn't fair, it isn't fair. She can hardly speak of what's troubling her. There has to be an answer somewhere, but she holds back from asking, out of pessimism, out of a conviction that asking will only hasten the catastrophe. At last her father, having made enquiries at the County Council, puts her out of her misery: bursaries, he says, you can get them these days to go to college if you get enough Highers. There's no question of her leaving school at fifteen; she must go on to Dumfries Academy and get her qualifications. It emerges now (why not before?) that both her father's sisters went to college on scholarships. He was the black sheep, idle, ended up as a mechanic. A revelation. But now you don't even have to win a scholarship, for there's the Means Test, and County Council Grants.

1959 brings newsreels of Fidel Castro riding into Havana on a tank, and she finds yet another hero. There are women, too, in this revolution: Haydée Santamaria, sternly glamorous in combat gear, if a little blurred at the edge of the picture (as so many of us will be, in our Army surplus, some ten years later on the streets of Europe.) But most of all it's the notion of the possibility of change, of upheaval, that captivates her, because now she can see a chance of escape for herself: she can *afford* to identify, now that the village will not, after all, strangle her.

She is Dux of the school, with her picture in the paper, and while the other village girls go to work as clerks, or waitresses, or join the Army, she goes on to the Academy at Dumfries, where you can tell the handful of working-class ones by the cheaper, rawer maroon of their Co-op blazers and the furrows of their parents' dreams on their faces. Sheila, being two years older, has already given up the Academy and taken a job in the British Linen Bank in Dumfries, so everything depends on her now, to show what the Fells can really do. Yielding to mother's pressure, Sheila joins the kirk, too — another defection of duty. She can't understand it, feels she has lost a fellow rebel. Supported by her father, who never did like padres and Bible-thumpers, she digs her heels in. It stirs nothing in her, anyway, this bleak religion without poetry or fire, this mere administrator of births, deaths and marriages. Its rituals sit on the year uneasy and prim as Sunday hats, ignoring all that she knows to be thunderous in the land, the light, the change of seasons. (Of course she has no name for these sensations, but the Highlands have obviously turned her into some kind of pagan or pantheist.) The upheavals of the seasons invade her and tug her this way and that; she feels too permeable, a continuum with them. Growth and death, joy and despair: things she can never say, they'll think she's off her rocker, lock her up in the Crichton Royal in Dumfries as likely as not.

Once again, words reach into the fog, a sudden blind alchemy of sounds and metaphor this time. Safeguards and promises, the words invent themselves; they have their own life and leap out ahead of her. At the Academy they tell her this is poetry, and good. In herself she knows it: it sings, it *answers*, it has to be right. She wins prizes, she's commissioned by *Scotland Magazine*. Her parents are tickled pink. A poet, by God, and in the same town as Rabbie Burns, too. 'Wee sleekit coo'erin tim'rous beastie' her father quotes, and 'A man's a man for a' that'. A good socialist, Burns was, the Russians love him: 'apart from Will Shakespeare, he's the only one worth bothering about'.

With studious obstinacy, she avoids her new peers, the middle-class, D.H. Lawrence-reading, bound-for-University girls, and clings to her old pals, who are working, who are working towards their engagements, their marriages, their babies, and who most certainly won't understand her.

TV has entered the house now, and every Saturday they hang over the set. Cliff Richard and 'Six Five Special'. It's the rebel voice of youth, amplified for the first time by capital investment. 'Got myself a cryin' walkin' sleepin' talkin' livin' doll' – herself, she prefers wild Elvis, or Billy Fury singing 'Halfway to Paradise' with his shirt open to the waist and his leather jacket slithering off his shoulders. At Lockerbie Rex she screams with the best of them at *Jailhouse Rock*, but only with an effort, for it feels false: secretly she'd prefer to *be* him. 'I'm evil, don't you mess around with me.'

The TV, the Pictures, Crolla's café with the jukebox: with a foot in two worlds, she blunders through the year. She begins to wonder about college. English or Art, Art or English? 'Commercial artist?' her father suggests, alert to the economics of it all. 'Or a journalist, maybe?' She can't make up her mind. Yes, she writes poetry, but she's beginning to wonder if she really likes English after all. So much of it seems to be Literature and reading *Macbeth* round the

21

class, and getting sniffed at for your accent and your glottal stop – as if it wasn't a Scottish play, too. And when it comes to the Dramatic Society, all the speaking parts in *The Taming of the Shrew* go to the ones with the English accents and the Prefect badges, and she has to content herself with singing the madrigals and strewing the sage and rosemary round the stage, and screaming and fainting for Mercutio, for the Drama teacher watches TV too and likes to be up to date.

No. Art looks like the answer. She'll be an artist with an older man as patron (platonic, of course, she won't marry), and she'll have a studio in Edinburgh and male models smooth as the marble Narcissus on the Art Room shelf. That'll give Rhoda and the others a shock. 'Art teaching?' her mother wonders, but she just nods and shrugs. Earning a living isn't something she can bring herself to think about. She's tried it, tried a summer in Maxwell's grocery chain in Lockerbie, selling potato scones and weighing out split peas, and no one, just no one would believe how awful it was and how she nearly went crazy having to wear stockings all the time and smile every minute of the day. But there's another worry, too: this new thing called 'career woman'. She doesn't want to wear this label, for isn't it all about chain smoking and tailored suits and being hard-boiled?

That year her parents have been saving all their pennies, and in August they set off with their borrowed tents and lilos for their first ever Continental holiday, to Carry-le-Rouet on the Mediterranean, where her father crash-landed in 1945 with a planeload of POWs from Italy. Granny, who hasn't strayed out of Scotland since her honeymoon in Scarborough, thinks they've got a screw loose. Herself, she just yearns, as she has already done on Lockerbie station seeing the school trip off to the Alps, and reads travel books and waits for her time to come. Her Geography marks shoot up, too.

At seventeen, school dances are full of Sandra Dees, sweetheart dresses, flatties, rustling petticoats. She opts for the Bad Girl look, in tight red or luminously striped dresses she runs up at home, and stilettos with long pointed toes which turn up and look at you. At last she has heard of Juliette Greco and the Left Bank with its candlelit cellars and existentialists, and so she grows her hair and bleaches it: it falls over one eye, both eyes, her mouth. 'Dirty beatniks,' her mother snorts, watching her paint black lines round her eyes. Bardot has arrived, too, and she learns how to pout – 'if you dinnae keep your mouth shut you'll catch flies,' Granny observes – and wears long black sweaters and black stockings in the Art Room, preparing to be a Bohemian. Brazen, she bets the astonished Head Girl – a sweetheart type if ever she saw one – that she can beat her to the Head Boy, who is clean limbed, kindly, and also Mercutio. A straight fight, all's fair in love and class war. At the Head Girl's birthday party she wins, but quite quickly the status palls, and Mercutio becomes *dead* boring. Really she wants someone like David Frost, snarling satire and opposition every weekend on 'That Was the Week That Was'.

Approximately Bardot, 1960

The first set of Highers are over, and she's got more than enough for University, let alone Art College, so why does she want to stay on into the Sixth Year? She can't answer this. Maybe she's scared of leaving home. Maybe she just wants to idle for a year and notch up some extra successes. Meanwhile with Rhoda and the others she dresses up and goes dancing every Saturday night at the Unionist Rooms in Dumfries, braving the Young Farmers' attempts at quicksteps and foxtrots and, oh the bliss of it!, the beginnings of jive. 'Stay away frae thae fairmers,' Granny cautions, 'they're too near to the coo's backside.'

Big Eric, though of respectable farming stock, has as bad a reputation as she could wish, so bad, in fact, that she puts on a sweetheart dress and flat pumps to go out with him. On the way home from *The King and I*, he stops the landrover in a layby beside the old aerodrome. He's six foot three, and in the moonlight a white tower of flesh erupts from his cavalry twills, tall as the Scott Monument and smelling of smoked haddock, and he's whining at her to do something for him. She can't believe it. She can hardly get a Tampax up, and who does he think he is, anyway? She's going to be a college girl, not just another village girl, another teenage shot-gun bride. Contraception? What's that? (Later, having fallen for an Art student, she'll prowl the Edinburgh surgical stores, feeling dirty, and force herself to ask about pessaries. In fact, the Pill explosion is only two years away.) Now, however, it's light years away, and they've got a place for her at Edinburgh Art College, her grant is in the pipeline, and there's no stopping her. The city glitters. Duffle coats and striped college scarves, drainpipes and jazz, bell-bottoms and the Beatles: the last of the Bohemians, the first of the Rock Generation. She sticks her nose in the air and orders Big Eric to drive her home immediately.

IN SPITE OF my staunch teenage vows against marriage, during the five years at Edinburgh I was married, divorced, and finally pregnant, so that in 1967 I found myself in Leeds as a faculty wife, mother, and depressive. In 1968 I got involved in the beginnings of the Welfare State theatre group, and then, in

1969, with one of the first Women's Liberation groups, which was a revelation, and saved me from a weight of guilt about how badly I fitted into my womanly role. It also provided outlets for daring. To speak at a male-dominated meeting or occupy a pub in those scornful days required a certain reckless edge. (Still does.) In 1970 I left the Welfare State and moved to London in search of all-woman theatre. The Women's Street Theatre group did its first performance on the 1971 Women's Day march, and members of the group later went on to found Monstrous Regiment, the Women's Theatre Group, etc. Then a report I'd done on our arrest at the right-wing 'Festival of Light' led to a job on *Ink*, one of the more radical papers of the underground press. So, by accident (or was it?), I was a journalist, just as my father had wanted. For me, the next few years were one long fever of feminist and libertarian politics, campaigning, militating, organising women's centres, working on *Red Rag*, the marxist feminist journal, and on the *Islington Gutter Press*. In 1974 a breakdown forced me to withdraw from activity for a year, but perhaps also gave me the inner permission I needed to write poetry again. In fact, that year marks the start of a serious commitment to writing.

Since then I've worked for four years on *Spare Rib*, and as a Writer-in-Residence in two London boroughs. In 1981 Collins published my children's novel *The Grey Dancer*, and in 1984 Virago brought out my adult novel *Every Move You Make* and my first individual poetry collection, *Kisses for Mayakovsky*. Currently I'm writing, teaching, and trying to believe I'm forty.

Julia Pascal

Prima Ballerina Assoluta

I would never die. It was a relief to know that. Men died – apart
from the First World War victims who staggered around Blackpool
on sticks – and animals died; I was always burying fish, birds and
still-born kittens in our back garden; but, at the age of five, I knew I
would never die. I had proof – the world was full of old women.

But if they did not die, they seemed to stay old and always be
alone. My Dublin grandmother used to visit us occasionally and her
husband died before I was born. I asked my parents what he did.
'Oh he bought and sold a few things.' And his father? 'He studied a
lot.' Minnie Fridjohn used to play the piano and I remember her
teaching me in our house at 204 West Park Drive, Blackpool. But
then she stopped coming. They said she had been ill with something
called a stroke. As far as I knew a stroke was something I did to the
cat, but from the way the word was said, I knew that it was
something else.

Minnie was spoken of with pride. She had pushed all her sons
through medical school at Dublin's Trinity College; pushed them
out of the tradition of poor talmud scholar into the English middle
class. I have a memory. I am lying in bed frightened of the dark,

frightened to go to sleep in case I don't waken, and I cry out to my father. He comes into my room and sits on the edge of the bed. He sings to me. 'Oh my baby. My curly headed baby.' His voice is wonderful and I tell him, 'I like your voice.' It's dark and an owl hoots outside. We live opposite a park and there are always owls. He tells me, 'I never wanted to be a doctor, I wanted to be a chazan, a cantor. But Ma used to say, "What sort of a job is a chazan? Be a doctor, make a decent living."' He continues to sing. I make him promise to stay with me all night and, safe in the knowledge, I sleep. When I wake in the morning he is gone. I feel betrayed. Fathers lie.

Another memory. I look up at the sun and it reminds me of free orange juice in a long glass bottle with a blue cap. The blue becomes the sun. I am standing in the garden with my brother David. I am seven, he is eleven. A plane flies overhead from Blackpool's Squires Gate airport. 'That's a Wellington bomber,' he tells me with authority. 'Do you know why it's called a Wellington bomber?' I look up at the plane and listen to the noise of the propeller. 'No,' I say. 'Because it drops wellingtons, silly.'

I love him fiercely even though he ignores me if his friends are around. We are on a bus going to the same primary school. He has a book of twopenny tickets and he gives me one. A friend of his comes on the bus and David turns away from me and shares his packet of Rolos with him. I feel terrible. They say he's naughty. My father straps him often with a leather belt. I never know why. One day I find him hiding in the toilet. Someone has just rung the door bell. It is a bus conductor. We live on a main road and buses are having their windows broken by someone throwing stones. They say it is David. He says he didn't throw the stones. I believe him and as they strap him I cry with the injustice. They send him away to school, Rossall School in Fleetwood. But at half term he is sent home. Expelled. For stealing, they say. I don't believe them.

I am glad he is home again. We share a room with twin beds. We talk a lot and then secretly take turns to read with the torch under the bedclothes. We promise never to get married to anyone else. Once we both made 'wedding dresses' with our sheets, stood up on our beds in our finery and made a pact to marry each other.

He is sent to cheder to learn Hebrew for his barmitzvah. My father was taught by his grandfather when he was a child of three in Dublin, but David at twelve shows little interest and is bribed to learn at sixpence a lesson. A milk bottle is soon filled with sixpenny bits. It doesn't seem to matter if I learn or not. I go to cheder briefly and learn the shema and the alphabet but I sense that my learning is not important and so I forget as quickly as I learn. David is thirteen and the barmitzvah approaches. My parents dread it – they don't want to 'waste all that money on a do'. Suddenly my father's brother, a liver specialist, ironically dies of liver cancer. My parents rush to London with David for the funeral. They return saying that it would not be correct to hold a barmitzvah celebration when Uncle Henry has just died and inform the family that David was barmitzvahed quietly in a London synagogue. They come back to Blackpool with relief that it is all over. My mother tells me, 'If you ever get married, run away and do it secretly.' They talk of vulgar Jewish weddings and barmitzvahs. A Jew parading wealth sickens them. They survived the European pogrom and the ghetto to assimilate in post-war England, but somewhere inside is a feeling of guilt. At survival? At the jump into comfortable middle-class 1950s life? I feel their anxiety but don't know what it is. They speak about 'The English' and at first it is a shock. Am I not English? My mother tells me that if anyone at school says that the Jews killed Jesus I am to say they did not and that it was the Romans. But it never happened like that. I am eight years old and coming in from break at Stanley Primary School when a girl with a blonde pony tail shouts at me out of the blue. 'You killed Jesus, you killed Jesus.' 'No, I didn't,' I shout back, 'I wasn't there.'

The image sticks in my mind. The little girl is frozen like a film still. Other memories are less obvious. The school rhythm of Christmas and Easter is worrying. Christmas is cribs and paintings of baby Jesus all over the school corridors and the inevitable daily prayers with 'Onward Christian Soldiers' filling me full of endless fear. I pretend to sing so as not to stand out, but the words do not come out of my lips. I am the only Jew in the school and that they shouldn't look at me is crucial. At Easter it's even worse. All those visions of Jesus hanging from the cross and every one accuses me.

Blackpool is full of gothic churches, and again the deathly cross, with his body hanging on it, dominates everything. And horrors, one church has a red, bleeding heart on the board outside. People pass eating fish and chips, rushing on to buses and trams, singing the latest George Formby or enjoying their summer holidays and I am frozen in front of the church gazing at the bloody heart.

'Be thankful,' my father tells me. 'You're living in the Welfare State. Free medicine, free dentistry.' It is the Golden Age for him. He praises Bevan and tells me of how he almost had to buy this practice in Blackpool for £6,000 but did not have the money, and now, thanks to Labour, the practice was his – free. His surgery is full of drug samples and books on the body. I look at the medical encyclopaedias, at the images of the skeleton and feel uneasy. On the wall opposite his desk is a picture he has had sketched of Anne Frank. Anne Frank's diary is given to me to read but I am too young and hardly understand it.

My mother helps him in the surgery and I am taught how to file letters which have come back from Victoria Hospital. I listen to his patients. Most of them are women. One comes in for a weight problem. He gives her a diet sheet then tells her a joke. 'I had a patient last year, a Mrs Sidebottom. She was fifteen stone so I gave her this diet. Then three months later I was going past her house on my rounds when she invites me in for a cup of char. So I go in and there she is with a huge dinner on the table and I says to her, "Mrs Sidebottom," I says, "what about your diet?" "Oh doctor," she says, "I've had my diet, now I'm going to have my dinner".'

Some girls are pregnant and come to him for help. There is nothing he can do and they are told they must have their baby. My mother tells me, 'Never go home with anyone after school. Never talk to any men.' I have dreams. I am walking down Beechfield Avenue, a long, tree-lined road where the trees still have white waists painted on them from the blackout, and a man is following me. I am frightened but he runs after me and I am unable to run fast because suddenly I have on a tight skirt and high stiletto heels which prevent me running freely. I wake up terrified. It is a continual dream which stays with me even now.

It is 1959 and I am nine. She tells me that soon I will have a period and that it will come every month. I don't believe her, it sounds too strange. But I am a mature nine. My breasts are beginning to grow so that I hide them under my navy school cardigan. No other girl has breasts yet. I don't like it. I tell the other girls that they can expect periods. They crowd round me at breaktime as I give them this secret knowledge and I feel important. My mother puts a roll-on on my bed – 'to hold you in'. She wears one and I hate it but, because she tells me, I wear it. I am five foot two at nine, one of the tallest in the class. I wear a roll-on and white ankle socks. Suddenly I feel I ought to wear stockings like my brother's girlfriends. But usually girls do not wear stockings until they're fourteen, what am I to do? I go with my brother to a party. I am the youngest one there. The girls of fourteen wear full skirts and sticky-out petticoats. Some wear tight skirts. All have big legs. I look at their legs and wonder if mine will ever grow so big. They are necking with the boys as The Platters sing and I am watching or eating food from the buffet. I go home and tell my mother. She says, 'They'll end up in Glenroyd.' Glenroyd is a maternity home in Whitegate Drive near the convent school where rich Jewish families send their daughters rather than to the local secondary modern when they fail their eleven-plus.

Meanwhile David is playing Cliff Richard's 'Living Doll' at least fifty times in succession and then sings it secretly in the bathroom. Everyone worries about him. What will he do? Why isn't he good at school? He could be a doctor like my father, there's the practice just waiting. Other boys aren't so lucky. But he does badly in school, fails his eleven-plus, is clearly never going to be a doctor. His only talent seems to be for petty thievery at this stage. The first grandchild, the only boy, oh my God, what is to be done? My mother takes him to the local education authority, anything rather than submit to the shame of the doctor's son going to the sec. mod. He ends up in Palatine Technical School where he will be encouraged to learn a trade, he may even take 'O' levels. But he makes no progress. His essays are returned with 'Rubbish' or 'Tommy Rot' written on them. There is a sense of gloom in the family. My father shows little interest but disappears for long periods of time with his Hebrew books or a migraine. David continues to learn Hebrew; there are more sixpenny bits in the milk bottle.

My mother seems to get thinner and continues to have bouts of mysterious illness which confine her to bed frequently. My eleven-plus approaches. Already the teachers are preparing us with intelligence tests. English and Arithmetic is fine but those strange tests comparing peculiar shapes mystify me. I want to pass. There are two schools: Collegiate, the grammar school on the hill, and Arnold, a fee-paying school. I know my parents will never pay for my education so I have to pass.

The results are out. About half the class has passed and I am one. The other half pretend I-don't-care-never-wanted-to-go-to-grammar-school-anyway. I feel happy that I am one of the chosen. I'm going to be a Collegiate girl and go to the red-brick school on the hill. Many of the others are crying. It's as if someone has ripped the class in half, and those small children thrown out from the chance of grammar school education know deep in their hearts that this is the crucial moment in their lives. The teacher mutters something about thirteen-plus and, if work is done then transfers to grammar schools can be made, but the children ignore this and pretend indifference. It's not anything they can articulate, just a knowledge that their new place in a secondary modern makes sure that for the rest of their lives they will feel secondary.

End of marbles and hula-hoop sessions in the concrete playground. End of sports days, standing around endlessly in navy knickers and white aertex T-shirt waiting for the ball to come in my direction when I am supposed to hit it with a rounders bat and in reality as it comes towards me all I want to do is duck. End of team games and terms like 'team spirit', or so I think. But it isn't. It progresses into the more sophisticated games of netball and hockey in grammar school, but what do I care which team wins? Why should throwing a ball through a net be so important? It all seems such a waste of time. Early days in primary school with music and movement were best. My first love affair is with dance.

Blackpool in the 1950s – pleasure beach for northern workers, a place of seaside showbiz and tat. I go to the Grand Theatre and see

Hilda Baker — she knows-you-know; I impersonate her and everyone laughs. Ken Dodd is at the end of the pier and the local paper has a Girl Of The Year contest. 'You should be Girl Of The Year,' my father tells me, 'when you're sixteen.' So I think I have a chance to enter a whole magic world of showbiz. A cousin of mine, Valerie Carton, comes to the Grand in a touring show. I sit in the audience and watch this blonde girl sing a song while hanging mid-air on a moon. It is strange and wonderful. At six I am dancing to the music on the radio, the lines on the carpet become lines of people applauding my performance.

Memory: I am in Victoria Hospital and a doctor is looking at my feet. I am given physiotherapy for flat feet and they teach me to pick up pens and marbles with my toes. 'But if you really want the arches to improve,' says the doctor, 'you should send her to ballet classes.' Paradise begins here. Laura Webb's Ballet School at the top of Whitegate Drive is freedom once a week, and soon I progress to tap and musical comedy. 'Casey would waltz with the strawberry blonde and the band plays on, he'd waltz cross the floor with the girl he adored and the band played on.' Pastiche-of-the-thirties waltzes and soft-shoe shuffles are taught to Blackpool's daughters as they compete for medals and fight to come first in the Blackpool Summer Dance Festival. I compete in ballet and wear a pink tutu and a band of pink rosebuds in my hair.

I came across a photo of a plump little Jewish girl in pink tulle recently and saw in her face that she wanted to be Margot Fonteyn. The little fattie was me. And as I came second in ballet I looked out in the hall for my mother — for what use success if nobody sees it? — but she wasn't there. She arrived late and I was mortified.

'Why weren't you there?' I asked. 'I was too busy, darling,' she told me. I felt miserable that she hadn't seen me step forward for my medal. She was my beloved mother but too often she was busy or else David or my father 'needed' her so she forgot me. It was the beginning of a pattern which I could not understand as a child. But it goes back much further.

'A lovely baby, just like a doll,' she used to tell me, but the doll was too demanding and the doll was given away. Soon after my birth she sent me to her parents in Manchester. 'You learned to walk

Me at ten — an overfed duck dreaming of becoming a swan

and talk with us,' said my grandmother with pride, and the early years are Manchester years in a large, damp house in Prestwich with two old people. I never understood why I was sent to them at 32 Hereford Drive; I must have done something terrible that my mother sent me away, but I never knew what this was. I remember lying in bed as a young child and my grandmother putting a chair at the side of the bed, 'so you won't fall out'. I remember being ill with scarlet fever and being taken to Bury Hospital in an ambulance and then being put in strict isolation. I felt panic. Not only was I sent away from my parents but now I was sent away from my grandparents.

Finally they came to see me and brought me a jigsaw and some books, but there was nothing I could say to them. I had got stuck in a shell of solitude where only the nurses talked to me and then it was to tell me off because I refused to eat the hospital greens and hid them under my plate. One nurse slapped me and I felt how unjust the world was. But there were moments of pleasure. Radios were installed in the isolation cubicles and I remember listening to 'Stranger In Paradise' on the earphones and now, whenever I hear that record, I am taken back to those weeks in isolation.

My parents were in Israel during this period. I must have been about six. When they heard I was ill they sent me a parcel of clothes: jumpers and dungarees. I was angry; not only had they not taken me with them, but they'd sent me dungarees and only boys or very young children wore those – I wanted a dress.

Now I realise that my mother sent me to her mother because emotionally she could not cope with having a daughter. Although she sent David to boarding school his early years were close to her whereas mine were not. Years later she told me, 'You're lucky not to have sisters', and I never knew why she said this so passionately. Only today do I understand her sibling rivalry with her two younger sisters and see that a daughter provoked early memories of internal conflict and jealousies.

She was always a little girl who refused to become a responsible woman; crises were met with bouts of mysterious illness confining her to bed, so that her volatile relationship with me shifted dramatically between being the loving mother of a 'little doll' to being the absent mother of the demanding child. I never knew which mother she would be – would she suddenly burst into tears and cry, 'I wish I was dead, I wish I was dead', or would she laugh and embrace me? All I knew was that if she didn't seem to love me it was my fault.

My grandmother then was my mother. The early years with her cemented an emotional bonding which I realised only at her death.

Memory: my grandparents are sitting in their living room in Manchester listening to the news and the Billy Cotton Band Show. My grandfather takes us out to town and I watch my first film with them on a rainy Saturday afternoon. It is *The Blue Angel* with Sammy Davis Junior and Mae Britt. 'He's a Jew,' they tell me and I wonder how a black man can be a Jew. But the film is very sad and the black Jew is alone while the blonde woman goes off with someone else. The sophistication of the film escapes me but the tone of it does not. My grandfather drives us home in his Ford Poplar and as we go down Corporation Street I look out of the window and see daubed on the wall 'SAVE THE ROSENBERGS'. I wonder who they are and hope they will be saved.

They go to Hallé Orchestra concerts in the Free Trade Hall and sometimes to weddings. I go to synagogue with them on Saturday mornings and am shown off as being the first grand-daughter. But their pride means little to me and I wonder how my mother is and when I am going to see her next. On Saturday afternoons my grandmother takes me to Lewis's in Market Street to 'try and find a bargain' and then we go to Kendal's. She takes me to the Ladies Powder Room. It is a vast space with lots of toilet cubicles and a large carpeted room with wide porcelain bowls and padded stools where Manchester ladies sit down to powder their noses in front of a curtained mirror. I stare in fascination at the powder and lipstick ritual and have to be dragged away.

At night I lie in bed counting the weeks until I can go home. It's dark and rainy and I'm in a single bed; my grandparents are next door. I can't sleep so I sit up and take an imaginary dagger and stick it in my chest, and in my head my mother's voice: 'I wish I was dead, I wish I was dead.' Childish morbidity or a playing out of my mother's fantasies? Whatever it was it was a displacement which was part of a longer chain of events.

My mother's parents came from Romania at the beginning of the century. Grandmother Esther had been married off to my grandfather against her wishes but he was the third suggestion so she had little choice. He, however, was passionately in love with his blonde, tall wife, and the pain of the marriage was his warmth and her coolness. They left a traditional Jewish middle-European culture for strange exile in Manchester. My grandmother, who loved Wagner and Strauss, wanted to settle in Germany, but my grandfather had family in Manchester and wanted to join them. So, she settled in foggy, rainy Manchester and pined for Bucharest – the sunny Paris of the Balkans. She retained memories of Europe which outshone the reality of the damp Manchester streets, and, although she was happy being a mother to her four children, she did not enforce any religious orthodoxy or strong sense of cultural bonding. My grandparents were the last of the Yiddish speakers and with the loss of the language there was the loss of a cultural heritage. They did not teach their children Romanian because they wanted them to assimilate.

But their children knew that although they were English they were also continentals. Either they sank into conservative provincial Jewish attitudes, worrying that their children might 'marry out', or they floated free, divorced from traditional values but caught in a no-man's land between the Yiddish past and the English post-war present. The fifties gave my parents an economic stability which their parents had never known and the jump from immigrant to middle-class English respectability was effected.

My mother's family were never radicals: her father came to Manchester and built up a textile business in Faulkner Street which today is Manchester's Chinatown. But my father's Lithuanian background was steeped in talmud study and a disdain for materialism. My father was something of a Fabian Jew, caring little for his good income which he occasionally gave to needy patients, much to my mother's rage. If they were mismatched it was because my mother had chosen my father for his status: she was attracted to the idea of being a doctor's wife. She expected the man to be 'a pillar of strength' to the woman, and when she discovered he was as weak as any other human being, she was bitterly disappointed.

Memory: sitting in the front row at the Palace Theatre, Manchester, watching The Royal Ballet. New stars, Lyn Seymour and Merle Park, dance in 'The Sleeping Beauty'. I am going to be a ballerina. I announce I am going to study seriously, am going to audition for The Royal Ballet School at White Lodge. This will mean going to London and, if I pass, boarding there. I tell my parents of my decision. The next morning my mother hardly speaks to me, my father takes me to one side. 'Your mother was up all night worrying about you. She doesn't want you to go away. What sort of a daughter thinks of leaving her mother, especially as she's always so ill? Put the idea out of your mind immediately.' My mother keeps silence for days. I stop talking about the audition but resolve to lose weight.

Memory: David calls me 'fattie' which isn't fair as he's fat too. I call him 'fattie' back but he doesn't seem to care. Mother's cooking is erratic. When she's happy meals are good but when she's upset –

which is most of the time – they are extraordinary. One teatime she makes stewed apple for herself and mashed potato and poached eggs for us. But she is flustered and gets it wrong so we are presented with a plateful of stewed apple and egg. I complain and she bursts into tears. 'I hope your children treat you the way you treat me,' she cries.

We devise ways of getting rid of food. David saves brown paper bags and we bring them down to meals in our pockets. When Mother isn't looking we hide most of the food in the bags and then sneak them down the toilet. But one day David hurls his bag out of the window and into the neighbour's garden: we are discovered.

Breakfast is less painful, though the amounts are always huge. Father makes breakfast and then brings Mother hers up on a tray. It's three courses of porridge, eggs, beans or spaghetti on toast, followed by more toast and several cups of tea. We go to school with lead in our stomachs. Victor Sylvester is on the radio and my father tells us that the bandleader has gone to the studio at six o'clock with his band to play especially for us. We don't realise he's having us on.

One morning he's cooking breakfast in his shorts – he's just been for an early-morning run around Stanley Park opposite where we live. 'Did you know that you have a fifty million to one chance of being you?' he asks. 'Millions of sperms fight to get to the egg and only one survives – all the others die.' I imagine fish swimming but I don't really know what he's talking about or why this is so fantastic. What does he mean I have a fifty million to one chance of being me? I am me – what more is there to say?

Memory: I am looking at myself in the mirror and in my ballet dress I look fat. I ask my mother, 'Can I please go on a diet? I'd like to lose weight.' She goes white with rage. 'On no account. You'll make yourself ill. You're lucky you've got food. Thousands haven't. If you go on a diet your nose will get even longer.' Quite a threat to a pubescent Jewish girl who longs to be blonde, thin and snub-nosed.

There was a secret garden in Stanley Park, a covered way with a shed in it. I imagine running away and hiding there but I never do. Instead I take a tram down to the sea and walk along the prom. It's blustery, even in spring and early summer, but I let the wind almost pull me over while I hang on to my skirt. Everywhere there are pigeons and seagulls. I like the gulls and want to put my hand up in the air and stroke their chests, but they are too far away. The sea is soothing and magic. Blackpool, out of season, is best without tourists and kiss-me-quick hats. One day the school takes us to Fleetwood. The town smells of fish because of Fleetwood kippers. We go into a trawler and have to bend our heads low to go into a cabin where there are pictures of bare women on the cabin wall.

Memory: King's Road School, Manchester. It's my first day in a new primary school during one of the long stays with my grandparents. Children play two-ball on the wall and I learn too. Others do hand stands but I'm afraid of falling so just watch. The teacher gives me a book to read all about an elephant; I read it before breaktime and the teacher is astonished. 'It's supposed to be read all week. Go back and read it again.' I'm pleased because my father taught me to read before going to school. He sat with me and showed me David's comics and the first line I read was 'Little Plum Your Redskin Chum' in the *Beezer*. Now, at school, I'm quicker at reading than anyone else but then it's boring because I've got to go back and read the same book all over again.

Lunchtime at King's Road School and a bus is hired to take the Jewish children to a kosher canteen. I go too. It's quite different from my Blackpool school – everyone seems more adult. On the coach they all sing 'Love and Marriage, Love and Marriage, they go together like a horse and carriage, you can't have one, you can't have one, you can't have one without the other.' I want to join in but don't because I don't really know anybody, though I'm not shy at singing.

My parents and grandparents are in Blackpool's Savoy Hotel one Sunday for tea. There is a small band playing Victor Sylvester style. I go up and ask if I can sing. The family all watch as I sing 'Che sera' without inhibition. Everybody loves me and pinches my cheeks hard, especially my grandparents who praise me in Yiddish and kiss me. Then David and I go and play in the lift until suddenly it stops between floors and I get frightened and cry. David isn't frightened.

He teases me. 'It'll be stuck for ever and we'll run out of air and die.' I'm hysterical and when it starts up again I rush out as soon as we reach the ground floor and run to my parents.

It's cold, always cold. Even though the Aga cooker is supposed to heat the house, it never does. One of my jobs is cleaning the flues. I don't mind this. It entails dipping a long square-bowled spoon down a long chimney and lifting out the soot. I then wrap the soot in a newspaper and throw it away. But even after cleaning the Aga every room is cold. And it's the same in Manchester. My grandmother's toilet is coldest of all. I rush out of it as quickly as possible and then suffer constipation pains. She gives me syrup of figs or Ex-Lax chocolate, and then the cramps start and it's back to the freezing toilet with knives in the stomach.

Memory: I am nine and in my grandmother's house with David. We have single beds in the same room. As we go to sleep he asks to see my tummy. I show it to him and then he rolls down his pyjama bottoms and shows me his and rubs his tummy against mine. I don't know why but I feel strangely uneasy. Then he goes to sleep. It becomes a regular occurrence and I wonder if this is how people make babies.

When I am ten he comes into my room late one night and asks me if I want to know how people make babies. I say yes. He tells me and I refuse to believe him. People don't do that. My parents don't do that. The next day I ask him how he knows. 'I've known for ages,' he tells me. 'Dad told me. One day he took me for a drive on the sea front and there was nobody else around. And he said, "Now you're a man you should know these things." So he told me. And I said I knew anyway. And he seemed pleased about that.' I wondered if my mother would ever tell me, but she never did.

David is in the bathroom. He shows me a razor blade. I tell him to put it down because it's dangerous. 'Don't be silly,' he says, 'it's not dangerous' and slides his finger over it. There is no cut. 'Now you do it,' he tells me. I do and the blood pours all over my dress. He laughs.

We are in Prestwich, outside Manchester's Heaton Park. There

40

are fields. He takes out a box of matches and sets fire to them. Then he takes my arm and makes me run away down Bury Old Road towards the village with him. 'Come on, run like Billio,' he yells as he drags me with him, and I wonder who Billio is.

In 1962 my grandfather is on holiday in London with my grandmother. He has a heart attack and there are frantic phone calls. I pray to God to let him live and if he does then I'll go on believing in him. Grandpa dies and that's the end of my faith.

My grandmother does not cry. My mother cries as if the world has ended. 'No one is like my daddy,' she cries, and my brother and she seem to get closer while my father shrinks into his Hebrew studies and I move to Collegiate and a new life.

My mother goes to Manchester rarely. I spend my holidays with my grandmother as she sits watching the Manchester rain, waiting for death. She wasn't happy in marriage and now she is unhappy without it. She has few friends and her English slips away from her. 'Whatever you do,' she tells me, 'get an education.' I write letters to family in America for her. 'I don't know what to say,' she tells me, 'you write something.' She takes up smoking and now her cooking is mainly tins. Tinned salmon at teatime is a favourite. Now there's nobody to cook for she has no aim. I watch her. I watch my mother. The quiet little girl just watches.

*I*N *1961* I went to Collegiate School for Girls, Blackpool, a grammar school weighed down in petty details of school uniform and model behaviour, but a place where I saw that women could hold positions of power and authority, where the pleasures of learning, particularly languages, could offer me a freedom. Here I learned about Shakespeare, and one of my favourite moments is a secret rehearsal with a friend, Judith Cohen, when we met in the deserted school hall one break to play a scene from *Julius Caesar*: she was Brutus and I was Cassius.

In 1964 my family tried unsuccessfully to emigrate to Israel. I spent two months in a Scottish missionary school in Jaffa and then we all moved to London where I was sent to Sydenham

Girls' School, which was an all-girls comprehensive with a much racier atmosphere than the protective grammar school in Blackpool. I took O levels there and then went to drama school in 1967, picking up A levels later on.

Looking back it seems a most peculiar childhood, but at the time I thought everybody's was the same. Most prominent is a sense of frustration. My father was pushed into a career he did not want, my grandmother into a marriage she did not want and my mother into the role of good mother, which she clearly did not want. Hardly great models of marital happiness for me to follow!

I studied at E15 Acting School which was formed by associates of Joan Littlewood and moulded in her spirit. I worked steadily as an actress but realised that I was more temperamentally suited to directing so in 1974 I went to London to read English at Bedford College, and in those three stimulating years began to make sense of my life. But this was in the face of parental opposition. My mother actively discouraged my going to university: 'It's too late, you should settle down,' she told me; whereas her sister, my aunt Edith Newman, now a widow and teacher in Manchester, said, 'Go ahead. You must complete your education.' And it is those words, said first by my grandmother, which hit home.

After university I joined the National Theatre as an actress in Robert Bolt's *State of Revolution* and became the NT's first woman director with my dramatisation of Dorothy Parker's stories, poems and reviews, *Men Seldom Make Passes*. A year as associate director of the Orange Tree followed and since then I have worked as a freelance theatre director, and as a freelance writer. All that love of dance has found a niche, if not total fulfilment, as dance editor for *City Limits*.

As a director I am attracted to dangerous writing which is usually seen as 'male territory'. Plays which confront issues of violence in Northern Ireland and the Middle East; plays which most women directors would not usually be asked to direct. But mine, like most women's, is a theatre of the fringe ghetto because the larger, state-subsidised stage denies access, preferring to employ the Oxbridge boys, even though women's taxes pay half their handsome salaries. Everywhere I look I see a 1980s England controlled by Oxbridge men with a few Oxbridge girls being let into the club. It is not an England which I like, so I will continue to direct plays which challenge the status quo and write about events which people would rather not recognise. And when I want to write purely for pleasure I watch dance.

Harriett Gilbert

Growing Pains

When I dragged my childhood down from the attic and started to shake off the dust, when I slotted the bits and pieces back into some sort of plausible shape, it appeared so awkward, lumpy and strange that I couldn't imagine what on earth it was about but itself.

My exposed position as the eldest of seven siblings gave it a quality that even *theirs* didn't share, while the character of my parents, their income, class position and race, and the part of the country in which I grew up (to name but some obvious moulds), distinguished it no less than the fact that I was born in 1948 – precisely three years, ten days, after the horrors of the Second World War had been slammed back into their box.

And yet, that date does seem to have had an effect. Something did draw 'my generation' together in the 1960s, did give us an identity that had all the cohesiveness of class. We even thought, with more or less conviction, that we might have abolished the latter altogether – along with most other traditional social divides.

The popular explanation for why we thought and behaved as we did was that we had simply failed to grow up. Pumped full of National Health orange juice, further education, our parents' relative prosperity, we were seen as a Peter Pan generation, naive, irresponsible hedonists. Even we who were part of it tend now to dismiss that era (nobody sneers at an old hippy as much as an old hippy), but I should like to suggest something different: that we 'pampered' kids of the fifties and sixties (who thought we could build Utopia in our lifetime) were, politically and ethically, extra-ordinarily 'grown up'.

Born to peace and apparently endless opportunity, we were also born to the stifled groans from Auschwitz, Belsen, Nagasaki and Hiroshima. Even if few of us knew what they were (were, indeed, deftly protected from knowing), our parents were perfectly well aware of the death camps, torture chambers, devastated cities, ruined lives and lives cut short that heaved beneath the ground on which we strode towards our bright tomorrow – and awareness only increased the resolution with which they hurried us forward, to prevent both us and themselves from having to listen.

My mother, the sheltered, youngest daughter of an army colonel stationed in India, had been wrenched from school in 1940 (before she could finish her education) to join her parents in an alien Delhi of point-to-points and *chota pegs*. Frustrated, she found herself work with military intelligence – a job that involved typing reports from soldiers who'd managed to escape from the Japanese in Burma. What she learnt turned her whole moral world inside out.

Certainly, she might herself have been the inmate of a death camp. Just as my father, instead of escaping from an Italian POW camp and legging it south, for sixty days, to join the British army at Campo Basso, might have lost his life on the Russian front. But what they didn't experience themselves, they either learnt about or guessed at (all that hearty propaganda, in cinemas and on the radio, must have imposed some terrible contortions on the nation's collective cre-dulity), while the end of the war outdid almost everyone's guesses, with the first news not only of Hitler's, but of Truman's final solution.

All 'that' was being bundled away by the time my parents met. My father, once more out of uniform and with a wartime majorship, a mention in dispatches and ribbons of campaign medals to his credit, was resuming his climb up the ladder of the legal profession.

What he himself was climbing away from was not entirely the war, but also the period that led to it – those unkind, hungry 1920s and thirties, when he and his sisters, their father gone, their mother battling to make ends meet, had had to cling by their fingertips to the basics of middle-class existence. Most notably, they hung on to their access to prep and public school education by winning as many scholarships as were needed to pay the fees. And later, my father studied at night for his law degree, earning a living by teaching during the day.

But, in 1947, the worst of the struggle was over. He had just had an offer for his first novel (written, in fact, before the war, in an effort to finance his law studies); he had got himself a job with a firm of London solicitors; he was earning £450 a year; he was thirty-six, and his senior partner had a beautiful, intelligent, twenty-four-year-old secretary.

In some ways, their marriage could not have been more Mills and Boon Romance. I've seen a home movie of the wedding – a hot July day with sprig-muslin bridesmaids and women in hats and calf-length dresses kissing each other with their eyes shut – and the bride and groom look sensational. He is lean and six foot three and is obviously going places; she comes somewhere up to his chest and, as they hover in the door of the church, looks as though she could happily lean on him for ever.

Of course, of course, it was not remotely like that. Apart from the fact that the bridesmaids' dresses were scraped together from begged and borrowed coupons, my mother's parents, so apparently benign in the flickering, black-and-white pictures, were actually apoplectic with rage at their daughter's unsuitable, moneyless 'no one' of a husband. My grandmother had a stroke two days after the wedding, making perfectly sure that my mother knew who was to blame.

My mother must have been rigid with the qualms of her defiance – and yet, with those echoes from the war at her back, those questions she didn't want to hear, where else was there to go but forward? Where else was there for *any* of them to go? Improvising wildly as they went along, the only thing of which they were sure was that tomorrow would be better.

The cine-camera belonged to some friend of a friend. After the wedding, we return to the frugality of snapshots. But here, too, the sun's always shining (no one, in those days, took pictures when it wasn't – the role of the early Box Brownie in falsifying popular memory might repay further study) and it certainly seems that my parents' life was moving forward as it should be. Arms wrapped around one another, they stand outside the semi-detached house in Hornsey Lane Gardens, North London, that they've bought (with my mother's post office savings, my father's war gratuity) for the sum of £3,000. My mother wears a nip-waisted, full-skirted suit, with her hair dragged back by two combs. My father is dressed in a sports jacket and baggy, flannel trousers.

Fourteen months after the wedding, their first-born begins to join them in the pictures. Swathed in lace, she ignores the grins at her christening. Egg-shaped buttocks thrust in the air, she clambers naked from the sandpit by the back kitchen door. Accompanied by a cocker spaniel, she staggers about in a dress with smocking, puffed sleeves and Peter Pan collar.

My only contact with that baby, that toddler, comes in a couple of visual flashes: I remember the vault of a high, high bridge as I'm rattled beneath it in my pushchair; I remember the hill curling down to our house as I wait at the window for Mother Mats (my father's mother) to take me to feed some ducks.

Other than that, she is out of reach – and much as I'd love to get in touch with her, this isn't really the place. Nor is it the place to leap to assumptions about her reaction when her sister was born – bringing an abrupt and violent end (the sister very nearly died) to that only-childhood that all eldest children retain at the core of themselves.

Here, I'm concerned to recapture only those things that have passed through my *conscious* mind, that have shaped my *conscious* attitudes towards the world and myself. The membrane, of course, is porous; knowledge will seep back and forth.

In the summer of 1951, when their eldest daughter was three years old, their second daughter fourteen months and their third well-progressed in the womb, my parents sold their London house (delighted, such was the curious state of the property market then, to get as much for it as they had paid) and moved to a vast, dilapidated, Victorian rectory in Kent. The asking price for this nine-bedroom house with its ten acres of land (two fields, a spinney, an orchard and a garden, a stable and some outhouses) was £5,500 – for which they put down a deposit and took out a mortgage on the rest. And this is the home in which I began to be aware of myself, to notice my family's idiosyncrasies. It is the background, and in some ways the symbol, of most of my growing up.

No one could understand why my parents had bought it. Even now it isn't precisely beautiful from the outside. Then, what rooms were habitable were dingy in the extreme; the roof leaked; there was no heating; the wiring exploded at the flick of a switch; the window frames shook in their sockets. Besides, it was so enormous.

My mother answered that she would fill it with children (which, certainly, she did), but I think that it meant far more to her, and to my father, than that. Whatever its defects, *because* of its defects, it had the overriding virtue of potential: as the nation started Never Having It So Good, mouse-scuttling attics could be cleaned, decorated, opened up into further bedrooms; bright new plumbing could be installed; sheds could be knocked into garages; ponies could occupy the stable; a tennis court could be laid in the orchard – our 'lifestyle', in short, could expand and expand *without our ever having to move*.

Spiritually, my parents had come to rest. Out there, the Cold War might very well be rubbing its hands together; politics (international and national) trying some new positions; the social order shuffling about and industry having its death fling. In here, in this house in the valley, none of that need impinge.

By 'rest', I don't mean my parents didn't work. My mother brought us up and managed the house (including papering and painting it) and gardened and cooked and washed and ironed and looked after the animals with only the most sporadic of domestic help. My father used his commuting hour to write another two pages of a novel, or put the last touches to a story, òr outline a radio play. When he took us with him for walks at weekends, we knew that we mustn't talk to him – he was 'plotting' the next piece of work, the next instalment on the mortgage.

None of this was gratuitous. Since my parents had neither family money nor capital, what earnings came in went out. And not, in those days, on the later frivolities of central heating or a tennis court. We certainly had a *car* when we moved to Kent – an old Ford Prefect that someone had sprayed with a coat of totally unsuitable paint (a matt navy blue that rubbed off on your clothes whenever you brushed against the bodywork) and that ripped the thighs with a spring that protruded from the middle of the back seat – but even that wasn't frivolous, since we lived, without public transport, three miles from the nearest shops. Mostly, the money went on food and clothes and various forms of private education for my parents' expanding family.

In conflict though it was with the national trend, to go on producing as though there were no contraception (my parents are not Roman Catholic), it was, of course, perfectly topical to have the kind of faith in the future that such production implies. That, however, I say with hindsight. At the time (meaning from the moment at which I began to go out to school), my growing awareness that the size of my family was abnormal was the first in a series of indications that perhaps we were Not Quite Right.

When I started school – a local, private primary school where we read Beacon Readers and learnt to count and cut things up with blunt scissors – there can only have been the first three of us, with perhaps the fourth on the way. Every eighteen months, however, another one came along and, with them, the exclamations about how 'extraordinary' my mother must be, not only to have all those children, but also to cope with that enormous house.

My reaction was mixed. Like all young children, I found it hard to imagine any other way of living but ours. Still, the more I looked around me, the more it seemed that perhaps we weren't *perfectly* normal.

Living in a village, I had quickly learnt about class. Those people who lived in the council houses and cottages, who went to work locally by bicycle and talked with a certain sort of accent, those I understood to be of a different, irrelevant species. The families with whom I compared my own were those who lived in the Big Houses, whose fathers commuted to London (or, at a pinch,

Gravesend), who came to drinks and dinner with my parents and called them by their Christian names.

And in none of those, it had to be conceded, was the father a 'writer', a person apparently always exposed to public comment and criticism (sometimes even in the newspapers). And none of those lived in pass-me-down clothes, or had such a horrible second-hand car, or washed in a bathroom the size, bareness and temperature of a morgue – in a tub that could have accommodated a horse. And none of them seemed to have so many books as we did. In my parents' house, there were (still are) books not only on the bookshelves and in the bookcases, but also on the lavatory windowsills, in the bathroom, stacked on the top of the fridge, lying around on chairs, on beds, in the dogs' basket, on the floor. Instead of books, my 'control' families had television sets and washing machines and much more pocket money than we were allowed.

But my studies weren't essentially concerned with who was better off. There were things about the way we lived – the space, the freedom of action and speech – that even at the time I appreciated. What worried me, increasingly, was both our peculiarity and the fact that my parents didn't *care*. When I asked my mother why she preferred to go on having these children instead of spending her money on some proper new clothes, for example, she would merely smile in a distant sort of way and say, 'Oh darling, you'd *hate* it if we were just a tiny little family.'

But what I would hate or otherwise wasn't at all the point. What mattered was that other people lived different, more regular lives – and it worried me that we were being so anarchic.

What I couldn't know was that we weren't alone. In the village where we lived there were only two families to compare with – the Etons, who lived up the road by the church, and the Clarrabuts, in the other direction, where the village curved away into farmland. None of their children was my sort of age, and the children with whom I went to primary school lived too far away to be played with, except in the formal circumstances of a birthday party.

This didn't mean that I was lonely. It merely meant that my sisters and I (and, as they arrived, my brothers) formed a tight and self-referential group – whether searching the attic for a hollow panel which, when pressed in the right place, would slide open on a secret staircase, or jumping from the apple trees with rope tied round our waists to get some practice flying, or 'camping' (i.e., eating picnics) in the spinney at the top of the garden, or hunched over sheets of foolscap paper that my father brought home from the office, drawing eternal comic strips with 'thinks' bubbles and captions. Or, consistently, reading.

And, of course, it was from books that I really acquired my conviction that we were strange. Not in *The Famous Five*, not in *The Secret Seven*, not in Jennings, not in E. Nesbit, not even in *Eagle* or in *Girl*, did any family behave itself like mine. We *children* might try to model ourselves on such stories – but where were our jolly grandparents; our even jollier cousins; our benevolent, pipe-smoking, dog-walking dad; our smiling, sweetly sewing mum? Where was our warm, secure and immutable world of grown-up certainties? I didn't know that those books were written before the war, or referred to the values of that period.

How on earth was I supposed to? I knew that The War had happened all right: at the top of our garden there were, for some time, the remnants of a bomb shelter, and a crater in the field in front of the house had been ploughed by a German plane. What I couldn't do was relate all of that to me. It was history, as surely as the Battle of Hastings or the Druids. Speaking with friends who were born in the course of the war, I know that their belief in its existence is totally different from mine. As one of them said, 'It wasn't *war* that was odd, but this thing that the grown-ups kept talking about called *peace*.' My parents never talked about peace; it was assumed. They lived in the present as though it were detached from history. Absorbing their concept of time, I accepted E. Nesbit and Enid Blyton as though their fantastic creations lived somewhere just over the hill.

That what was really happening over the hill (and in thousands of middle-class and 'upwardly mobile' working-class families in the land) was the same sort of improvising pragmatism as my parents' was also kept secret from me by the fact that I hadn't any cousins, aunts or uncles in the vicinity. My extended family met at weddings and funerals alone. My nuclear family may have been large, but it was the self-same hermetic unit as all those others that were struggling alone to invent a post-war lifestyle.

One of my mother's quandaries was how a woman lived the middle-class life without servants. She could afford the occasional char and, later, hearing of such things from friends, even tip-toed into the world of foreign 'au pair girls' – but the cook, gardener, housemaid, nursemaid and parlourmaid of her childhood were out, not only for reasons of expense but because it appeared that such things had perished with the war.

When I was turning six, then, and my fourth sister about to be born, and my mother going crazy with sleeplessness and physical exhaustion, she hit upon the expedient of removing me from my primary school and sending me, from Mondays to Fridays, to live with Mother Mats – my paternal grandmother; the one who used to take me to feed the ducks. From her mansion flat in Paddington, I was to venture out each day to the French Lycée in South Kensington.

The reason for that school's existence was a hard core of French diplomatic (or otherwise exiled) children – the French educational system is jealous; it spreads its tentacles wider than any in the world. In my year, in 1954, maybe 30 per cent of the children came from this sort of background; the rest of us were middle-class Brits whose parents, like mine, were all improvising. Some were attracted to the Lycée because it provided a good education (i.e., an academic one) for considerably less than the cost of an ordinary, private, English day school. It was, besides (for those with the stirrings of egalitarian conscience), not *precisely* private, being part, if not of ours, then at least of the French state system.

There was also a general lack of certainty, now that those post-war babies were coming of school age, about what it was, exactly, for which they were all to be educated. What would the brave new democratic, technocratic world require? There was, it appeared, a national eruption of educational opportunity – but how did one judge what was good and what bad in all that?

This problem of choice, I am aware, was essentially middle class. The question of what one did with one's daughters, however, was more widely spread. After that first scurry back to the kitchen when the nation's protectors returned from battle to reclaim their rightful jobs, it seemed as though women were once again to be tempted out into the workplace. The new boom economy needed them: to produce, to earn, to spend.

Our mothers were torn between vicarious pleasure at what we might enjoy and achieve and a fear (born of their own experience) that the bubble might once again burst, that their educated daughters might find themselves discarded. For my mother, in any case, the conflict was never resolved. While never doubting my right to whatever the best education might be (hers had not only been aborted but had, in any case, revolved mainly around riding and darning socks), or my ability to profit from it, she would still ask, 'Who'll ever marry you?' as I lost my temper, shouted too much or behaved in some other 'hoydenish' way, or would warn, 'You'll never have children,' as I staggered across the stable yard with some heavy object or other. Marriage and children were still, it was perfectly clear, the only safe goal. Training began early on – the nadir of preposterousness being the day that I was forbidden to go out swimming in bathing trunks. I must have been sevenish and flat as a razor blade, but girls must cover their nipples and that was that.

Like everything else, however, the message was ambiguous. For a start, a great many 'un-girlish' things were not only permitted but encouraged in the privacy of home. Arguing, asking questions, putting my own point of view – all these were perfectly fine at a family meal, though not to be indulged in at other people's houses or when we had people to visit. Similarly, in the matter of clothes, we could all wear (or not wear) whatever we chose – unless it was thought we'd be seen. Just as we were allowed to be physically adventurous – up to a point; the point more often than not being reached when other children were around.

Sometimes I found this double standard, this evidence that my parents hadn't a clue what they were doing, very funny indeed. Once, when I had been out riding with a girl whom I scarcely knew (she just happened to live in the neighbourhood and have, like me, a pony), my mother was in the stable as we rode in. My pony came to a halt at the gate and lifted its tail to shit. When my friend turned to

'Un-girlish' things were encouraged – but only in the privacy of home

see where I had got to, I explained, in the only word I knew for the process of defecation. 'Darling,' declared my mother through very clenched teeth. 'You do *not*,' she explained, when we were alone, 'say "shit" to people just like that.'

'But I do. So do you. We *all* do.'

'*Not*,' she insisted, 'in public.'

'Then what?' I said. 'Big jobs? Do you want me to say "big jobs"?'

And we both cracked up at the thought.

This in-jokiness was warm and cosy, but it became very frail when confronted by the Outside World. There, I felt that I constantly needed to bluff, constantly needed to be on my toes for clues as to what was expected. Certainly, I'd been given and absorbed such 'timeless' ethical concepts as honesty, fairness, courage, kindness. What no one could tell me was how such concepts were to be interpreted. That, I had to keep re-inventing for myself.

Later, when I started going to parties, when I started getting letters from boys, when I started to think about what I might do after school, the need became even more obvious. 'Well *I* don't know,' my mother would say. 'In *my* day we wouldn't wear trousers/ ring the boy first/ go to drama school, but I dare say you know better than me what's acceptable now.'

She didn't really believe that I'd any idea. But she *was* being honest when she said that she hadn't, either. Even in my first term at the Lycée there were limits to what guidance either she or my father could give. Not just the contents of the syllabus (there, even Latin was taught with a French accent) but what was expected from me in terms of attitude and behaviour were totally alien to them.

Mother Mats was no better informed. Nor was my father's sister Flick, nor his second cousin Lizzy – both of whom had bedrooms in my grandmother's flat. In fact, although they gave me a lot, these women, they were, in this respect, part of the problem: another set of alien people with whom I had to tread cautiously, working out, by trial and error, what was acceptable to them and why.

Physical boisterousness wasn't. Lizzy and Flick must have been in their early forties, Mother Mats her late sixties, and none of them had been recently used to the thunder of heavily walking-shod feet, the slamming of doors, the crashing of glass, the clatter of anything vaguely metallic – the noises that accompany the progress of a six-year-old child. Such violent intrusions into their world were discouraged.

On the other hand, they were all intelligent, independent-minded women: women who not only argued and discussed among themselves – assuming their right to opinions on politics (Mother Mats was a Fabian), on literature (they all liked thrillers) and religion – but who tirelessly answered my questions and fed me esoteric facts.

'William the Conqueror,' my grandmother said. 'You're learning about William the Conqueror, are you? Have they told you that he was a bastard? It means that his parents didn't marry, my dear. You'll find that a lot of great people were bastards.'

All either widows or spinsters, and all of them professional women (two civil servants, one journalist), they were vaguely dismissive of the men with whom they came into contact. Even their admiration for my mother ('Honestly, how does she cope?') was tinged with an ambivalence of which I was not unaware.

I tucked all this under my cap. Just as I tucked there the sweet-stealing expeditions, for which Eric Horsley and I slipped out of Geography. Just as I tucked there my knowledge of French when playing with children (other than my family) back in Kent. Just as I tucked there my country ways when dealing with the street-wise Lycée-ites.

I don't suppose for a second that I was the only fraud around. What matters is that I thought I was, and that this belief entailed a sense of permanent anxiety and watchfulness.

This wasn't in any way practical. On the physical levels of parental (or *in loco* parental) care, I was fed, clothed, bathed, nursed, entertained and treated with a thoroughness that ought to have left me breathless with gratitude. That it didn't was partly because I was very rarely told to be grateful; but even if I'd been constantly told, it wouldn't have meant a great deal – I'd no experience of hunger, or any real deprivation, with which to compare my lot.

Ignorance, then, made me careless of *what* was going to happen. When, two years after I'd started there myself, my second sister joined me at the Lycée, I assumed, with more pride than trepidation, my aunt Flick's role as the chaperone. She armed me with advice about sweets from strangers and staying out after dark, but it never really occurred to me that anything awful would happen. On the contrary, I enjoyed bossing poor old Vicky: telling her to hurry; coping with our changes of bus. But, more importantly, I needed someone to whom I could interpret this world. It was this that frightened me more than the sweets or the darkness – the social and moral chaos I could sense. I needed to give it a structure, to explain to myself *why* things happened.

We used to tell ourselves stories in bed as headlights swept across the moulded ceiling and Mother Mats grumbled at the *Guardian* crossword down the corridor. Vicky's were fantasies of flying and escape told in the third person and featuring an obnoxious little boy who looked a lot like Le Petit Prince. Mine were first-person churnings, dark and violent and aggressive, obsessively going over and over almost identical incidents.

In the morning we ate our cornflakes and spam (Mother Mats wasn't known for her cooking), then sauntered out with skipping-ropes and satchels to school: a couple of fair-haired, red-cheeked, privileged brats. On Friday evenings our father met us at Victoria and the weekend existence began – no less privileged, yet no less accompanied by night-time stories and sleepwalks and waking screams.

At around this time, when I was nine or ten, we started going to Brittany for summer holidays. One year, besides my parents, six of us were involved – the youngest, Laura, scarcely more than a toddler. Merely organising the luggage, making sure that children kept hold of whatever they'd been given to carry, must have been trying on the nerves. Somewhere between Southampton and St Malo, however, our ferry hit a bit of 'turbulence' and everyone started being sick. Stewards were called, bunks were changed, tears were wiped – and anyone who looked as though they might be recovering promptly started vomiting again. By the time we arrived at the hotel, tension was snapping its fingers.

'Tell them our name and that we've booked three rooms,' said my father.

'I can't,' I said – not because I couldn't, but because it seemed incredibly unfair. Nowhere, not in *The Famous Five*, not in any family of which I could conceive, would a child be asked to explain her parents to a hotel proprietor.

'I thought you spoke French. Now do it,' he said. My mother nodded at me to obey. In times of conflict, they clanged together as tightly as magnetic mines.

That night (I'd done it; what else was there to do?) the sister with whom I was sharing a bed, and who was still feeling seasick, woke me up shivering and sobbing.

'Go to sleep, Libby.'

'I'm frightened to.'

'What do you mean?'

'I mean, if I do, I'm frightened I'll never wake up.'

I knew what I was supposed to answer – I wasn't the eldest sister for nothing – but when she asked me to *swear* to her, to *promise* that she'd wake up, I found that I couldn't say it. There was, I was perfectly well aware, the tiniest chance, maybe one in a trillion, that she wouldn't.

'You *almost* certainly will,' I said.

It took my mother to sweep in, to cuddle her and to promise it would all be all right.

So it was; we all woke up in the morning. But beneath the *pain grillé* and apricot jam that met us in the hotel dining room, beyond the beach and the rock pools and the flashes of sun on the Atlantic, almost concealed by those gifts that our parents were pouring like myrrh on our heads, there were still the gaps, the cover-ups, the evasions and moral ambiguities.

Of course, I like to think that I was fearless in searching them out, that I displayed exceptional courage, imagination and integrity in tearing and finally ripping through my parents' Picture of Life. But I only did what such a childhood makes possible – what such a childhood, I would even suggest, makes necessary.

First, I rejected university. This may not seem the most intelligent move, but, by the time I was sixteen, the need to construct a picture of my own was becoming more and more urgent, and higher education was too much part of my parents' and teachers' expectations to be any use to me at all.

Drama school, where I went instead, taught me that I would never be an actress.

It also taught me (which I'd started to suspect) that my middle-class values, cultural references, lifestyle and expectations weren't the only ones that mattered – might not even matter at all. But, perhaps more important still, it gave me a framework in which to explore my sexuality – allowed me, most immediately, to acknowledge my homosexuality, and also showed me patterns of sexual and emotional inter-relationship (between students of whichever gender) in which all the prescribed behaviour patterns were questioned, subverted, shaken up.

The new picture that was emerging was horribly confused and messy. Sensing this on my visits back home, my parents grew quietly anxious – and, although I pretended to them that everything was under control, those student days were *not* (and I understate) the happiest of my life. Later, when I discovered writing, lurve and a sense of perspective, I was often tempted to disown them. But they *did* provide me with the marks and colours that my introduction to feminist theory – not to mention to socialist theory and socialists and feminists themselves – helped me to shape into something which, because it is mine, I can trust.

Or, more precisely, find plausible. Because I suspect that neither I, nor any of my fellow 'post-war babies', were ever too hot on trust: were never, in that sense, children.

WHEN 1968 erupted, I was finishing drama school. In between learning audition speeches, getting 'publicity photographs' taken, writing off to provincial reps and rehearsing for the end-of-course show, I certainly heard of the riot shields and cobblestones clashing in Paris – but none of that was as real or important as trying to persuade the Nottingham Playhouse at least to *hear* my unique rendition of Bertolt Brecht's Mother Courage.

I might as well have saved myself the stamps. In the end, the only jobs I ever got in the theatre were a week at the Oval, Kennington, and two hideous months in a company that trudged around Britain's primary schools with a dramatisation of Kipling's *Just So Stories*.

Mainly, I subsided into unemployment, the friendship of other 'resting' actors, a communal house in South-west London sub-let (illegally, it turned out) by a stripper who specialised in S&M, hippiedom, dope, the Beatles' *White Album*, the Electric Cinema, the loss of my virginity (yes, I was backward there too) – until, at the age of twenty-one, as the sixties slid into the seventies, two things happened simultaneously: I had my first affair with a woman and I started writing a novel.

Sexually and emotionally, I felt rescued. Creatively, I began to do something which little by little restored my pride – a process in no way diminished when the novel, followed by others, got published. Intellectually, I came into contact with Woolf, de Beauvoir, Greer and Millet.

Self-employed (with in-and-out raids on charing, modelling, etc.) and safe inside a supportive lesbian circle, I felt that I'd managed to sidestep the need for a struggle with the status quo. It might be perfectly disgusting, but it wasn't bothering *me*.

Then, in 1977, ejected from the nursery of that long-term affair, homeless, suddenly noticing my age, I found myself having to reconsider this assumption. In need of a rather more solid financial subsidy for my writing, I started to do some freelance reviewing for *Time Out* magazine. And it was there, in that intellectual, political and physical environment (one which became even more exciting when, in 1981, the co-operative magazine *City Limits* was founded by some of the staff), that I acquired the conceptual frameworks for a Reconsideration of My Life.

Of course, I'd *known* about feminism and socialism before, had vaguely believed them the only fair and intelligent political scaffoldings, but I'd realised neither that I needed their support nor, conversely, that I owed them mine. They gave me a context not only for my homosexuality but for the (more difficult) heterosexuality with which I was beginning to engage; not only for my fiction but for my journalism; not only for my friendships but for my wider political involvements.

And if all of those things get progressively more and more complex, that's not such a terrible thing. My childhood may make me sometimes yearn for simplicity; it's also taught me to suspect it.

I now work at the *New Statesman* as deputy literary editor. My last novel was *The Riding Mistress*, published in 1983.

Valerie Walkerdine

Dreams from an Ordinary Childhood

It was the summer of 1983. In a suburb of Derby I sat in the car and looked at the inter-war semi that had been my home since I was born. A little girl on a tricycle cycled along the drive and out on to the pavement. It was as though I were seeing myself in a time warp.

This was the first time that I had been able to go back and look at this place, the house that was the basis of my childhood memories and dreams, the last remaining testament to that secret past of a proletarian provincial childhood. I had wanted to keep its nooks and crannies, its supreme ordinariness, safe as a place I could remember, where the past would not be lost.

And yet, everything about it, its sense of safety, had felt for so long like a trap, the site and origin of an ordinariness both hated and desired. It was the place in which, if I were not careful and being so vigilant, I might turn into my mother.

It was in that moment, in the fifties, when I felt set up, set up to want, to want to be different, special, when I was chosen to be one of the children of the post-war boom, who would leave the safe innocence of the suburbs for the stripped-pine promises of the new middle class, for the glamour of the metropolis and the desperate lure of the academy.

For years, in the midst of other people's confident sophistication, I felt trapped by a wall of silence about the very ordinariness of my past. I imagined that my new-found acquaintances in the intellectual élite had different and exciting childhoods. Indeed, casual conversation at parties always seemed to act as confirmation of this, making me sink into a depression, feeling that absolutely nothing about my childhood was worthy of comment. But more that the embarrassment of that past was a topic to be kept well hidden. I didn't have an affair at fourteen, join the Communist Party at sixteen, go off to paint in Paris, or live in a ashram in India. Childhood fantasies of getting out, of being rich and famous abounded, but in the circles I moved in there had been only two ways to turn the fantasy into the dream-lived-as-real of bourgeois life, and they were to marry out or work my way out. It is the latter which, for that first moment of the fifties, lay open to me. For that moment of the post-war educational expansion fuelled my puny and innocent little dreams as I grew up, the epitome of the hard-working, conservative and respectable working-class girl.

Becoming middle class in the seventies was like entering a new world peopled by those who designated themselves as special. I felt split, fragmented, cut off from that suburban semi, where I couldn't tell my mother what was happening. Where nobody knew what academic work was (and where it would have been better to announce that I was going to produce a baby, not a thesis). I felt, in the old place, as in the new, that if I opened my mouth it would be to say the wrong thing. Yet, I desired so much, so very much, to produce utterances which, if said in one context, would not lead to rejection in the other.

Yet, in all of this, it was the supreme ordinariness which I found so difficult to talk about in the circles in which I had begun to move. My version of a working-class childhood simply did not fit the illusion of the proletariat as a steaming cauldron of revolutionary fervour. The suburban semi could hardly be described as a backstreet slum from which I could have claimed a romantic poverty. No, I came from among the serried ranks of what my mother was fond of describing as 'ordinary working people'. It is that conservative and respectable ordinariness which I want to reclaim. The ordinariness of manners, of please-and-thank-you'd politeness, of being a nice girl, who went to Brownies and Guides, and for whom the competitions in the annual Produce Association show provided one of the most exciting occasions of the year. Reclaim that, name it, speak it, for in it lies a childhood like so many, and yet all too easily explained away in a pathologisation of difference. It is as though those stories which are 'nothing to write home about', in all their ordinary obviousness, were not themselves both constituted by, and constitutive of, a history which has to be told. It was the pattern of daily life which gave this adult that I have become her specificity.

There, caught in the threads of that ordinary life, is the basis for understanding what my subjectivity might be about.

Proto-fascist organisations are embarrassing to those who stand outside the familiarity of one of the mainstays of suburban life. Yet, it was the church, the school, the Brownies, the Guides and the fêtes and competitions which helped provide the building blocks of my formation. Or, holidays in Skegness, brought sharply into focus one day in the early seventies when, walking with friends in another seaside town, we passed a row of cafés, watching the ordinary working families eating fish and chips inside, off plastic tables, with tomato sauce.

'How can they do it?' How to reply that they had been me, that I liked tomato sauce (indeed, it was from Brown sauce that I got a first French lesson: *cette sauce de haute qualité est une mélange d'épices orientaux* ...)? How to evoke the happy holiday memories here at once disdained as nothing? But what I failed to recognise was the fascination of gazing at the working class, and the question these friends so very much wanted an answer to: what was it like to *be* like that, the fantasised Other, repository of simultaneous fears and dreams of radical subversion. Yet gazing further, looking through the window of the past, I glimpse the happiness of sunny days at the tea table, laughter, hopes and fears and pain, pain of loss, pain of leaving, of wanting. Fear of the reproduction of that ordinariness inside myself. To be ordinary is to be a woman; to be ordinary is to be a worker: terror and desire.

I have a terrible fear of the suburbs: I cannot bear the provinces, and especially the edges of conurbations. Just like home. The safe familiarity of the bay windows, the neat gardens, safety like a trap, ready to ensnare in its enfolding arms. The price, having to live in London, the fear and lure of elsewhere, of always working, never stopping, for working was the way out, the only guarantee, the safeguard against the necessity to accept, to return, to give up. I cannot explain what it feels like to be in another place because of that work, for embedded in it is the necessary fear of giving up, the terrifying doubts that very soon they will find out that you have no talent. To stop is to turn, like Cinderella, from riches back to rags. But my home is paid for by my mental labour. What else, except the slippery slide-path back to being ordinary, at home with children in a suburb?

But they set me up to want, fashioned my desires, and then held out the promise that, if I were a good girl, by dint of my own efforts, it could all come true. And here, the dreams of the prince, of being rich, of the exotic, the different, and being clever, mingle into one.

Three-year-old Valerie Walkerdine, one of the 'fairies' in the fancy dress parade at Mickleover children's sports and field day last night. (*Derby Evening Telegraph*, Summer, 1950)

There are many versions of the press photograph accompanying this text among our family snapshots. It is one of my favourites, an image I cannot erase from my mind. It shows a little girl dressed as a bluebell fairy, a pale blue dress with puff sleeves and a frilly skirt, a bluebell hat, fairy wings and wand. She smiles, hesitantly, towards someone near the camera but not holding it. Whose gaze? In whose vision was I created to look like this, to display the winning charms, so that posing before the judges, they too, like the camera, would be won over? It is my first memory of what winning meant. But towards whom am I looking, who dressed me like this? Like all the fairy fantasies rolled into one? I wanted to be like one of the Flower Fairies in the book of that name, of which I still have a copy. How I too gazed at those fragile and ethereal little fairies, who were not

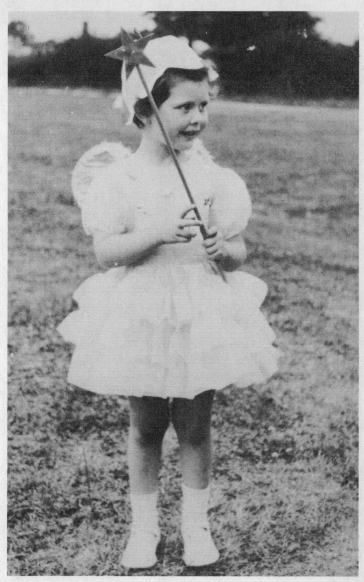

Me as a bluebell fairy at three, 1950

quite of this world; the sickly and underweight child, object and source of those fragile and yet devastating fantasies. It was somebody's dream, their fantasy, my fantasy, meeting in the mutuality of the returned look; the gentle and uncertain smile created there too. Charming little fairies who have good and beautiful powers to transform, fuelling the flames of an omnipotence, to cast spells, work magic. But then, the magic might fade ... for, if some central piece of myself was formed in the crystallising moment of that gaze, were not the will-o-the-wisp charms threatened by growing up, growing big?

'A day-early birthday present'. The day of my birth was the day before my father's birthday, and so here I was, in the circuit of exchange, given by my mother to my father. Tinkerbell, he called me: Tinky, the bluebell fairy, not quite of this world. A sick man's dream – he was always ill – of another who would make him well, whole again, give him life, the laughter in the soul, to take away the ever-present threat of death. Tinkerbell, who so lived for the life of Peter Pan that she drank his poison, and who only the belief in fairies would keep alive:

Hook poisoned it ... He lifted the glass, but Tink still hovered over it. There was no time to argue. She perched on the rim, her light shone inside it, and dropped down and down until the glass was empty. Down to the very last drop, Tink drained the glass ...

It was poisoned, she repeated faintly, and I think I'm going to be dead now ... All of you out there, if you believe in fairies, clap your hands. Clap them hard and go on clapping. If you don't, Tinkerbell will die.

There was hardly a moment before, suddenly and miraculously, the silence was broken by a tremendous clapping of hands.

He wanted me to be a doctor, the magician of science, substituting medicine for magical cures, but still with the wish-fulfilment of my capacity to cure him, to make him whole, complete. I never wanted to be a doctor. I remembered toying with the idea of being a nurse, but I didn't like blood. A casual remark. The wish of a working-class father for his daughter. But how else to explain that 1975 found me telling his shadow in a corner of the churchyard that

I had got my PhD? I was a doctor, and yet the kind that couldn't have cured him even if he were alive. Nothing would succeed in bringing him back, for wherever he seemed to be, in whatever guise, there around every corner was loss. At sixteen, a month before I took my O levels, he died suddenly in the middle of the night, there and then gone. And I struggled with those O levels, wanting somehow to show him that I would not give up.

I must have been about six. They took me into hospital. I had always been a rather sickly and underweight child, constantly absent from school with tonsilitis. I am told that in hospital I was a model patient, who sang to the nurses. But this charming episode was to mark the end of the reign of the bluebell fairy. Delicacy was to make way for an awkward lumpiness, a terror of my body that has always stayed with me. But I felt cheated in the hospital. They told me that I was ill and would be better, that I could eat what I liked. But who was to know the terrifying gains that had been made from that illness?

They told me that I could have jelly and ice cream after the operation. The kind of food reserved for special treats like parties, birthdays and Christmas. So, they set it up to be a celebration, the triumph over illness. But they didn't tell me that the pain would be so great that jelly and ice cream was all that I would be able to swallow. I had lost a lot more than my tonsils.

After that I seemed to eat a lot. I certainly put on a lot of weight, so that I find it almost unbearable to look at photographs of myself from that time on. They called it 'puppy fat', attributed it to my glands. The charming little girl, who was so frail and fragile that she could not be expected to be physical, had turned into a huge and clumsy lump. I could no longer be excused physicality through illness, but in fact lived in a state of terror about my body. I couldn't do the kind of sports that were expected. So instead of the active young girl of the pre-adolescent feminist myth, I was frightened and clumsy and seemed to have lost, with my tonsils, the magical powers, the capacity to be a fairy. Just because you are big, they imagine you are not afraid. Big and small, active and passive. The longed-for femininity. But that lumpen docility could be put to good use in the classroom. It was still possible there to win, to become the object of that other, laudatory gaze, in the place from which once again I might be chosen.

They don't just sell you a dream in school, they pin you down with truth. In the classroom the truth of a position is produced, holding you fast and steady, keeping the wanting going. When you have a position to keep up, winning and losing take on an altogether different meaning. When I was six, Miss Wedd, the class teacher, told me that if I didn't get a scholarship they would enter me for an Art Scholarship. I spent all my spare time drawing. It fitted well with the quiet and well-behaved little girl. She could let her imagination run riot with a pencil and paper. Where other people read books, I filled in the hours with this kind of solitary occupation. 'Valerie seems quite gifted,' said my school report. Gifts, it seemed, were everywhere; on my birth I had been a gift and now I had a gift. It was given and I was chosen. I don't think I knew what an Art Scholarship was, but my desire to be a teacher seems to date from that time. It was an art teacher at first. Later, in that other dream of difference, it became a French teacher. I became neither. I became that much more accept-able thing, a teacher of young children. But nevertheless it was a teacher I wanted to be, like the teachers who had chosen me. I knew no other teachers except my own, and had no sense of an ambition outside the possibility that, if you were good at something, then one day you might be good enough to teach it. When it came later, to the point of applications for college, I put down six choices, all of them in London, for teaching was to be my passport out of the suburbs.

Reading my reports of that time I find everywhere the facticity of those choices:

Junior 1   *No in class: 52*   *Age*: 8.4
Position in class: 3rd
Conduct: excellent
Progress: most satisfactory in all subjects
Remarks: a very good report. Valerie is a steady, reliable worker, with
    an ability above the average. If she continues as she has started she
    should do very well indeed.

But, when I read it now I could tear it up. I have spent enough time studying the ways in which girls' and boys' performance is understood to recognise the pejorative as well as positive connotations of being a 'steady, reliable worker'. Later, my head teacher was to call me a 'plodder'. Boring, ordinary, lumpish, snail-like. Yet the phrase, steady, reliable worker, could have been written by a personnel manager in a factory. Reliable doesn't rock the boat, and yet and of course the position: third out of fifty-two. Conduct, excellent: what else to keep you there, thinking, dreaming, one day, one day, the reward would arrive, the dream come true? They pin you down with facts: 'an ability above the average'. A dream, a fantasy to be sure, but so powerful in its effects and implications.

Psychologists claim that it is possible at a very early age to predict with some degree of accuracy the ultimate level of a child's general intelligence … Since the ratio of each child's mental age to his chronological age remains the same, while his chronological age increases, the mental differences between one child and another will grow larger and larger and will reach a maximum during adolescence. It is accordingly evident that different children from the age of eleven, if justice is to be done to their varying capacities, require types of education varying in certain important respects. (Board of Education, Consultative Committee on Secondary Education, 1938, pp. 357–8)

Psychologists may well make claims, but teachers have to put into practice those fragile illusions of truth. They classify and position. But let's make no mistake, the double bind of this double standard is that it got me where I am today. Those little moments in the dream: of being a teacher, third in class, the excellent conduct. Contradictory, painful, alluring. There but not quite yet. The constant search, the constant fear of rejection. But what, in that system, would I swap? Could I honestly say that I would rather have been forty-third than third?

Trying, crying, gaining, winning and, of course, ever present the barely whispered fear that I might not be good *enough* to avoid and evade failure and loss. But you told me, you told me if I tried …

But everywhere there was competition. Together, my younger sister and I competed. The most memorable competitions were on

71

holiday. At the seaside there were always competitions sponsored by children's comics and food manufacturers. We tried our hardest to win these and usually did. Often they were artistic, such as making castles and pictures in the sand. The local Produce Association annual show always had sections for children: 'posy in an eggcup' or, more difficult, 'design a cup and saucer'. I still have the prize certificates.

One form of winning which knitted together money and the dream of riches was Purpose Day. This was the Brownie and Guide equivalent of the Scouts' Bob-a-Job week. We only got a day. The main aim was to collect as much money as possible by doing simple household chores. My sister and I worked out fairly quickly that if we stayed around where we lived we wouldn't get much money, but by walking quite some way to a private avenue of very large houses it was possible to earn much larger sums. Here lived what we took to be the wealthy. Not only did they have more money, but there was a double and even more enticing bonus: we could get to see how the other half lived. In cleaning the shoes and washing the floors of the rich, there was a vicarious pleasure. We could find out what it was like to live like that. And so the dreams of being like that too were given some substance. A bit like the upstairs parlourmaid. Ironically, being inside the houses was in some sense enough. It was to be included. It is not difficult to understand how the mixture of desire and resentment should render occupations inside well-to-do households as glamorous. Sharing in the magic is almost like possessing the magic yourself.

It was my Granny who most fed these dreams. My maternal grandmother, who lived with us, had her own fantasies and dreams of grandeur. The arch conservative of the working class, who hated everything to do with proletarianism, she spent at least part of most evenings as the centrepiece of the local pub, drinking Double Diamond like an early version of Ena Sharples at the Rovers Return. But while she might have looked like Ena, her aspirations were more in line with those of Annie Walker.

The Midland Drapery was the largest department store in Derby. I loved it when she took me there for tea. They had waitresses, music, and mannequins swirling around between the tables. Granny and I played this little game together. We had sandwiches in little triangles with the crusts cut off, toasted teacakes and tea in heavy, pewter pots. Then we would look around the shop and fantasise about what we might have bought. Granny seemed a funny old lady, but she had class!

She seemed almost to perform the function of a fairy godmother. One of the things she made happen was visits to the home of her brother who lived in Chesterfield. The family story had it that he had worked his way from rags to riches, from office boy to managing director of a local firm. We used to go sometimes to the large house, set in its own grounds, which had the ultimate in decadence, a revolving summer house. You could turn it round to catch every last flicker of the sun's warmth. Everything there seemed to be tinged with sophistication. I had never before eaten biscuits sandwiched together with real chocolate or tasted ravioli.

The suburb of Derby was not always a suburb. Mickleover was once a village. That is how I first remember it. It is the village I want to preserve inside my imagination. Everyone knew everyone else. But, gradually, the suburban expansion of the post-war reconstruction began to encroach on the fields in which I had once played. New housing estates sprang up. The old Victorian school building burst at the seams. A new school was built, which I moved to while in the Juniors. This was the 1950s. When I made that journey home in 1983, it still seemed like the 'New School'. It was on the 'New Estate'. Its architecture was modern. I could not fit this time of post-war expansion of thirty years ago with the idea of the new school. The *Derby Evening Telegraph* reported the new school along with the year's award of swimming certificates:

Mr J.W. Best, the headmaster, spoke of the growing number of children (425) attending the school, and said that with the opening of the new school at Mickleover the position would be eased.

The encroachment of the new housing estates seemed to match the waning both of the countryside and of my childhood. But things were changing; we felt it in the new estates, we heard it on the radio, we saw it on the television, bought especially for the

Coronation. Separation was difference. Change was moving out.

In my school they asked me what my father's work was. I replied with some pride that he was a mechanised fettler. It had taken me a long time to learn that. The teacher wrote down 'Works for Rolls Royce'. Most fathers worked there or for British Railways, the two major employers in Derby. Some people's mothers were nurses and domestics at the county mental hospital in the village. My grandmother worked there until she was seventy-two, when they forced her at last to retire. She died a year later. My mother did no paid employment until after my father died. In the post-war respectable working class, it was clear where a mother's place ought to be.

To be special and to be ordinary: the home, the safety, the woman, the worker, the difference, there held out sparkling in the palm of an outstretched hand. To be clever is to be chosen. To leave the safety for the lure of those promises.

As part of the expansion, new grammar schools were built in villages further outside Derby. In 1958 I passed the eleven-plus. Ten years later I became a teacher. To want to be clever is to desire to win. It is both to be different and to long for acceptance. To be attractive enough, to be clever enough, to have enough money. I wanted them all. The new grammar school was part of what winning and being chosen meant.

They held out a dream. Come, they told me. It is yours. You are chosen. They didn't tell me, however, that for years I would no longer feel any sense of belonging, nor any sense of safety. That I didn't belong in the new place, any more than I now belonged in the old. So, around every corner of apparent choice lurked doubt and uncertainty.

Leaving one's class was to be both admired and scorned. My mother described its pejorative connotations as typified by a change of accent which she referred to as 'lasting and pasting'. The fear in this working-class morality of putting on airs and graces was the fear of being found to be an imposter. The terror was not a simple matter of working-class pride. It was all right to talk like that if you had a right to belong to that class. In 1983, I lasted and pasted it. Few would have recognised my accent as local. In London they still constantly remark on my 'northern accent', as though it were a mark of quaint and charming working-class authenticity.

To be neither, in no place, with no sense of belonging. For if the long vowel sounds are fraudulent, so would be the continued maintenance of the inappropriate authenticity. Valerie, the clever working-class girl from Derby, the trumped-up little teacher. These personages lurk fearfully in the insecurities of imagined failure and rejection. What if winning in one place is simultaneously always a loss? What if the fear of losing so fires you that you never dare to try? Other lives, other stories, but tangible and important histories.

And finally, where shall I look for cause in this history? The circuit of exchange in which a sick man accepted a gift? (To Stan and Rosemary the precious gift of a daughter.) But who gave it? The Lord giveth and the Lord taketh away. The man who wanted so desperately to hang on to the possibility of life that he found in his daughter. The woman who gave her children everything, hoping to find there some fragment of herself. My mother in this history has no history. She lurks silently in the kitchen. She is safety. She is danger. She is the suburbs. She is morality. I cannot find her in my dream because the kitchen is where I am most afraid to look.

Or what about that moment in history, the dream held out in the palm of an outstretched hand? They held out the knowledge, the position to me, and told me that I could claim it as mine, if I worked for it and had the ability. So what of that dream? Should I have adapted to reality? If so, which of the realities would you have me adapt to? The dream of difference, of the exotic, out of my class, out of my gender? The reality of the factory, the office, the kitchen, the cradle, workers and women, ordinary people? Did anyone really expect me to adapt to those realities, to swap poverty for wealth, when they faced you with a dream? Who in their Valium-induced haze would want to swap that version of reality for the glittering landscape of the dream?

Look, children of the post-war boom, over there at the new day dawning, the sun rising over the bright future of the new housing estates where, by our abilities and aptitudes we would be chosen to take our place in the land of opportunity. But how can we hope if we do not have dreams; how can we build if we do not have a future? What dream, what future, what here, what now? You should never have educated us, the ordinary girls of the fifties, for we are dangerous. We are set on becoming, and you will not stop us now. But it is not the individuals you sought to make of us who believe we have made it, leaving all the pain and uncertainty behind in that other place. No, not that. We are beginning to speak of our histories, and as we do it will be to reveal the burden of pain and desire that formed us, and, in so doing, expose the terrifying fraudulence of our subjugation.

*I*N 1965 I left Derby for good. That is to say, I never returned home to live in any real sense, making my bid for the high life by beginning primary school teacher training in London. Everything which smacked of provincialism was hated by comparison with the glittering sophistication I imagined in London.

The years of teacher training were a strange mixture of hard work and total failure to understand how on earth to study. 1968 found me changed, but not in the startling way of many of my contemporaries ... simply the desperate avoidance of what was expected by so many other would-be teachers: the engagement ring and return to the provinces to marry.

I wanted to teach in London, and the school in Mile End fuelled my urge – or rather missionary zeal – to 'work with the poor', itself hiding a fear of teaching middle-class children which far outweighed the difficulties of controlling my 'problem class' in the East End. Soon missionary zeal was replaced by my role as libertarian earth mother and revolutionary guardian; my classroom was the very centrepiece of free expression, a place in which my illiterate ten-year-olds would become inner-city poets, helped by my increasingly anti-school position.

In 1970 I left teaching to return to full-time study, still in London; from that moment I never looked back. Suddenly and inexplicably I understood how to read. Nothing, except the paid work I had to do to finance my studies, could tear me away from the library.

By 1972 I was starting a PhD at Bristol University. Now I teach and do research at London University's Institute of Education.

I came to radical politics and Marxism before I became a feminist and only later began to work on schooling and explorations of subjectivity informed at first by post-structuralism and later by psychoanalysis. It is this work which gave me the way to look from the vantage point of the present to the fantastic shores of the past.

Stef Pixner

The Oyster
and the Shadow

PRIVATE   !!!!!!!!!!
        MY DIARY

                        PRIVATE!!

        1957
Keep your nose out of it
                        HANDS OFF!

My diary is a sort of reflection of myself, and that is why he is essentially a boy. I would rather be a boy. He hasn't a name. He's memory's and thoughts for no one but him and me.

So began 2,000–odd pages, scrawled (often in bed by the light of streetlamps) in exercise books and on loose sheets of paper, which seem to me now like a long note corked into a bottle and thrown into the sea. The sea was my future. The note said, amongst advice and warnings for the grown-up I would become: DON'T FORGET.

But my route back to the early fifties is different. There are no written records; no embarrassing childhood voice fixed to the page …

The man comes round to light the gas lamps at 3 p.m. with a long stick; an action both comforting and forlorn. We sit, girl-boy, girl-boy, at ink-stained desks fixed to the floor on iron runners. Round the china inkwells, the ink has dried with rainbow colours on its surface. We write now with pencils, and with chalks on little wooden framed slates, but soon we will learn to use the scratchy dip pens that blob on the first word and run out of ink on the third. It's my first class at primary school, so it must be the winter of '49–'50, and I'm four years old. There are more than forty of us in the class; my mother often remarks on how large it is. We're the first year of the 'bulge', she says, the post-war baby boom. We're post-war babies; you can't forget it. You know it under your skin.

For one thing, my best friend Sally is away. (Sally has dark hair, and we play 'Little Witches' together at playtime in imaginary tunnels under the playground, emerging only to shoot people who don't know they've been shot.) One day, Sally goes to Vienna with her mother and never comes back. Vienna is where people go when they don't come back, and it's all to do with the war being over; like my father, who went in '46 never to return.

For another thing, we get malt and cod-liver oil in the hall by the cloakroom at morning playtime; also milk, and syrupy orange juice in medicine-shaped bottles. It's all connected somehow. We're the Post-War Generation, and we're tall for our age, and healthy, and will grow bigger than the grown-ups, and (though I don't know this yet) menstruate earlier and have everything on a plate, and the world is our oyster. But the war is our shadow, as are the hungry years before it.

The war is the great divide. Time began with the end of it, and not just because I was born on VE Day. All the bad things built up to it, it happened, and then things started; the world began. But the shadows don't go. Underneath my fiercely held utopian convictions of the late fifties, I go on expecting the next great recession, the next great war. Even through the sixties I know that hard times will return. But in the early fifties, it's wartime austerity cookbooks, and my brother's advice not to eat a lot of butter: you might get used to it and then find it hard to go without. A message distinct somehow from the immediate constraints of economic hardship – using matches twice, not putting soap in water, turning sheets side to middle when the middles get two sides to them – because it's more about not letting yourself enjoy luxuries you will one day have to forgo.

Brown lino, blackout curtains with coloured tape sewn on the bottoms, a patchwork tweed blanket, and a toy elephant of the same wartime patchwork tweed. A potato sack which does for a bathmat, well-washed muslin flourbags which do for hankies (and for disposing of unwanted school dinners under the table). The context of the memories is a roomy flat at the top of a large Victorian house where I live with my mother and brother and other people who come and go. Buttons in each room for calling servants give the house a sense of past grandeur; very much pre-war. Other things have the same pre-war feel, like horses. It's because soon they're going to be 'put out to grass', as Mum says of the Co-op milkman's horse with fluffy feet and yellow teeth that I feed on Saturdays when we pay the milkman and tell him our share number so Mum will get the 'divi'. There's a Co-op laundry service, too. You can leave your dirty clothes in a bundle on the front step, and they come back in brown paper with string round it, though Mum also washes by hand, boiling things in a zinc bucket on the gas stove.

I have few memories of grown-ups at this time. They make my hair into 'plates' in the morning before school, and talk about things like 'spring' and 'the Labour Party'. They forbid us children to play in the bombsite two doors down, but we do anyway. We squeeze in through a hole in the wall. It's like being in a house with the lid off; like a doll's house with extra walls missing. This also is connected to the war somehow.

A year later we are evicted from the large top flat, and re-housed by the council in one partitioned room a mile or two away. It's another grand house fallen on hard times, with lofty moulded ceilings, a wood-panelled galleried staircase, and a curving front drive with gravel in it but no cars. (Or horses.) We share a kitchen with two other families; three gas stoves, three sinks, one main table and three smaller ones. We have a brown bakelite wireless and a wind-up gramophone for 78 rpm records; things like Danny Kaye singing 'Tubby the Tuba', Paul Robeson singing 'Ol' Man River', and the massed male voices of the Red Army Choir.

My mother works in an office nine to six and Saturday mornings as she has done all our babyhood and childhood. She also teaches typing and shorthand at evening classes twice a week. On those evenings Granny puts us to bed, but this stops when I am about seven, and we do for ourselves. Neighbours help out if we are ill, or we go on the bus to Granny's, as we do most holidays and some weekends. Granny has a television, a telephone, a Hoover, and carpets on all the floors (none of which we acquire in the fifties or even the sixties, except for a telephone) but these aren't the important things.

What I like about Granny's is the allotments and the trains at the back (in 1984, the allotments have long since been run over by the southernmost reaches of the M1), and the macaroni cheese she makes with brown macaroni and yeast extract. She's a vegetarian. We all are; my mother and brother and me, and my aunt, who's engaged to be married. Even the man who's going to marry her will become a 'veggie' when he does. I remember the ration books with 'extra cheese' written over the 'bacon' squares. Granny was the first to be a vegetarian, though, and the family jokes about her because she's so fanatical. At Christmas time she buys a nut turkey from Shearns (the posh vegetarian restaurant in Bloomsbury) that's shaped just like a real dead bird.

Her being there all day gives me a snug, secure feeling. Not that I see her; I'm off for hours, hiding in the allotments, or making mud soup with Doreen, or skipping with my imaginary friend Susan (who is just like me only not as good at skipping), or watching trains with my brother, if he'll let me tag along.

Back at home, he teaches me how to read a clock, how to tie shoelaces, and how long is a second. We play conkers, and he wins. The 'we' is always him and me. Although with a family in every room there are a lot of children, I don't remember them. I play alone a lot, with the fairies who live in the black and white tiled WC, or the people who come to my shop with cancelled ration

Me and my brother, 1956

books so I can ring up things like one and ninepence on the tin cash register.

We stay two years in the 'Halfway House', though the maximum stay is supposed to be six months. In that time, two tragedies stand out. The first is the approach of my sixth birthday, which is on 'Empire Day', because then I will get a blue ration book with tea coupons in it and be too old to listen to 'Little Miss Mother' at a quarter to two: 'the programme for children with green ration books'.

The second is the approach of my eighth birthday, when overnight I will grow too big to crawl through child-sized holes in things. I cry and cry because I want to stay seven forever. Somewhere inside I promise myself I will never forget. I won't become like the grown-ups you can't imagine ever having been young, that make you feel growing up is like dying; that mock and punish and say no and don't understand. I won't forget the language that babies and little children understand and speak in, that I just about remember. We children can see adults clearly, even though they hide so much from us. We see them muck up and complicate their lives. I won't lose this vision as I cross over to the other side.

But being eight isn't so bad, as it turns out. Like sweets have just come off the ration and now I will get an extra shilling a week pocket money in addition to the eightpence (a penny for each year of my age) I already get, to buy my own gobstoppers, liquorice sticks, honeycomb and sherbert.

It's 1953. Year of the Coronation and the climbing of Mount Everest. Last year Princess Elizabeth was called back from her tour of the pink bits of the map we were following in morning classes, and ascended the throne. This year she is to be crowned. We get given a silk handkerchief with Buckingham Palace on it, a silver spoon, and a tin of chocolates.

1953 is also the year we move from the temporary accommodation for homeless families to another top flat in another big old house not far from the first one, painted council cream and council brown, and temporary again. In fact we stay there seven years, but it's always with the threat of a sudden move. I have my own room at last, and there's a big kitchen with a coal fire, and a long view of trees.

I walk the mile home from school alone, but I'm not lonely. I make friends with fence posts, and leaves feel glad when I touch them. I often forget my key. Then, if my brother is out, I have to ring Mrs Miller's bell. I know she will sigh and tighten her lips, and say: 'You'd forget your head if it wasn't screwed on', so I sit by the front door and pray. 'Please Morona, Please Ronona (my goddesses – of whose existence Mum has been informed just in case I go into hospital so they can send me a card), Let Another Neighbour Come Out Soon.'

Later in the fifties I hear Mum talk about the new ideas suggesting that broken homes and working mothers turn 'latchkey' children into juvenile delinquents. She dismisses them with scorn, but she's worried when we're on our own (even though she knows the neighbours can be relied on to cope with crises) and hedges us round with rules.

At school, despite Morona and Ronona and unaware of any inconsistency, I am decidedly anti-religious. Mum has often told us about my brother's first rendering of the Lord's Prayer: 'Our Father which art in Heaven, Halibut be thy name.' Her laughter says: of course! How can children understand all this hocus pocus? I'm not sure what halibut is either, if truth be told, but it's the 'trespasses' that bother me; I think they must be something like 'christmasses' (a kind of Christmas tree, perhaps?) – but why do they need to be forgiven? I stand with my eyes open in morning assembly; why is everyone talking to someone who clearly isn't there? In the playground one day I am taunted and called a heathen. It hurts, but I'm proud of my difference, my unbelief.

Almost as unpopular as not believing in God, but less threatening to my schoolmates because more obviously ridiculous, is my claim that babies are not delivered by storks or bought in shops, but grow in mothers' tummies. I'm laughed out of court. How do the babies get out, for one thing? And for another, how do they get in? Clearly, I'm on sticky ground. But I know Mum is right. She has given me a book with diagrams, called *How Life is Handed On*, that shows once we looked like blackberries and then we looked like tadpoles.

I have an Indian friend at school called Himalata, whose family lives in one room in a block of houses in our street that's full of Indian families each in one room. Her house is mysterious and smells of curry, and when I stay the night she and her parents snore at different volumes, loud, medium and soft, like the three bears. She teaches me how to make necklaces from coloured birthday-candle wax that you drip onto cold water. It makes little round flat beads you can thread together with a needle. She also teaches me to move my head from side to side without moving my neck, like Indian dancers do.

Inspired by Himalata, and encouraged by my mother, I have my ears pierced. Granny objects. (She objects to operations, too, like when I had my tonsils and adenoids out; a 'fashion', she calls it, among 'knife-happy surgeons'.) Pierced ears were fashionable too when she was young, like bottom-long hair, but not now, thank heaven. It's barbaric, having holes made in your ears – like a savage; nobody does it these days. But Mummy buys me a pretty pair of earrings that I wear at children's parties; two silver bells that tinkle when you toss your head.

I wear them when an Indian boy in our class asks me to a party. He lives in a whole house in Kilburn. There are pictures in frames on a cloth in the middle of the floor, with food and things, that we throw rice onto. He also invites me into the bathroom, because his father has told him it's good for his health if I pull my knickers down and he touches me with his penis. I'm not as interested as he is in his health, but I don't like to be rude. Oh, but suddenly his father's knocking loudly on the door: what are we doing in there? Come out at *once*! When Mum arrives to collect me, I have a red spot in the centre of my forehead, and bits of rice are still stuck to it. 'Like a little Indian girl,' she says.

The school towers amongst back alleys, sandwiched between a hospital and a 1930s estate. It's the usual handsome redbrick prison of the early 1900s, with a high wall round and three tarmac playgrounds: Infants', Girls' and Boys'. There's not a tree or a blade of grass in sight, though it's near Hampsted Heath where we go once a year in autumn for nature walks, and once in summer for egg and spoon races. In nearby Flask Walk, a narrow sloping street with small neglected houses, there are notices stuck on trees and in the windows about tenants' meetings to fight evictions. Mum tells me the landlords' plan to put bathrooms in, and then sell the houses for thousands of pounds! (In 1984 the estate still stands, invisible unless you explore the back alleys, incongruous amongst the opulence of the nearby streets. Once bathless, the now beautiful cottages of Flask Walk have pink and blue front doors. The public wash house, where once a year Mum washed a pramful of blankets, now has curtains at the windows, like a converted railway station. The school too still stands, still towers.)

'Pass it on! Pass it on!' Rituals of exclusion, pollution,

conformity, taboo. Inside its high wall, the girls' playground is a world of its own; a world of hand-stands and Shirley Temple, and rhymes about willies eight feet long. In the classroom, us girls are called 'Barbara', or 'Julie', but the boys are called 'Clark', or 'Cooper', or 'Bell'. Still we sit girl-boy, girl-boy, in rough order of our success in tests; the best in the class sit at the front on the window side. You sit next to a boy, but you mustn't touch him. If you touch a boy, by mistake, or for a dare, you must 'pass it on' as if it's a contagious quality you can pick up and then get rid of. You wipe your hands on the nearest girl, and then she has to 'pass it on' herself.

This bad magic doesn't only belong to the boys. The two poorest girls in the class, who are also the ones who can't read and whose clothes are the tattiest, are untouchables too. We bump into them, accidentally-on-purpose, and rush away to 'wipe it off'. They are part of our walled-in girl-world, but we won't let them join in our games of skipping, two balls, five stones, or 'The Big Ship Sails Through the Alley-alley-oo'. There's no counter ritual, either, as there is between girls and boys at going-home time. That's when the kiss chases begin in the cloakrooms and the Underground tunnels, when you run and run and scream and scream. I don't want to get caught (unless it's by John Clark), but I want to be chased, because I want to be wanted, and thought pretty.

In the top class of primary school, I make friends with Anya, who keeps straw in an enamel bucket filled with water, because she wants to create pond life in her bedroom. Like me, she lives with her mother and her brother. Her father, who escaped from fighting for Hitler through a window, comes to visit on Sundays.

Anya and I draw and paint all day long whenever we can. We wander over the Heath barefoot looking for birds' nests, and are potty about Van Gogh and horses. She plays with the kids that live in my house and street, my 'home gang', where we scramble across other people's gardens and run away, or pelt each other with guinea pigs' droppings, and are tomboys (or try to be). We've got a gang at school, too, that has boys in it; we call them by their first names, on purpose. If we touch, we don't pass it on. There are no kiss chases. We don't care when other girls accuse us: 'You love X'. The six of us go climbing the walls behind Peter's Dad's pub, and dawdle the long way home from school by the willow trees.

But then we all go to different schools. Anya doesn't go to the new comprehensive school I choose to go to. She goes to a 'central' school, which comes between secondary modern and grammar. We go on being best friends for a year or so though, walking to our new schools together in all weathers over Parliament Hill, where still the tallest thing you can see when you look out over London is church spires, and cranes sticking up far away by the river.

I like my new school (though Granny complains: 'People won't know you got grammar'.) It's all girls, and what I like is the field at the back, and the tennis courts and the roses. *I think now, of the time before I came to Parli. as if I had lived in a dream — all my thoughts were shallow. I seemed to be blind to the good things of life, though I had great fun at that age*, I write at the end of my first year there. It has an old building from when it was a grammar school, and a new building in the modern style with lots of glass. A lot of teachers didn't want it to be a comprehensive (it's one of the first, and we're the first year), like the headmistress, who tells us to wear our berets and not push in bus queues and keep up the reputation of the school. I like all the glass; it makes you feel less cooped up.

You know it's comprehensive because it's so big and sometimes girls change streams without having to change schools if they're 'late developers'. The classes are according to how you did in the eleven-plus exam, and I'm in the top class. We mostly get the teachers who've been there a long time, like Miss Edington and Miss Saltmarsh and Miss Pollard. There aren't many married ones because then, Miss Edington tells us, like nurses, you had to choose between marriage and a career.

I make new friends at school, like Jud and Jan, and Sandra who is tall and has slanting eyes and lives near me. Like my Mum, her Mum and Dad are in the Communist Party, and she joins the Hampstead Socialist Sunday School, which I've joined because I want to go on the hikes they have once a month. *I'm longing for the hike tomorrow and Sunday. I don't believe in God. I just can't think anyone's looking after us anywhere. My mother is a communist, and I agree with it's point of view. Communism is for the worker, and against the people who make money from their toil. It's awfully good fun in the SSS (Socialist Sunday School). We do not only have talks on socialism, but they are very interesting.*

Our SSS was started last year, in 1956, so it's very new. It has a children's committee, and is less formal than the other schools, which have been going since the nineteenth century. Still, we keep up some of the old traditions at first, like the song you're supposed to sing at the beginning of each meeting. It's like a hymn, with words like 'joyous' and 'kindly', 'righteous' and 'hearts sincere'.

We get given a pink booklet ('Aims, Objects, and Organisation'), that has in it the main ideas and how meetings should be run and the Declaration which goes: 'We desire to be just and loving to all our fellow men and women, to work together as brothers and sisters, to be kind to every living creature and so help to form a New Society with Justice as its foundation and Love its Law.'

Also it has the ten Precepts, which have things in them about labour, and not despising other nations, and working for 'one fatherland' in which men and women will all be free citizens. 'Honour the good, be courteous to all, bow down to none.' There is one really good one that I like that says: 'Observe and think in order to discover the truth. Do not believe what is contrary to reason, and never deceive yourself or others.' (It doesn't tell you, though, how difficult all this is going to turn out to be.)

Some of the SSS grown-ups are in the Labour Party and some are in the Communist Party. They do different kinds of jobs, like working in Collett's Chinese Bookshop, and for the Moscow-Narodny Bank and the Soviet News Agency, Tass. Betty is a social worker in the East End, and Clare's Dad is a Labour MP. There's a railway worker, too, who is in the NUR, and a Hollywood film maker who's been blacklisted from working over there because of McCarthyite witch-hunting and 'reds under the beds'. There are non-parents, too, like Fiona who is in the Workers' Music Association: *she has a terrific bust, and her glasses seem extremely close to her face, but she is very nice*, and Marjory who is an actress and very 'volatile' (as my brother keeps saying since he started doing chemistry), and wears a false bun. The grown-ups have their own committee. They run things really, I suppose, but I remember it as a world of children.

My first year at school is strange and wild. I like school, but other things call stronger, especially in the summer when I start my diary; the long hot summer of 1957. The call of mud between bare toes. The call of poster paint, and Conte crayons, and clay. The call of the countryside ... *Victoria – huge and grey and ugly. Mummy said I was ungrateful to cry over coming back. David and her had not even been away. But they don't long for it like I do. When I grow up I shall never live in the town. I detest London with all my heart and with all my might!!!!!!*

I take a week off school (because I feel wobbly and keep crying all over the place) and spend hours on my bed drawing self-portraits from the dressing-table mirror. I play with the hamster Anya gave me for my birthday, the clay that Jud gave me, and the new plastic farm animals from Sandra. I'm also writing a story that has magic in it, and discussions of heaven and hell. Sandra does her homework in my room after school, and brings me library books. *It's funny to think that I was perfectly well in the country and so utterly unwell in London. In a week I seem to have grown a lot older. Hardly anything is solid – it's all whirling. (Only in my mind.) Mummy was very comforting and said my blood was wrong because of the Glandular Fever and that's why I'm miserable. When I'm lying down like this I can't see anything out of the window except miles and miles of deepest blue sky.*

Week after week I don't go to school. Officially I am suffering from the after-effects of glandular fever; privately I am suffering from 'home sickness'. 'Home', in mine and Anya's world, is the country, which I visited for five days with Sandra. It's everything unfettered and growing and free. If I'm ill enough, they'll have to send me 'home' to convalesce. And if you wish something hard enough, surely it will come true?

I paint wild women with strong faces and mad faces in big brush strokes, and sweet innocent-faced girls with shining hair; then I paint more wild women. One day Anya comes after school to cheer me up, and we do a picture together. *It was very bright with purple and green, red and yellow and white and dozens of queer mixtures, with the sea, a waterfall, sand, hills, the sun, the moon, and all alive!* After that I do a fountain in pale colours that's like Paradise, and Anya paints The

End of the World. I paint a bloodstained sea with staring eyes above it, and a black tree against a dismal sky. The pictures have a force of doom or evil about them, especially after Anya has gone; and I'm frightened to look again. My brother hides them at the bottom of a drawer, but I'm gripped in a storm of fear and sorrow I don't understand, and I sob and sob until Mum comes home about nine o'clock. She strokes my hair, and soothes the storm away. Later, when I'm in bed but not asleep, I swear I see a white horse flying into the sky, with a pale young man and young woman astride it, riding up and up and off and away ...

But the day comes when my blood test says normal and I have to go back to school and face the exams (for which I've done no work) and the discipline of 'the pips' that divide the day; the unmoveable fact of the world existing outside and beyond me.

Winter comes too, choked with fog, and bringing a bad kind of flu that everyone gets; a killer called Asian Flu. I stay in bed with it, feet wrapped in jumpers, head buried in *War and Peace*. Before she goes to work, Mum lights the old black paraffin stove and leaves a jar of honey by the bed (a creaking iron thing with a flock mattress that sags in the middle). When she comes home, she brings a pack of plastic playing cards as a treat – a sample from the trading company she works for. Granny says everything's getting to be plastic these days. She doesn't like it because it's not 'the real thing'. I agree with her, except where farm animals are concerned. Somehow, though, I don't play with my farm animals as much as I did last year.

I am growing up, and it is such a nice feeling, soon I'll be a woman! On Saturday Mummy bought me a brassière. It is rather big and I haven't worn it yet, but somehow it makes me feel grownup and different, even though otherwise it is rather a nuisance. Mummy says if you don't give your breasts support when you're young, they'll sag when you're old like the lady next door's, who props hers up on the windowsill.

I rush round to Sandra's house, and lift up my jumper to show. But she raises one eyebrow and is rather sniffy, as if to say: what's all the fuss about, you're not big enough yet. She isn't the only one who is sniffy though. *I am really a dreadful hypocrite. I lie on my hair every night in a certain way to make it look nice, and comb it in a wave with a wet comb (not that it makes any difference) and then I scorn Valerie*

Beezam's way of frizzing her hair, and when she said it had turned natural because her hair been washed and it stayed, I said to Sandra, 'she probably uses a wet comb', in a scornful tone. I'm sure Sandra would think me terrible if she knew.

Sandra is my idol and we see each other a lot, and do things together, like dressing up, or putting damp bread on a plate and waiting till things grow on it. We go to SSS meetings together too, but I have been elected on to the SSS committee (I'm chairman), and she hasn't. *I am rather embarrassed because I am the only girl on the committee, and there are 5 boys*, although there are more girls than boys in the club.

It's terrible, though, the fog we have this winter. It's yellow, and you have to put your scarf over your face or it chokes you. You can hardly see where the road is, or the next lampost, even in the day. It's called a 'smog', and it's because of pollution (our SSS is going to write a letter about it, to get the air cleaned up again), and it makes you feel trapped and closed in and think of the nineteenth century when the streets were hardly lit at all. *I have started writing a play about the terrible working conditions in the 19 hundreds.*

In Naples, we might as well not be living in civilized times the way the poor people live. And yet in other ways humanity is so advanced; the Sputnik, for instance, and being able to send up a dog in it.

I must tell you my views on the tiny amount of polotics that I know about. The Tories keep sending round ridiculous pamphlets telling dreadful lies. One said 'we don't want rationing again'. But of course food had to be rationed! Another thing is this terrible H-bomb. Russia wants to stop them, but if the other countries (England and America) don't, they will have nothing for defence or attack in case of war. Oh! that it will be destroyed by man, before man is destroyed by it!

Sandra and I have an awful quarrel about water pressure *and I have pangs of thinking I hate her. Jud and I are having a battle over Sandra.* Still, on Saturday mornings we go together to rehearse for the SSS Drama Festival. The play we're doing tells how at the end of the war children without parents roamed Europe in bands. Some made their way to special homes in Switzerland called 'Pestalozzi villages', after a man who thought children learn best if they do things for themselves. In our play the children arrive two by two, girl-boy, girl-boy, from all the Allied countries. But then a pair of German children arrive: will we let them in? We do in the end, after a lot of discussion amongst ourselves, and us shouting at the German kids, and them shouting back. An image from 'Pestalozzi' stays with me through the years – of children together without adults, organising things, quarrelling, fighting, looking after each other.

After rehearsing the play we practise verse speaking. We're standing in a row (I'm in between two boys), and I wonder if I've got B.O. I can't smell anything, but maybe the boys next to me can? I have very little to do with boys, except that recently John and Mark (who are on the committee) asked me to see *Robin Hood* at Unity Theatre. *It was a Panto, but with great political digs. There was Sheriff Mac (MacMillan) etc and a terrible arrow equal with the H-bomb.*

On the subject of boys, there's a bit in the play where I have to quarrel with John, and we catch each other's eye. His eyes are sparkly brown, with long lashes. Also, he has a crew cut, and is quiet. John and Mark are in the YLC (Young Communist League – I'm not old enough to join yet, but as soon as I'm old enough I will!) On his membership card it says: *'Man's dearest possession is life'. How true! To think – all the millions of cells and contrivances that collaborate together to form YOU – out of all the things you own those are the most valuable and priceless. And I have the power to make all this WORTHWHILE. To have a life which I can feel at the end was worth living. Worth the trouble my mother has had in bringing me up. I have all my life in front of me, it is up to ME to make my existence worth anything, and by heaven i'll try!*

I think Sandra was rather jealous about me going to Unity. I'm beginning to grumble and curse her, and I don't go into such ecstasies over her anymore. Jan has just been to tea, and I'm convinced I like her best. But suddenly Sandra's in a good mood again, and *silly me, i'm going to contradict what I told you yesterday and say that I like Sandra a tiny bit better than Jan after all. Why should I be attracted to her again? Last night I felt I could have given her up without a pang, and Jud could have her all her schooldays.*

Me and Sandra have a lot in common, like our likes and dislikes in politics, religion, literature and art. We have a long talk about all this one time on an SSS hike in Epping Forest, and discover something else we have in common: in nearly all our dreams, the boys are there.

At school the other girls get browned off with us talking about our 'little romances' all the time, but we have good fun in our 'set', like when we crawl under the desks all through Geography. I get sent to see the assistant headmistress. If I wasn't naughty, she says, the others wouldn't be: I should set a good example. My socks look like they're my father's, my hair looks like a bird's nest, and couldn't I bring my books to school in something better than a wartime gas-mask bag?

Mum is tired these days and worried about money. She was crying today because we are going to be moved from this house very soon. Mrs Grant from downstairs bet me two bob we will have to move out in two months. It's this damned Rent Act that will come into force. *Our rent will go up, and hundreds of people have already had notice to quit. So my brother thought of throwing a home-made bomb at Henry Brooke the housing minister's expensive house. This is not to murder anyone, but to frighten Tory home breaker Brooke. David once made a bomb which he did not know the strength of. He was too near and was almost deafened! This is what comes of mucking about with chemicals.* Once we had an idea to creep into Buckingham Palace and kill all the Royal Family, so that then there would be a republic, which is fairer. It was just an idea, though, and I don't agree with it now. Talking of fairness, *why in this country do men get more money for the same job than women? I think this is bad.*

There's a wall on the way to school, where it was written: 'Get Out Communists!' Me and Sandra crossed out 'Communists' and put 'Tories' and then: 'NO U.S. BASES HERE'. Lots of people don't like Communists. They say the word with a sneer, as if it means something evil, or dirty, and say things like: 'Better dead than red.' You can lose your job if you are one, and there were the Rosenbergs, too, that were killed by the electric chair in America, where it's worse than here.

It may not sound much – politics – but it is your view of life, not just a vague thing going on in the house of commons and the newspaper that is difficult to get worked up about because it seems so remote, and seems always to happen in other countries, though really it doesn't only. It is difficult to keep up a very strong warm friendship when you and your friend are of completely different opinions of life in that you and your friend can never have a satisfying talk in which it is satisfying when you realize you are right and your friend agrees which is comforting.

I'm having guitar lessons at school, but instead of practising scales I pick out the tune of 'The Red Flag' (which I know off by heart, all six verses), or dream about being in a skiffle group, with Mrs Miller's Michael on Mum's washboard, and my brother on broomhandle bass. I like pop songs too, but some girls go crazy over pop stars, and I think that's stupid. My brother has got some Elvis records, like 'Blue Suede Shoes', and also a crazy one by Little Richard. It's wild and it's rock and roll.

'Last night I had the strangest dream / I've ever dreamed before / I dreamed the world had all agreed / To put an end to war' sings a tall American girl with a pony tail and bright blue stockings (she turns out to be Pete Seeger's sister Peggy), as we wind along between hedges and fields. It's Easter 1958, and *a four-day march is in progress. It is a protest march to Aldermaston against the terrible H-bomb.* Mummy won't let me go all four days – she says I'm not old enough yet. It's not fair. But I go for two days, and I love every minute of it. I see John one time when we stop for a break; he's with the YCL, standing next to the trad jazz band where people are jiving, looking a bit lost. *He smiled and came over tho' I hadn't much to say or anything and I just kept rolling the Challenge* (YCL paper) *up and down in my pocket.*

I don't even tell my diary just how much I'm beginning to think and dream about John. He asks me to see a play at Unity, and calls round to sell *The Young Socialist* – surely he likes me too? It's hard to know when *boys and girls hardly ever exchange a word, let alone an intimate one.*

There's an expresso bar that's opened up called 'The Loft'. It's in one of the cobbled mews nearby (once the home of horses and grooms for the big houses, now full of broken-down cars) and I start to go there with other SSS girls, hoping to meet the boys. *The low ceiling was draped with dark fish net, and among that, orange lights glowed. A man was playing the guitar.* We sit at black tables drinking orange squash, waiting for footsteps on the stairs.

Another coffee bar has opened up, too, in the village (where the fishmongers used to be), called 'The Witches Cauldron'. You can go in and order one plate of spaghetti between six; they just bring you six forks. Spaghetti is a big joke, because nobody knows properly how to eat it. There are other changes in the village, like the double-fronted chemist's that had big bottles of coloured water in the windows – red and blue, with glass stoppers – is a Do-It-Yourself shop now. The delicatessen's still the same, though, with its barrels of gefüllte fish and gherkins, and heart-shaped gingerbread covered in chocolate, and a rich mixed smell of everything. (In 1984 the 'deli' is an open-plan magazine shop. The Express Dairy is a boutique, and the DIY shop sells tandoori chicken.)

There aren't any local supermarkets yet. On Saturdays I go with Mum to the market in Camden Town, and the Co-op department store they have there. For cheese we go to Sainsbury's on Haverstock Hill, a small shop with beautiful old tiles where the women wear muslin round their hair and cut the cheese with a wire. You have to wait ages, though, to be served, so I stand in the queue while Mum does other shopping. We kiss when she goes, and we kiss when she comes back, too. We're always kissing. Sometimes she buys something new or special, like strudel pastry, and she enjoys buying me things that are about beginning to be a woman, like nylon stockings. As I get older, though, I don't want to spend Saturdays with her any more. It gets tiresome, and I feel sulky. *Mummy thinks I am very moody and hoity-toity, but she treats me as if I'm so young.*

I want to tell you that i've changed my mind about wanting to be a boy, and I think I wrote a lot of rubbish at the front. Of course then I was very un-mature. Anyway, now I have periods, and my bust is the same size as mummy's.

In the summer of 1958 there's a bus strike that lasts for weeks and weeks. It means the boys have to walk to school, like we do, and we meet them – by accident at first, then by design.

We go to the running track a lot, to practise for the SSS Sports Festival. Sometimes I know John's going to be there, and sometimes I don't. But I find out that he likes me best! The days become the days between seeing him.

Sandra, too, says she likes me best; *We really love each other now. We can voice our feelings and usually they are the same.* When she came to tea we looked up in a book about the signs of the zodiac. *Jesus Christ is Aquarius – 'plodding, painstaking, apt to look on the gloomy side and brood over fancied slights.'*

I think about religion a lot. What you believe is so important. But sometimes you can't be sure what you believe, like with *Peter Manuel, who is to be hung for 7 murders in 16 months. There is a struggle in my mind, do I think he should he hanged? Even for 7 murders, should his life be taken?*

In *The British Road to Socialism* (I've read it all the way through, and I couldn't agree more with its aims, which are for everyone's good, and all its ideas and policy), it says how the communists will abolish capital punishment when they take power in England. It will be different from in Russia, where they have just executed the former Hungarian Prime Minister. I go to a Labour meeting which gets heckled by the communists, *with people shouting about the British's mass murders in Korea and Cyprus, the bloody massacre of over a thousand, and then they protest at one. I also think he should not have been executed, but England's murders are ghastly in comparison.*

We talk about hanging in school, too. In the autumn we have a debate in the History lesson. *Lots of people in the class disagreed with me that capital punishment should be abolished. Also, many girls thought that the amount of coloured people coming into this country should be restricted.* Only two girls in the class believe what I do: Suzanne (Jewish), and Andrea (devout Christian). 'One thousand and nine hundred years ago, Christ taught all men to be brothers,' says Andrea earnestly. *Why can't everyone go from country to country as they please? England doesn't belong to the English, it belongs to the world.*

The colour bar bothers me more than the thing about hanging, especially in South Africa where *all whites and blacks must now be separated, even if they are married! (Whites may not even speak friendlily to a negro.) It is called the 'Apartheid'.*

After the History lesson debate I'm bitter and upset with my friends. *Recently there has been some indecision within myself, as to whether Communism is really too extreme or not, though I felt Labour was really too weak and undecided in policy, but now I am decided. During History we talked about politics, and Jud and Jan scoffed at Communism –*

and it hurt me, I knew I really believed in it, I couldn't bear them to scoff at my ideals and principles – they didn't even know what they were talking about. John is my ideal, he believes in what I believe in, and I love him as my dearest friend.

But am I in love with him? At the beginning of the summer, *I'm sure I'd know if I was really in love, and don't think I am now*. I remember it as a turquoise, sunlit summer, the summer when I became known as John's girl; full of swimming-pool water with bendy light patterns on it. One time, after an SSS meeting, *the boys asked the girls to go swimming but mummy wouldn't let me. How bitter and indignant I was, and even now I am so sad. At this moment they are in the lovely turquoise water* and Jud is probably talking to John. The people charged of High Treason by breaking Apartheid, that I mentioned before, are still in prison. *The sentences they might receive, vary from one year to death. And yet life in Hampstead is just the same. The cars and the people go by, and the sun streams in at the windows, casting a peaceful glance at a Stefanie whose heart is rebelling at the injustice of the white Parliament in South Africa, and the fussiness and beastliness of mothers.*

There's a really big crowd of us now. As well as me and Sandra, Jan and Jud, there's Jane and Clare and Laura, and lots of other girls. Not only are the boys in the minority, but there are only four that have girls crazy over them, and they have about three girls each. It's a drifting, shifting crowd, connected with the SSS, Forest School Camps (that we go to in summer) and our various schools. We start having 'socials' at people's houses, where we play chess and pontoon and learn to jive to trad jazz.

John lives in the flat we used to live in when I was small. At first I call on him with Sandra on various pretexts. Then, when I don't seem to see much of Sandra anymore – *how fickle is love and friendship!* – I call on him alone, despite its being a boy's job to call, not the girl's. We sit on his bed and talk about committee meetings and whether your mind exists or not (he thinks it doesn't), and he puts his arm round me, in the attic room that was once my father's studio, and where my mother used to listen to the bombs over in France while drying her hair. We haven't kissed though. *No girl has ever been kissed yet in our SSS – it's a sort of sacred thing really. That John will ever kiss me is something to be hoped and hoped for, dreamed and dreamed about.* Will it ever happen?

Nowadays all I write about in this diary is boys boys boys. I had better change the subject. I wonder if World War III is on the way, it certainly seems like it, doesn't it? The future is like a great gloomy cloud looming ahead that will swallow us up. It could be Formosa, it could be the Lebanon or Berlin, the flash-point that ignites it all. *But before the end, there will be a lovely world, in a socialist society, where everyone* **wants** *socialism and everyone is happy.*

So many millions of things happen this summer. There's camp, which is wonderful, with wood fires, and cocoa at night. I go to Devon with Sandra, where we play jacks and two-balls and have moods and write our diaries in the bath together (in fits of laughter), and our own women's magazine stories. More and more, though, I feel a new kind of loneliness, even when I'm with my friends. Nothing stops it, or the new boredom, except being with John, or dreaming about him. After the holiday I drift away from Sandra, and the other girls in our class. *Sometimes I feel sad I haven't an especial friend, but not very, because I like John best.*

It's at the leaflet-dishing that my dreams come true. The leaflets are anti-Rent Act, and we dish them out in exchange for supper. Afterwards John takes me home, *and he kissed me on the lips! And then he sort of cleared his throat cos he was embarassed, and went, and I'm so happy. He had no jumper or anything just a short sleeved shirt, and oh, I love him!*

Mummy has started teaching typing in a school. She seems tireder than when she was working in an office, and the pay is not so good because it's two part-time jobs.

We have arguments about everything, like housework, and what time I come in. Still, she buys me a duffle coat, some colourless nail varnish – and a pair of black stockings. I've got a big beatnik jumper too, and tight jeans that I've taken in at the seams. I'm nervous of being stared at, but I'm proud of living round here, where lots of people aren't ordinary; *in Hampstead one sees bohemian women, with tight slacks, large bottoms, striped tops with plunging necklines, and piles of straggling hair.*

Still, there are things you just don't do. There's a girl at school who's only thirteen like me, and who's six months pregnant! *It's horrible to think of the sexiness that goes on between boys and girls of only 12 and 13. The girls are physically mature but not mentally, they like it when the boys take off their brassières and give them love bites. Half of them will turn out prostitutes probably, or have a family of bastards. Is this society's fault? Mummy thinks all this will be solved under socialism – I sure hope so!*

But then *in Art we drew Jan, and I had a funny kind of feeling. She was sitting there all complete. And it looked nice to see her pink petticoat underneath the skirt because it reminded you of things that are young and pretty, and some boy would find out one day that Jan was made to be hugged and kissed.*

We win the Music Festival again. *'It makes me proud to see Socialist children doing as well as anyone else,'* says Jack Allen when he presents the banner. I'm happy, with my duffle coat and black stockings, the applause I get for my song, and my boyfriend sitting next to me; *when I forgot the banner I just dumped everything in his arms.*

But then it all changes, quite suddenly, in the New Year of 1959. There's something different about the way he looks at me, and I know his feelings have changed, though I don't know why.

Nothing is said between us. He's always friendly. We do things together. People tell me I'm still John's girl. But I know, and he knows. For months life is aching and grey, and I think of little else. *What use is geometry when all I want to know is how he feels about me?* Sometimes it feels like he'll come back to me, like the weekend in a tent by the river, where we kiss all night, and I wouldn't mind how far he goes. I get swept up by strong new feelings that change very fast, from 'utter melancholy' to 'an ecstatic joy of everything existing' – like the kitchen table, or lighted windows in dark roofs at night. *I s'pose I'm just a crazy mixed up kid.*

Easter comes round again. This year the Aldermaston march is really big. I am allowed to go all four days, but I am miserable because there's a girl on the march that John obviously likes more than me. Still, I felt exultant *as we marched across Parliament Square, singing 'Glory glory what a hell of a way to die!'* There are so many of us: we're sure to win. *Cars along the march had their wirelesses on full blast so that we could hear the boat race, and in the evening, the Atomic*

Blues was being played over the loudspeaker: 'Hiroshima, Nagasaki, Alamagordo, Bikini …'

One night in high summer, I'm lying in John's arms. It's a three-day hike; some of the boys have invited girls to be with them for the evening. We've hardly begun to kiss when he tells me, kindly: 'finita'. The next night, the boys ask different girls. Back at the Youth Hostel, the girls' dormitory is full of the sound of crying.

In my diary I write a heading in capitals. *THE DISSOLUSION-MENT. Are all boys like this? Do they think of girls as being humans too?* It's the last straw. We didn't protest at private socials to which girls were 'invited' (each one hoping she would be one of *'the select' as Tom says 'the elite' as David says 'the clique' as Mark says*); we allowed ourselves to be turned away from train carriages and outman-oeuvred in elections. But now the boys kiss girls they don't even pretend to love! This is a cardinal sin. The next heading in my diary is *THE SEGREGATION HIKE. We girls resolved we would no longer be treated like dishcloths, one a week, and decided to give the boys the brush off. It was called CSB. Campain for the Suppression of Boys, and it lasts all of one day.* On the way home, packed into our train carriage, we sing at the tops of our voices (hoping that they'll hear):

This story ain't got no moral
This story ain't got no end
Just goes to show
THERE AIN'T NO GOOD IN MEN

The diary carries on for a few more pages and peters out. *I won't bother to record events any more. Sorry for style an' all that, but I'm sure you don't care, 'cos I don't, and you're me indirectly.*

It's at about this time that the council gives us permanent accommodation at last, and we move to a nicely painted flat round the corner. Mum has a new job as a political secretary to a nice man, and is much happier. She buys us all divan beds and dunlopillo pillows. Also we get a cat, and a telephone!

I am fourteen years old now, and I try to sort out who I am and my position in life (it must be possible to sit down and work it out). I decide that *life isn't all 'jam and honey' as prophesied by an optimistic young heart, full of dreams of a fiction world* and conclude, once again, that growing up is like dying: *after the thrill of motherhood there's nothing new or exciting* ...

But then – *perhaps I should explain* – I write in September – *I am no longer crazy over John. Oh hell, perhaps I am. I still like him tremendously, but not so blindly, shutting out other things. My horizons widen as each new day dawns.*

At the beginning of 1960 I make ten New Year resolutions. Most of them are about working hard at school, helping Mum with housework, having baths and going to bed early. Here is resolution number five: *To read good books knit and sow as much as poss. Actively support CND, YCL etc and all peace demonstrations. YHA and as much country as poss. Learn to Ballroom dance.*

I feel unstable as if I am in a temporary period between falling over a brink into the future. There's what's behind me and what is now – and I can't make out now properly, and the future will suddenly happen and I will be a different me.

I washed 2 petticoats and sang and sang and sang.

I WAS educated at Leeds University and the London School of Economics. I have worked as a polytechnic lecturer, waitress, artists' model, gardener, writer and feminist therapist. I live in London, and have given up New Year resolutions.

My poetry, stories, drawings, reviews and songs have appeared in: *Licking the bed clean* (Teeth Imprints, 1978), *Smile smile smile smile* (Sheba Feminist Publishers, 1980), *One foot on the mountain* (Onlywomen Press, 1979), *Hard feelings* (Women's Press, 1979), *Bread and roses* (Virago, 1982), *Apples and Snakes* (Pluto Press, 1984), *Spare Rib*, *Big Bang*, *City Limits*, *Gallery*, and *New Songs New Times* (Hackney and Islington Music Workshop)

*

Special thanks to Nadine Cartner whose humorous acceptance of the girl I once was helped me select from the diaries and shape a wood from the trees. Thanks also to Hilary Arnott, Jocylyne May and the adults and children of the Hampstead Socialist Sunday School circa 1957–59.

Carolyn Steedman

Landscape for a Good Woman

When I was three, before my sister was born, I had a dream. It remains quite clear across the years, the topography absolutely plain, so precise in details of dress that I can use them to place the dream in historical time. We were in a street, the street so wide and the houses so distant across the other side that it might not have been a street at all; and the houses lay low with gaps between them, so that the sky filled a large part of the picture. Here, at the front, on this side of the wide road, a woman hurried along, having crossed from the houses behind. The perspective of the dream must have shifted several times, for I saw her once as if from above, moving through a kind of square, or crossing place, and then again from the fixed point of the dream where I stood watching her, left forefront.

She wore the New Look, a coat of beige gaberdine which fell in two swaying, graceful pleats from her waist at the back (the swaying must have come from very high heels, but I didn't notice her shoes), a hat tipped forward from hair swept up. She hurried, something jerky about her movements, a titupping, agitated walk, glancing round at me as she moved across the foreground. Several times she turned and came some way back towards me, admonishing, shaking her finger. Encouraging me to follow in this way perhaps, but moving too fast for me to believe that she wanted me to do that, she entered a revolving door of dark polished wood, mahogany and glass, and started to go round and round, looking out at me as she turned. I wish I knew what she was doing, and what she wanted me to do.

This book is about childhood, a time when only the surroundings show, and nothing is explained. It is also about a period of recent history, the 1950s, and about the way in which those years shaped individual lives and collective ideas. But children do not possess a *social* analysis of what is happening to them, or around them, so the landscape and the pictures it presents have to remain a background, taking on meaning later, from different circumstances. Understanding of the dream built up in layers, over a long period of time. Its strange, lowered vista, for instance (which now reminds the adult more than anything else of George Herriman's *Krazy Kat*, where buildings disappear and reappear from frame to frame[1]) is an obvious representation of London in the late forties and fifties: all the houses had gaps in between, because of the bombs, and the sky came closer to the ground than seemed right. I understood what I had seen in the dream when I learned the words 'gaberdine' and 'mahogany'; and I was born in the year of the New Look, understood by 1951 and the birth of my sister, that dresses needing twenty yards for a skirt were items as expensive as children – more expensive really, because after 1948 babies came relatively cheap, on tides of free milk and orange juice, but good cloth in any quantity was hard to find for a very long time.

Detail like this provides retrospective labelling, but it is not evidence about a historical period. The only *evidence* from that dream is the feeling of childhood – all childhoods, probably: the puzzlement of the child watching from the pavement, wondering what's going on, what they, the adults are up to, what they want from you, and what they expect you to do.

Worked upon and reinterpreted, the landscape becomes an historical landscape, but only through continual and active reworking. 'The essence of the historical process,' says Tamara Hareven in *Family Time and Industrial Time*, is the meeting between an individual's or a group's life history and the historical moment. People's responses to the historical conditions they encounter are shaped both by the point in their lives at which they encounter those conditions and by the equipment they bring with them from earlier life experiences ...[2]

But children possess very little of that equipment, and in the process of acquiring it, the baggage is continually reorganised and reinterpreted. Memory simply can't resurrect those years, because it is memory itself that shapes them, long after the historical time has passed. So to present the decade through the filter of my parents' story, and my growing awareness of the odd typicality of my childhood, is the result of a decision to see the 1950s as a political moment when hope was promised, and then deferred. We rework past time to give current events meaning, and that reworking provides an understanding that the child at the time can't possess: it's only in the last few months that I've understood who the woman in the New Look coat was.

Now, later, I see the time of my childhood as a point between two worlds, an older 'during the war', 'before the war', 'in the Depression', 'then', and the place we inhabit now. The war was so palpable a presence in the first five years of my life that I still find it hard to believe that I didn't live through it. There were bombsites everywhere, prefabs on waste land, most things still rationed, my mother tearing up the ration book over my sister's pram outside the library in the High Road when meat came off points in the summer of 1951, a gesture that still fills me with the desire to do something so defiant and final; and then looking across the street at a woman wearing a full-skirted dress, and then down at the forties straight-skirted navy blue suit she was still wearing, and longing, irritatedly, for the New Look, and then at us, the two living barriers to twenty yards of cloth. Back home, she said, she'd be able to get it from the side door of the mill, but not here; not with you two ... I was three in 1950, only twelve when the decade ended, just a child, a repository for other people's history; and my mother gave me her version long before my father did.

By the time my father could sit down with me in a pub, slightly drunk, tell me and my friends about Real Life, crack a joke about a Pakistani that silenced a whole table once, and talk about the farm labourer's – his grandfather's – journey up from Eye in Suffolk working on the building of the Great North Western Railway to Rawtenstall on the Lancashire–Yorkshire border, I was doing history at Sussex, and knew more than he did about the date and timing of journeys like that. My father, old but gritty, glamorous in the eyes of the class of '68, a South London wide boy with an authentic background, described his grandfather's funeral, about 1912, when a whole other family, wife, children, grandchildren, turned up out of the blue from somewhere further down the line where they'd been established on the navvy's journey north. (This was a circumstance paralleled at his own funeral, when the friends and relations of the woman he'd been living with for part of the week since the early 1960s stole the show from us, the pathetic huddle of the family of his middle years.) My mother's story on the other hand was told to me much earlier, in bits and pieces throughout the fifties, and it wasn't delivered to entertain but rather to teach me lessons. There was a child, an eleven-year-old from a farm seven miles south of Coventry, sent off to be a maid-of-all-work in a parsonage in Burnley. She had her tin trunk, and she cried, waiting on the platform with her family seeing her off, for the through train to Manchester. They'd sent her fare, the people in Burnley; 'but think how she felt, such a little girl, she was only eleven, with nothing but her little tin box. Oh she did cry.' I cry now over accounts of childhood like this, weeping furtively over the reports of nineteenth-century commissions of inquiry into child labour, abandoning myself to the luxuriance of grief in libraries, tears staining the pages where Mayhew's little watercress girl tells her story. The lesson was, of course, that I must never, ever cry for myself, for I was a lucky little girl; my tears should be for all the strong, brave women who gave me life. This story, which embodied fierce resentment against the unfairness of things, was carried through seventy years and three generations, and all of them, all the good women, dissolved into the figure of my mother who was, as she told us, *a good mother*. She didn't go out drinking or

Post-war picnic, 1950, me and my mother

dancing; she didn't do as one mother she'd known (in a story of maternal neglect that I remember feeling was over the top at the time) and tie a piece of string round my big toe, dangle it through the window and down the front of the house, so that the drunken mother, returning from her carousing, could tug at it, wake the child, get the front door opened and send it down the shop for a basin of pie and peas. I still put myself to sleep by thinking about *not* lying on a cold pavement covered with newspapers. She must have told me once that I was lucky to have a warm bed to lie in at night.

What she did, in fact, the eleven-year-old who cried on Coventry station, was hate being a servant. She got out as soon as she could, and found work in the weaving sheds – 'she was a good weaver; six looms under her by the time she was sixteen' – marry, produce nine children, eight of whom emigrated to the cotton mills of Massachusetts before the First World War, managed, 'never went before the Guardians'.[3] It was much, much later that I learned from *One Hand Tied Behind Us* that four was the usual number of looms for a Lancashire weaver; Burnley weavers were not well organised, and my great-grandmother had six not because she was a good weaver but because she was exploited.[4] In 1916, when her daughter Carrie's husband was killed at the Somme, she managed that too, looking after the three-year-old, my mother, so that Carrie could go on working at the mill.

But long before the narrative fell into place, before I could dress the eleven-year-old of my imagination in the clothing of the 1870s, I knew perfectly well what that child had done, and how she had felt. She cried, because tears are cheap; and then she'd stopped, and got by, because nobody gives you anything in this world. What was given to her, passed on to all of us, was a powerful and terrible endurance, the self-destructive defiance of those doing the best they can with what life hands out to them.

From a cotton town, my mother had a heightened awareness of fabric and weave, and I can date events by the clothes I wore as a child, and the material they were made of. Post-war children had few clothes, because of rationing; but not only scarcity, rather names like barathea, worsted, gaberdine, twill, jersey … fix them in my mind. The dream of the New Look has to have taken place during or after the summer of 1950, because in it I wore one of my two summer dresses, one of green and one of blue gingham, that were made that year and that lasted me, with letting down, until I went to school. Sometime during 1950, I think before the summer, before the dresses were made, I was taken north to Burnley and into the sheds. My mother was visiting someone who worked there whom she'd known as a child. The woman smiled and nodded at me through the noise that made a surrounding silence. Later, my mother told me they had to lip read: they couldn't hear each other speak for the noise of the looms. But I didn't notice the noise. She wore high platform-soled black shoes that I still believe I heard click on the bright polished floor as she walked between her looms. When I hear the word 'tending' I think always of that confident attentiveness to the needs of the machines, the control over work that was unceasing, with half a mind and hands engaged but the looms always demanding attention. When I worked as a primary school teacher I sometimes retrieved that feeling with a particular clarity, walking between the tables on the hard floor, all the little looms working but needing my constant adjustment. The woman wore a dress that seemed very short when I recalled the picture through the next few years: broad shoulders, a straight skirt that hung the way it did – I know now – because it had some rayon in it. No New Look here in Burnley either. The post-war years were full of women longing for a full skirt and unable to make it. I wanted to walk like that, a short skirt, high heels, bright red lipstick, in charge of all that machinery.

It's extremely difficult for me to think of women as people who do not work; their work, moreover, is visible and comprehensible; they can explain, or show to children what they do and how – unlike men, whose process of getting money is mysterious and hidden from view. There's been recent reassessment of the traditional picture of the enforced flight from the labour force to domesticity on the part of women just after the war, and far from a flight, large-scale recruitment to the new industries in the early 1950s now seems to present a more historically accurate picture. It's probable that the memory of most children of our generation is of women as workers.[5] I had no awareness of the supposed stereotypical mother of that era – lipsticked and aproned, waiting at the door – and don't think I even encountered a picture of her, in books, comics or film, until the early 1960s.

As a teenage worker my mother had broken a recently established pattern. When she left school in 1927 she hadn't gone into the sheds. She lied to me, though, when I asked at about the age of eight what she'd done: she said she'd worked in an office, done clerical work. Ten years later, on a visit to Burnley and practising the skills of the oral historian, I talked to my grandmother, and she, puzzled, told me that Edna had never worked in any office, had in fact been apprenticed to a dry cleaning firm that did tailoring and mending. On the same visit, the first since my early childhood, I found a reference written by a local doctor for my mother, who about 1930 applied for a job as a ward maid at the local asylum, confirming that she was clean, strong, honest and intelligent. I wept over that of course, for a world where some people might doubt her – my – cleanliness. I didn't care much about the honesty, and I knew I was strong; but there are people everywhere waiting for you to slip up, to show signs of dirtiness and stupidity, so that they can send you back where you belong.

She didn't finish her apprenticeship – I deduce that, rather than know it – sometime, it must have been in 1934, came south, worked in Woolworths on the Edgware Road, spent the war years in Roehampton, a ward maid again, at the hospital where they mended fighter pilots' ruined faces. Now I can feel the deliberate vagueness in her accounts of those years: 'Where did you meet Daddy?' 'Oh, at a dance, at home.' There were no photographs. Who came to London first? I wish now I'd asked that question. He worked on the buses when he arrived, showed me a canopy in front of a hotel that he'd brought down on his first solo drive. He was too old to be called up (a lost generation of men who were too young for the first war, too old for the second). There's a photograph of him standing in front of the cabbages that he'd grown for victory wearing his Home Guard uniform. But what did he *do*? Too late to find out.

During the post-war housing shortage my father got an office job with a property company, and the flat that went with it. I was born in March 1947, at the peak of the Bulge: more babies born that month than ever before or after, and carried through the terrible winter of 1946–47. We moved to Streatham Hill in June 1951, to an estate owned by the same company, later to be taken over by Lambeth Council. A few years later, my father got what he wanted, which was to be in charge of the company's boiler maintenance. On his death certificate it says 'heating engineer'.

In the 1950s my mother took in lodgers. Streatham Hill Theatre (now a bingo hall) was on the pre-West End circuit, and we had chorus girls staying with us for weeks at a time. I was woken up in the night sometimes, the spare bed in my room being made up for someone they'd met down the Club, the other lodger's room already occupied. I like the idea of being the daughter of a theatrical landlady, but this enterprise provides my most startling and problematic memories. Did the girl from Aberdeen really say, 'Och, no, not on the table!' as my father flattened a bluebottle with his hand, and did he *really* put down a newspaper on the same table to eat his breakfast? I feel a fraud, a bit-part player in a soft and southern version of *The Road To Wigan Pier*.

I remember incidents like these, I think, because I was about seven, the age at which children start to notice social detail and social distinction, but also more particularly because the long lesson in hatred for my father had begun, and the early stages were in the traditional mode, to be found in the opening chapters of *Sons and Lovers* and Lawrence's description of the inculcated dislike of Mr Morrell, of female loathing for coarse male habits. The newspaper on the table is problematic for me because it was problematic for my mother, a symbol of all she'd hoped to escape and all she'd landed herself in. (It was at this time, I think, that she told me that her own mother, means-tested in the late twenties, had won the sympathy of the relieving officer, who ignored the presence of the saleable piano because she kept a clean house, with a cloth on the table.)

Now, thirty years later, I feel a great regret for the father of my first four years, who took me out, and who probably loved me, irresponsibly ('it's all right for him; he doesn't have to look after you'), and I wish I could tell him now, even though he was, in my sister's words, a sod, that I'm sorry for my years of rejection and dislike. But we had to choose, early on, which side we belonged to, and children have to come down on the side that brings the food home and gets it on the table. By 1955 I was beginning to hate him – because *he* was to blame, for the lack of money, for my mother's terrible dissatisfaction at the way things were working out.

The new consumer goods came into the household slowly – because of *him*. We had the first fridge in our section of the street (he got it cheap – contacts) but were late to get a television. The vacuum cleaner was welcomed at first because it meant no longer having to do the stairs with a stiff brush. But in fact it added to my Saturday work because I was expected to clean more with the new machine. I enjoy shocking people by describing how goods were introduced into households under the guise of gifts for children: the fridge in the house of the children we played with over the road was given to the youngest as a birthday present – the last thing an eight-year-old wants. My mother laughed at this, scornfully; but in fact she gave us Christmas and birthday presents of clothes and shoes, and the record player came into the house in this way, as my eleventh birthday present. But I wasn't allowed to take it with me when I left; it wasn't really mine at all.

I remember walking up the hill from school with my mother after an open day, and asking her what class we were; or rather, I asked her if we were middle class, and she was evasive. She was smiling a pleased smile, and working things out; I think it must have been the afternoon (the only time she visited my primary school) she was told that I'd be going into the eleven-plus class and so (because everyone in the class passed the exam) would be going to grammar school. I was working out well, an investment with the promise of paying out. I answered my own question, and said that I thought we must be middle class, and reflected very precisely in that moment on my mother's black waisted coat with the astrakhan collar, and her high-heeled black suede shoes, her lipstick. She *looked* so much better than the fat, spreading South London mothers around us, that I thought we had to be middle class.

The coat and the lipstick came from her own work. 'If you want something, you have to go out and work for it. Nobody gives you anything; nothing comes free in this world.' About 1956 or 1957 she got an evening job in one of the espresso bars opening along the High Road, making sandwiches and frying eggs. She saved up enough money to take a manicuring course and in 1958 got her diploma, thus achieving a certified skill for the first time in her forty-five years. When I registered her death I was surpised to find myself giving this as her trade, because learned history implies that only the traditional ones – tailoring, weaving, joining, welding – are real. She always worked in good places, in the West End; the hands she did were in *Vogue* once. She came home with stories and imitations of her 'ladies'. When I was about twelve she told me how she'd 'flung' a sixpenny piece back at a titled woman who'd given it her as a tip: 'If you can't afford any more than that Madam, I suggest you keep it.' Wonderful! – like tearing up the ration books. From her job, supported by the magazines she brought home, and her older skill of tailoring and dressmaking, we learned how the goods of the earth might be appropriated, with a certain voice, the cut and fall of a skirt, a good winter coat; with leather shoes too, but above all by clothes, the best boundary between you and a cold world.

We weren't, I now realise by doing the sums, badly off. My father paid the rent, all the bills, gave us our pocket money, and a fixed sum of £7 a week housekeeping money – quite a lot in the late 1950s – went on being handed over every Friday until his death, even when estrangement was obvious, and he was living most of the time with someone else. My mother must have made quite big money in tips, for the records of her savings, no longer a secret, show quite fabulous sums being stored away in the early sixties. Poverty hovered as a belief. It existed in stories of the thirties, in a family history. Even now when a bank statement comes that shows I'm overdrawn, or the gas bill for the central heating seems enormous, my mind turns to quite inappropriate strategies, like boiling down the ends of soap, and lighting fires with candle ends and spills of screwed-up newspaper to save buying wood. I think about these things because they were domestic economies that we practised in the 1950s. We believed we were poor because we children were expensive items, and all the arrangements had been made for us. 'If it wasn't for you two,' my mother told us, 'I could be off somewhere else.' After going out manicuring she started spending Sunday afternoons in bed and we couldn't stay in the house nor play on the doorstep for fear of disturbing her. The house was full of her terrible tiredness, her terrible resentment; and I knew it was all my fault.

When I came across Kathleen Woodward's *Jipping Street*[6] I read it with the shocked amazement of one who had never seen what she knew written down before. Kathleen Woodward's mother of the 1890s was the one I knew: mothers were people who told you how long they were in labour with you, how much you hurt, how hard it was to have you ('twenty hours with you,' my mother frequently reminded me) and who told you to accept the impossible contradiction of being both desired and being a burden, and not to complain. This ungiving endurance is admired by working-class boys who grow up to write about their mothers' flinty courage. But the daughter's silence on this matter is a measure of the price you have to pay for survival. I don't think the baggage will ever lighten, for me or my sister. We were born, and had no choice in that matter; but we were burdens, expensive, never grateful enough. There was nothing we could do to pay back the debt of our existence. 'Never have children, dear,' she said. 'They ruin your life.'

Later, in 1977 after my father's death, we found out that they were never married, that we were illegitimate. In 1934 my father left his wife and two-year-old daughter in the north, and came to London. He and my mother had been together for at least ten years when I was born, and we think now that I was her hostage to fortune, the factor that might persuade him to get a divorce and marry her. But the ploy failed.

Just before my mother's death, playing around with the photographs on the bedroom mantelpiece, my niece discovered an old photograph underneath one of me at three. A woman holds a tiny baby. It's the early 1930s, a picture of the half-sister, left behind. But I think I knew about her and her mother long before I looked them both in the face, or heard about their existence; knew that the half-understood adult conversations around me, the quarrels about 'her', the litany of 'she', 'she', 'she' from behind closed doors made the figure in the New Look coat, hurrying away, wearing the clothes my mother wanted to wear, angry with me yet nervously inviting me to follow, caught finally in the revolving door. We have proper birth certificates, because my mother must have told a simple lie to the registrar, a discovery about the verisimilitude of documents that worries me a lot as a historian.

In 1954 *The Pirates of Penzance* was playing at the Streatham Hill Theatre, and we had one of the baritones as a lodger instead of the usual girls. He was different from them, didn't eat in the kitchen with us, but had my mother bake him potatoes and grate carrots that he ate in the isolation of the dining room. He converted my mother to Food Reform, and when she made a salad of grated vegetables for Christmas dinner in 1955, my father walked out and I wish he'd taken us with him.

I've talked to other people whose mothers came to naturopathy in the fifties, and it's been explained as a way of eating posh for those who don't know about Continental food. I think it did have a lot to do with the status that being different conferred, for in spite of the austerity of our childhood, we believed that we were better than other people, the food we ate being a mark of this, because our mother told us so – so successfully that even now I have to work hard at actually seeing the deprivations. But more than difference, our diet was to do with the desperate need, wrenched from restricted circumstances, to be in charge of the body. Food Reform promised an end to sickness if certain procedures were followed, a promise that was not, of course, fulfilled. I spent a childhood afraid to fall ill, because being ill meant my mother had to stay off work, and lose money.

But more than this, I think a precise though unconscious costing of our childhood lay behind our eating habits. Brussels sprouts, baked potatoes, grated cheese, the variation of vegetables in the summer, a tin of vegetarian steak pudding on Sundays and a piece of fruit afterwards is a monotonous but healthy diet, and I can't think of many cheaper ways to feed two children and feel you're doing your best for them at the same time. My mother brought the food home at night, buying it each day when she got off the bus from work. My sister's job was to meet her at the bus stop with the wheel basket so she didn't have to carry it up the road. We ate a day's supply at a time, so there was never anything much in the house overnight except bread for breakfast and the staples that were bought on Saturday. When I started to think about these things I was in a position to interpret this way of living and eating as a variation on the spending patterns of poverty described in Booth's and Rowntree's surveys; but now I think it was the cheapness of it that propelled the practice. We were a finely balanced investment, threatening constantly to topple over into the realms of demand and expenditure. I don't think, though, that until we left home, we ever cost more to feed and clothe than that £7 handed over each week.

Now I see the pattern of our nourishment laid down like our usefulness, by an old set of rules. At six I was old enough to go on errands, at seven to go further to pay the rent and rates, make the long, dreary trip to the Co-op for the divi. By eight I was old enough to clean the house and do the weekend shopping. At eleven it was understood that I washed the breakfast things and scrubbed the kitchen floor before I started my homework. At fifteen, when I could legally go out to work, I got a Saturday job which paid for my clothes (except my school uniform, which was part of the deal, somehow). I think that until I drop I will clean wherever I happen to be on Saturday morning. I take a furtive and secret pride in the fact that I can do all these things, that I am physically strong, can lift and carry things that defeat other women, wonder with some scorn what it must be like to have to learn to clean a house when adult, not have the ability laid down as part of the growing self. Like going to sleep by contrasting a bed with a pavement, I sometimes find myself thinking that if the worst comes to the worst I can always earn a living by my hands; I can scrub, clean, cook and sew; all you have in the end is your labour.

I was a better investment than my sister, because I passed the eleven-plus, went to grammar school, would get a good job (university was later seen to offer the same arena of advantages), marry a man who would, as she said, buy 'me a house, and you a house. There's no virtue in poverty.' The dreary curtailment of our childhood was, we discovered after my mother's death, the result of the most fantastic saving – for a house, a dream house that was never bought. When I was about seventeen I learned that V.S. Naipaul wrote *A House for Mr Biswas* in Streatham Hill.[7] I think of the poetic neatness of the novel about the compulsive, enduring desire for a house of one's own being composed only a few streets away from where someone with infinitely fewer resources tried to mobilise the same dream. It was at least an important dream, a literary dream, that dictated the pattern of our days.

It seems now a joyless childhood. My sister reminds me of our isolation, the neighbours who fed us meat and sweets, the tea parties we went out to but which we were never allowed to return. I remember the awful depression of Sunday afternoons, my mother with a migraine in the front bedroom, the house an absolute stillness. But I don't *remember* the oddness; it's a reconstruction. What I recall is what I read, and my playing Annie Oakley by myself all summer afternoon at the recreation ground, running up and down the hill in my brown gingham dress, wearing a cowboy hat and carrying a rifle. Saturday morning pictures provided confirming images of women who not only worked hard, earned a living, but who carried a gun into the bargain.

The essence of being a good child is taking on the perspective of those who are more powerful than you, and I was good in this way as my sister never was. A house up the road, Sunday afternoon about 1958, plates of roast lamb offered. My sister ate, but I refused, not out of sacrifice nor because I was resisting temptation (I firmly believed that meat would make me ill, as my mother said), but because I knew – though this formulation is the adult's rather than the ten-year-old's – that the price of the meal was condemnation of my mother's oddness, and I wasn't having that. If people give you things, they should give freely, extracting nothing in return. I was a very upright child. At eight I had my first migraine (I could not please her, I might as well join her; they stopped soon after I left home), and I started to get rapidly and relentlessly short-sighted. I literally stopped seeing for a very long time.

School taught me how to read early, and I found out for myself how to do it fast. I read all the time, rapidly and voraciously. You couldn't join the library until you were seven, and before that I read my Hans Christian Anderson back to front when I'd read it twenty times from start to finish. Kay was the name that I was called at home, my middle name, one of my father's names, and I knew that Kay, the boy in *The Snow Queen*, was me, who had a lump of ice in her heart. I knew that one day I might be asked to walk on the edge of knives like the little mermaid, and was afraid that I might not be able to bear the pain. Foxe's *Book of Martyrs* was in the old library, a one-volume edition for nineteenth-century children with coloured illustrations and the text pruned to a litany of death by flame. My imagination was furnished with the passionate martyrdom of the Protestant north.

I see now the relentless laying down of guilt, and I feel a faint surprise that I must interpret it that way. My sister, younger than me, with children of her own and perhaps thereby with a clearer measure of what we lacked, reminds me of a mother who never played with us, whose eruptions from irritation into violence were the most terrifying of experiences, and she is there, the figure of

117

nightmares, though I do find it difficult to think about in this way. My mind turns instead to the communality of this experience, of all those post-war babies competently handled but generally left alone, down the bottom of the garden in their prams, in the fresh air and out of the way. Expectations of childhood and ways of treating babies changed rapidly in the 1950s, and perhaps the difference in perception between me and my sister is no more than four years' difference in age, and a reflection of a change in expectation on the part of children themselves, learned from the altered practice of adults around. Against this learned account, I have to weigh what it felt like at the time, and the message of the history that was delivered up to me in small doses: that not being hungry and having a bed to sleep in at night, we had a good childhood, were better than other people, were *lucky* little girls.

My mother had wanted to marry a king. That was the best of my father's stories, told in the pub in the 1960s, of how difficult it had been to live with her in 1937, during the Abdication months. Mrs Simpson was no prettier than her, no more clever than her, no better than her. It wasn't fair that a king should give up his throne for her, and not for the weaver's daughter. From a traditional Labour background, my mother rejected the politics of solidarity and communality, always voted Conservative, for the left could not embody her desire for things to be *really* fair, for a full skirt that took twenty yards of cloth, for a half-timbered cottage in the country, for the prince who did not come. My childhood was the place where, for my mother, the fairy tales failed, and through the glass of that childhood I now see that failure as part of a longer and more enduring one.

The 1950s was a period when state intervention in childhood was highly visible. The calculated, dictated fairness that the ration book represented went on into the new decade, and when we moved from Hammersmith to Streatham Hill in 1951 there were medicine bottles of orange juice and jars of Virol to pick up from the baby clinic for my sister. This overt intervention in our lives was experienced by me as entirely beneficent, so I find it difficult to match an analysis of the welfare policies of the late forties which calls 'the post-war Labour government ... the last and most glorious flowering of late Victorian liberal philanthropy',[8] which I know to be correct, with the sense of self that those policies imparted. If it had been only philanthropy, would it have felt like it did? I think I would be a very different person now if orange juice and milk and dinners at school hadn't told me, in a covert way, that I had a right to exist, was worth something.

My inheritance from those years is the belief, maintained with some difficulty, that I do have a right to the earth. I think that had I grown up with my parents only twenty years before, I would not now believe this. For I was also an episode in someone else's narrative, not my own person, my mother's child, and brought into being for a particular purpose. Being a child when the state was publicly engaged in making children healthy and literate was a support against my particular circumstances, its central benefit being that, unlike my mother, the state asked for nothing in return. Psychic structures are shaped by these huge historical labels: 'charity', 'philanthropy', 'state intervention'.

It was a considerable achievement for a society to pour so much milk, so much orange juice, so many vitamins down the throats of its children, for the height and weight of those children to outstrip so fast the measurements of only a decade before. But the 1950s divided people from each other; large-scale benevolence maintained individualism, and reveals its basis in the philanthropy described above. The statistics of healthy and intelligent childhood were stretched out along the curve of achievement, and only some were allowed to travel through the narrow gate at eleven, towards the golden city. This particular political failure of the post-war welfare policies, to provide equality and not just the opportunity for individual achievement, was set in its turn against the dislocation that my mother's 1950s represent: welfarism in one country did not embody the desire people felt for the world that had shaped them.

From a current vantage point I see my childhood as evidence that can be used. I think it's particularly useful as a way of gaining entry to ideas about childhood – what children are *for*, why to have them – that aren't written about in the official records, that is, in the textbooks of child analysis and child psychology, and in sociological descriptions of childhood. This public assertion of my childhood's usefulness stands side by side with the painful personal knowledge, I think the knowledge of all of us, going as far back as the story lets us, that it would have been better if it hadn't happened that way, hadn't happened at all.

People said at the time that the war had been fought for the children, for a better future, and the 1950s represent a watershed in the historical process by which children have come to be thought of as repositories of hope, and objects of desire. Accounts like Jeremy Seabrook's in *Working Class Childhood* see in the material affection displayed towards children of our and more recent generations, the roots of a political failure on the part of the Labour movement to confront the inculcated desires of the market place. 'Instead of the children of the working class being subjected to rigorous self-denial in preparation for a life-time in mill or mine,' he writes, 'they have been offered instead the promise of the easy and immediate gratification which, in the end, can sabotage human development and achievement just as effectively as the poverty and hunger of the past.'[9] There hovers in *Working Class Childhood* the ghostly presence of more decent and upright children, serving their time in the restriction of poverty and family solidarity: 'the old defensive culture of poverty gave working class children ... a sense of security which is denied the present generation ...'[10]

But in this sterner, older world, the iron entered into the children's soul, and many of them had to learn that being alive ought simply to be enough, a gift that must be ultimately paid for. Under conditions of material poverty the cost of most childhoods has been most precisely reckoned, and only life has been given freely. (One of the least attractive features of *Working Class Childhood* is its denial of the evidence it presents, its interpretations of people's consciousness of grim childhoods in terms of regret and loss.) After that initial investment, no one gave me and my sister anything. The landscape of feeling that this measured upbringing inculcated in countless children has yet to be surveyed; we should start, perhaps, with the burden of being good, and the painful watchful attention towards the needs of others rather than oneself.

I carry with me the tattered remnants of this psychic structure: there is no way of not working hard, nothing in the end but an endurance that will allow me to absorb everything by the way of difficulty, to the grave. This psychology must have served capitalism at least as well as a desire for the things of the market. At least Jeremy Seabrook's cut-out cardboard teenage figures of abject horror and pity know, as they sit sniffing glue and planning how to knock off a video recorder, that the world owes them something, that they have a right to the earth, an attitude at least as subversive as the endurance that is the result of not being ever given very much.[11]

It's a mistake, I think, to confuse the gift relationship with mindless material indulgence, for it is only by being given things that anyone ever learns that they have a place in the world. I want to reinterpret the metaphor of the fifties, of childhood as a community's investment in the future, and find its material base in the individual circumstances that help interpret historical developments. My sister and I were investments that didn't pay off, for the income that is derived from investment is *unearned* income: having made that initial payment, the investor need make no further effort. An older history brought this idea forward to a new era: we were brought up to be simply grateful for being alive, guilty at the fact of our existence.

Two weeks before my mother's death, I went to see her. It was the first meeting in nine years – for the day of my father's funeral doesn't really count. The letter announcing my visit lay unopened on the mat when she opened the door, and an hour later I came away believing that I admired a woman who could, under these circumstances and in some pain, treat me as if I had just stepped round the corner for a packet of tea ten minutes before, and talk to me about this and that, and nothing at all. But I was really a ghost who came to call. Talking to my sister on the phone about the visit she insisted that the feeling of being absent in my mother's presence was nothing to do with the illness, was the emotional underpinning of our childhood. We were truly *illegitimate*, our selves *not there*. Our unconscious acknowledgement of this at the time lay in taking up as little space as possible, not being a nuisance. Paradoxically, this denial of the known self makes its boundaries stronger.

As I went out, past the shrouded furniture in the front room (things made ready these twenty years past for the move that never came) I noticed a Lowry reproduction hanging over the mantelpiece that hadn't been there on my last visit. Why did she go out and buy that obvious representation of a landscape she wanted to escape, the figures moving noiselessly under the shadow of the mill? 'They know each other, recognise each other,' says John Berger of these figures. 'They are not, as is sometimes said, like lost souls in limbo; they are fellow travellers through a life which is impervious to most of their choices ...'[12] Perhaps she did buy that picture because it is concerned with loneliness, with 'the contemplation of time passing without meaning',[13] and moved then, momentarily, hesitantly, towards all the other lost travellers.

Where is the place that you move into the landscape and can see yourself? When I want to find myself in the dream of the New Look, I have to reconstruct the picture, look down at my sandals and the hem of my dress, for in the dream itself I am only an eye, watching. Remembering the visit to the cotton mill, on the other hand, I can see myself watching from the polished floor; I am in the picture. To see yourself in this way is a representation of the child's move into historical time, one of the places where vision establishes the child's understanding of herself as part of the world. In its turn, this social understanding interprets the dream landscape.

When I was about nine I grew positively hungry for poetry. I learned enormous quantities to say to myself in bed at night. The poetry book I had was Stevenson's *A Child's Garden of Verses*, and I read it obsessively, once going in to Smith's in the High Road to ask if he'd written any other poems. I liked the one on the last page best, 'To Any Reader', and its imparting of the sad, elegiac information that the child seen through the pages of the book

> ... has grown up and gone away,
> And it is but a child of air
> That lingers in the garden there.

You're nostalgic for childhood whilst it happens to you because the dreams show you the landscape you're passing through, but you don't know yet that you want to escape.

This is for Claire MacKensie, my only witness.

I WENT to the University of Sussex in 1965 to read history, a statistical component of the Robbins generation: my grammar school had sent one girl to university in 1964; sent seventeen of us, the children of 1946–47, a year later. In 1969, after a year spent teaching adults in Edinburgh, I went to Newnham College Cambridge to do research on the policing of mid nineteenth-century provincial communities. It was the working-class men who became policemen who interested me; I still want to know about the resistance involved in becoming what those who are more powerful than you expect you to be. There's a story in *Akenfield* (probably not true; it doesn't matter) of farm labourers threatened with eviction and unemployment because of fault found with their ploughing, some time before the First World War. They made no protest; listened silently to the farmer; turned round and made a series of perfect furrows. The farmer tried to boast about his achievement in the pub afterwards, but knew that something was wrong, that in some way he'd been outdone.[14] I think a lot about that story; it has taken on the telling proportions of a myth. Nineteenth-century policemen are interesting because they show that silent defiance so clearly, and because, I now realise, policing was so *feminine* an activity: a system of organised and institutionalised passivity within the nineteenth-century state.

My thesis was rejected in 1973, and I entered violently the imaginative territory of stupid/not stupid. I'd not thought clearly in those terms before: with our mother you were never praised for doing well, only given a hard time for doing badly. You were expected to be competent; to iron a blouse, scrub a floor, pass an exam; and I was. From my early teens an outraged sense of justice was my response to my mother's stance over many things, particularly her treatment of my sister. This outrage was easily translated into a social egalitarianism: as I was just the same as everyone else, I was doing only what everyone else could do. I'd never thought of myself as clever because no one had ever said I was; now I believed that I'd been told I was stupid. I was – and am – the first person in my family ever to have stayed at school beyond the compulsory leaving age; I thought someone ought to have alerted me to my unworthiness long before 1973.

I cried (for two days) and got by. I went out and got a job, supply teaching, easy to do in 1973 if you had a degree and as easy to manage as ten years before walking down the High Street and getting a job filling shelves in the VG Store. Within a month or so, I was sent to a Social Priority primary school. I knew, with an early clarity, that I shouldn't stay, but I did – for eight years. All I knew – of nineteenth-century history, the unknown struggles of people getting by under impossible circumstances – swam into sharp focus. The striking acknowledgement of my first weeks, that tired and depressed eight-year-olds doing their sums and writing their news were engaged on the same kind of intellectual task as I had been, never left me. It's not the sort of thing you can say at parties, but – it did seem a way of being a socialist in everyday life.

But it was very bad for me. Hard physical labour stops you thinking, and I didn't, for a long time. I was never a real teacher (this in spite of being a good colleague, a good friend, a good trade unionist) because I was too well educated, worked too hard. Slumming, I have to think of it as now (and it would be easier for others to accept as a valid past if I had filled shelves in a supermarket all those years instead of working at the nether end of the intellectual world). I think one reason I didn't see my mother during that time is that I knew what she thought: was it all for this? A teacher – like being a nurse or a policeman; something I could have done anyway, without her sacrifice. For the first time, I'd let her down.

She died at the end of 1983. I still feel worry draining away, water into pebbled ground, though this may have something to do with the fact that for the first time in ten years I don't have a job that keeps me awake at night, rigid with anxiety and self-denigration. I had a year off in 1980–81, wrote *The Tidy House*, started to think again, got a job at the Institute of Education. My thesis was published as *Policing the Victorian Community* by Routledge & Kegan Paul in 1984. This year I have research money to write a biography of Margaret McMillan, whose work on defining children as new objects of desire in the period 1890–1930 connects a lot with the concerns of my working life and historical practice.

I got married in 1971 – already an established relationship. No children, nor shall have any now, I think: 'the little thing was very sweet to kiss', said Hannah Cullwick of her baby nephew in 1872, 'but I was glad I wasn't the mother of a little family … for after all however natural its very troublesome & after they grow up generally a great anxiety'.[15] My sister had her first baby at seventeen, her second nine years later. She's done it all by herself, on social security. We're both daughters of the state, but she's poor and I'm not.

Having been given the extraordinary power of responsibility for the nuisance to others that my existence constitutes, I spend a lot of time removing my troublesome presence from events and situations. I have stood, alienated, envious, watching the political currents of my generation, feeling a particular distance from both the politics of liberation and the heavy-metal labourism of the late 1960s. I remember sitting in the snack bar at Sussex explaining post-seminar that my mother – from her background – voted Conservative, out of her own experience, and someone in IMG wondering if I couldn't have a word with her and get her to vote with her class. That was the last time I ever spoke about my background, except to very close friends. Now, there are feminisms, soft and sentimental, that would have my mother returned to me, and make us sisters in adversity.

I want a politics that will take all of this, all these secret and impossible stories, recognise what has been made out on the margins, and then, recognising it, refuse to celebrate it; a politics that will, watching that past say: 'so what?'; and abandon it to the dark.

Notes

1. George Herriman's Krazy Kat cartoons, syndicated throughout the US from 1913 onwards, are reproduced in *Krazy Kat Komix*, vols. 1–4, Real Free Press, Amsterdam, 1974–1975.

2. Tamara Hareven, *Family Time and Industrial Time: The Relationship Between the Family and Work in a New England Industrial Community*, Cambridge University Press, New York, 1982, p.355.

3. That is, never applied to the Guardians of the parish for financial help under the Poor Law.

4. Jill Liddington and Jill Norris, *One Hand Tied Behind Us: The Rise of the Women's Suffrage Movement*, Virago, London, 1978, pp. 93-95.

5. See Denise Riley, *War in the Nursery*, Virago, London, 1983, pp. 145–149 for working women in the post-war years.

6. Kathleen Woodward, *Jipping Street* (1928), Virago, London, 1983.

7. V.S. Naipaul, *A House for Mr Biswas*, Andre Deutsch, London, 1961. Naipaul has recently written about the book's composition in Streatham Hill in the *New York Review of Books*, November 24, 1983.

8. Gareth Stedman Jones, *Languages of Class: Studies in English Working Class History 1832–1982*, Cambridge University Press, Cambridge, 1983, p.246.

9. Jeremy Seabrook, *Working Class Childhood*, Gollancz, London, 1982, p.147.

10. ibid, p.202.

11. ibid, pp. 21-36.

12. John Berger, *About Looking*, Writers and Readers, London, 1980, pp. 90–91.

13. ibid, p.94.

14. Ronald Blythe, *Akenfield*, Penguin, 1969, p.130-131. It has recently become clear that *Akenfield* doesn't represent the transcribed words of its subjects but a kind of meta-narrative created by Blythe himself. This may make the words no less truthful.

15. Liz Stanley (ed.), *The Diaries of Hannah Cullwick*, Virago, London, 1984, p.238.

Alison Hennegan

... And Battles Long Ago

In my mother's Surrey garden (not the garden of my childhood) grows a sturdy fuchsia, a 'Lady's Ear-ring', the delicately flamboyant yet hardy shrub beloved by cottagers. This now vigorous specimen came originally as a cutting from my Great-aunt Jinny. Her own plant, flourishing in the tiny back yard of the nineteenth-century terraced house in Teddington which she occupied for more than sixty years, was taken from the majestic shrub which dominated the garden of the Hampshire cottage where my great-great-grandmother lived and raised six children in the second half of the last century. Her mother had had a cutting ...

By the time you read this – if my mother's shown her usual wizardry with growing things – a healthy slip of that same bush will be flourishing here in Cambridge: the offspring of one plant, tended by five generations of women, in the gardens of four counties, for more than a hundred years.

I was born in 1948 but before I can make for you any sense of myself and the child that I was throughout the fifties, we have to go back – to Cork in 1848, to Hampshire at the turn of the century, to

Edwardian Lambeth and to Wandsworth in the years before, during and just after the First World War.

For a fifties childhood may be less deeply influenced by the Festival of Britain, 'Contemporary' furniture, working-class affluence and Thirteen Years of Tory Misrule than by a Victorian grandparent, an Edwardian father and a cluster of potent family legends and memories which stretch back to the middle of the last century.

But let me begin with the house. Our house was white. It was detached. It stood at the very top of the hill and it was called Number One. Its owner occupied it. All these things distinguished it from the (mainly) rented pebbledashed semis and concrete-fronted terraces straggling away beneath it.

At the bottom of the garden was an untidy jumble of wooden buildings. There was the shed where my grandfather mended the family boots and shoes and kept a magnificent assortment of junk and treasures. ('Keep a thing for seven years and you're bound to find a use for it' was his motto. It became mine, too, as the overflowing contents of my house testify.) Next to the shed was a curious ramshackle and tunnel-like structure which had started life as a lean-to. Whatever it had leant against had long since disappeared but the adjunct remained, defying gravity and leaning, it seemed, upon the very air itself.

Here grandfather had once brewed and stored lethally potent country wines until the occasion when my five-year-old brother regaled himself upon a particularly fine parsnip vintage and erupted minutes later, rampageously drunk and foul mouthed, into the house where, most unusually, the vicar was being given tea. By maternal *fiat* the still was dismantled. Nothing but the folk memory remained for me.

Just a few feet away the hens resided, rather grandly, in *two* houses: one large and square, where they laid; the other, long and low and gabled, where they roosted. Quite often I roosted there of an afternoon, too, with warmly plump, fussily friendly hens jostling on either side and the satisfying smell of their droppings filling the tiny space with a pungently heady aroma.

On the other side of the brick path was the hutch containing my shamefully neglected (by me) rabbit. If my grandfather hadn't taken pity on him and shoved home-grown cabbage leaves in, the wretched beast would have succumbed early to starvation. To my utter mortification, I can't even remember his name.

I remember his source, though. He came from Number Three, where my friend Brenda lived. She too had a grandfather, a blind one. They had only one outhouse: a square, concrete building, three of its four walls covered in a wiffling, nibbling, twitching mass of rabbits. From floor to ceiling their hutches were banked, scores of them. The rabbits came in all colours − black, grey, brown, brindled, blue and albino − many species, all ages and sizes.

The blind man knew them all in their hundreds. He'd unlatch a cage, reach in, feel gently for its inhabitant and, with swift assurance, hoick it out and hold it to his chest, fondling the long ears, gently scratching its chin, murmuring and crooning to it while it lay, quiet, relaxed, trusting. Across his face flitted a host of rapidly changing emotions: pleasure in a coat's fine texture; surprise at an unexpectedly good gain in weight; delight in the lively wrigglings of a healthily inquisitive youngster. I see him yet, standing motionless, rapt, removed. His unseeing eyes becoming bright, his face glowing with content provided one of my childhood's most poignant images.

I was born in the white house. My mother was very firm about that. 'Home's the place for births and deaths,' she said (a sentiment I find myself echoing ever more faithfully as I learn more about the ways of institutional medicine). But although my parents, my brother and I all lived together in a house I'd now find too tiny just for me, it wasn't ours. It belonged to my mother's widowed father and he lived there with us. Or, rather, we lived there with him. A vital distinction which would prove to be of unforeseen significance later.

Throughout my infant-schooldays it was Grandad I returned to at lunch and it was he who cooked it. And it was to him I returned at the end of the day. My (primary) school-teacher mother lunched with her colleagues, or did her stint of Dinner Duty, and came home after me.

When I was still 'too young' to go to school, I'd gone just the same, accompanying my mother in the years when she was a supply teacher and filled in for periods of a few days, weeks or months as needed. Headley remains my idea of near perfection. Its tiny village school in the Surrey Downs boasted one long, ecclesiastically vaulted room and two classes, one of them taken by the headmistress. Each class held children of varying ages: five to eight and nine to eleven, if I remember rightly. An informal monitor system evolved naturally as older children, bossily efficient but genuinely kind, helped younger ones who were often siblings or cousins.

Remarkably docile babies, tucked into carry cots with a teddy bear on one side and a bottle of milk on the other, were occasionally left beside my mother's desk by hard-pressed parents. They'd gallop in, deposit the infant, give my mother a breathless and embarrassedly apologetic explanation of a family emergency and gallop out again, their vehement thanks still hanging on the air as the door swung behind them and the trailing toddler clinging to their skirts (or trousers: quite often it was fathers who came and the emergency was an even newer baby at home).

I was myself little more than three then. It was a time of blissful warmth, relaxed affection and peace. The children did well. Do you wonder?

Grandad kept us all in vegetables from his allotment just over a mile away. He'd go there in his heavy boots and earth-stained corduroys, smoking a blackened pipe which belched evil-smelling clouds of shag, looking like the old countryman he was. I'd go with him in the curious trot-skip-hop-lurch gait which I was always forced to adopt when walking with the men of the family who never seemed to make any allowances for my shorter legs. We went via the badlands of the neighbouring council estate where many of my schoolfellows lived. I rarely traversed it alone. Few of us did: we went in safe bands of three or more. Children from the estate made equally cautious, properly reconnoitred sorties into our territory. There was little active hostility, just a cat-like wariness.

Linking the two technically neutral states was a long, asphalted road bounded by fields on one side and by a high brick wall on the other. It was ideal for roller skating (on metal wheels which made a good, loud, satisfying and gritty scrunch). There I learned to perfect the much favoured Russian Dancer position (crouched on your haunches, bottom three inches off the ground and one leg dashingly and daringly thrust forward, well off the road, with wheels still spinning). And there those of us with bicycles (but not me, because my cousin had been killed years earlier on his twelfth birthday, riding his gleaming new birthday present), learned to conquer them. First came the 'Look, no hands!', followed by that dizzying, dazzling trick whereby you braked hard, threw your weight backwards and suddenly found yourself mounted on a bucking, shying monocycle.

Number One Woodbridge Grove was my grandfather's last but one home and he lived there for almost thirty years. He had been born in a small Hampshire village in the late 1870s, one of a large but healthy cottage family, and began his working life as an ostler until the agrarian depression drove him, with thousands of others, to the cities. He came to London and turned, as did so many of the men in my mother's family, to that all-embracing employer, the Railways: suitable that a family called Watts should boast so many plate-layers, guards and porters. And some – cause for great family pride and rejoicing – even joined that proud band of engine drivers who, as I was constantly reminded by great-aunts, were the true aristocrats of the working classes.

George Watts, my grandfather, ended his working life as an Inspector of the Permanent Way on what was then the London and South Western Railway. In 1929 he moved, from Wandsworth in South London where he'd lived since 1917, to Leatherhead in Surrey, just half-way down the line between Waterloo and Horsham.

With him was the wife who had become engaged to him when she was sixteen. I never knew her but I wear always her engagement ring: a simple but substantial piece of plaited gold, pleasingly evocative of a harvest loaf. Gemstones were, financially, quite out of the question. She married him at seventeen, a country girl and his first cousin, raised in the same village as he. At thirteen she'd gone straight from school into domestic service, leaving it only for her early marriage and the uprooting exodus to London.

Not to Wandsworth – a comparatively genteel lower middle-class suburb – but to Lambeth where my mother was born in 1909: 'dahn Lambeff way', as she says, half in mockery, half in memory.

In neither Wandsworth nor Lambeth were there dusty London pavements in July and August – not, at any rate, for my mother. For she, like many a little first generation Townee, became a country child during the summer months, going with my grandmother back to the Hampshire village which was still really Home. There they'd stay for weeks at a time, with my grandfather coming down at the weekends (on his God-sent concessionary tickets). Mother and Grandma walked endless miles to see relatives scattered across a handful of villages or, sometimes, like Auntie Kate, sitting peacefully in a solitary house dumped in the middle of a field two miles from the nearest neighbour.

During the Second World War my brother was to repeat the pattern of Town Child in the Winter, Country Child in the Summer. Half his childhood, like my mother's, was made up of the village bakery (where an uncle baked bread and Hampshire's lusciously oozing, sugar-encrusted Lardy cakes), village cricket (where another uncle was captain of the XI) and Harvest Home, when he was hoisted up on to the offspring of the same vast, sofa-backed shires which had carried my mother twenty-five years before.

Sadly, the baking uncle no longer makes his loaves; the cricketing one finally severed his connection with the team last year, after more than sixty years of varied association with it. And his forty-year-old son, my cousin, retired from his captaincy at the same time. The village now is filled with the commuting middle classes and the nature of the team and club has changed. He hasn't said it in so many words – he's a gentle man – but I *think* he means there's no place left for villagers in the village team.

My own first childhood home hovered uneasily between town and country. Behind the houses were open fields where Keith Jones and I made and played with our bows and arrows, climbed trees, recreated Robin Hood and Davy Crockett and ambushed Cowboys *and* Indians, Roundheads *and* Cavaliers with a fine and generous impartiality. Today the air hums with the noise of constant traffic coming from a new stretch of the M 25, its construction, ironically, supervised by a male cousin whose mother has just returned to the family village and the family house.

If it seems curious that I should spend so much time and space on childhoods not my own, on an experience of the true countryside which was not mine. I do it partly because that sprawling country past makes me so passionately aware that cities, whatever their inhabitants may like to believe, are not the centre of the universe; that, in the end, towns need the country more than the country needs towns, and that 'working class' is not – or should not be – synonymous with 'urban working classes', although you'd never guess it from the townee arrogance of most theorists and polemicists.

I do it, too, because that country past gave me my first sense of belonging to a network, stretching across time and space, in which women played the chief part in gathering, storing and disseminating its legends, lore and history. That I know so much of my mother's family, so little of my father's, seems no accident.

Much of that knowledge comes from the family photographs, spilling out of an elegant inlaid box, the gift of someone's Mistress – an employer, not a paramour. It was the favourite treat of a rainy Saturday afternoon to go through them, catechising my mother: 'Who's *she*? Is he still alive? Do *I* know them?' And, most important of all, 'What relation are *they* to *me*?' I listened spellbound as the intricacies of the generations, of third cousinship twice removed, were delicately unravelled.

More than a century of people and places: highly formal and luxurious *cartes de visite* from the 1860s, satin-glossy employers as plumply upholstered as their button-back chairs; family groups stiffly posed in the bizarre studio fantasies of high street photographers in the eighties; from the turn of the century come bevies of great-aunts – as cooks, dairymaids, housekeepers and gate house keepers to great estates, brides and proud new mothers. And – dozens of these, it seemed – young men: alone, in couples, in groups of three or four linked by hands on arms or shoulders, some with an air of uncertain swagger, others with a gentle resignation and tired, tired eyes. All of them in uniform, on leave. And in answer to my ritual question, 'Who are *they*?', came always, it seemed, the same reply: 'You didn't know them. They died in the war.' 'In Daddy's war?' 'No, no. The First one, the *Great* War, *the* war.'

And *the* war it remains for me, despite the significance of the Second, despite the fact that there have been at least fifty others since then. During those early childhood years I took deep down into myself a conviction that somehow the world, the *real* world, had ended in 1918 and everything that followed was merely a tiresome and irrelevant postscript.

Not until my early twenties would I willingly read contemporary novels, take a newspaper, begin to fill the vast gaps in my political knowledge of the previous half century.

Such stubborn and long-lasting refusal to acknowledge the present stemmed in part perhaps from easily identifiable causes: I was raised as a quasi only child by comparatively elderly people; I turned early to a fantasy world fed by those photographs and supplemented by the numerous but mainly Victorian and Edwardian family books.

But I think I also resisted the present so vehemently because I was already uncomfortably aware that I wasn't going to fit it. I didn't consciously define myself as lesbian until I was thirteen, when I met the word for the first time and recognized that it and I belonged together. But long before that I felt chafed, excluded, cramped by the assumptions about boys and girls, men and women, which I sensed crowding in from the world outside.

I liked boys, played with them, joined their gangs, took my own place in their loosely knit fellowship. I had boy friends but no boyfriend. Yet all around me, it seemed, the air was heavy with the knowing glances and *doubles entendres* exchanged by adults as they watched each other's sons and daughters at play. 'Boy talk' was already rife amongst my seven-year-old girl friends. I found it disturbing, distressing – and indecent: not because it was sex but because, as I was already dimly aware, it was for me the wrong sex.

Gradually I made a series of archetypal retreats: into fantasy; into books; into safely de-sexing fat; into tomboyery; negatively, but usefully, into a sharp-tongued verbal dexterity which kept mockers at bay; positively, and better far than merely 'useful', into the

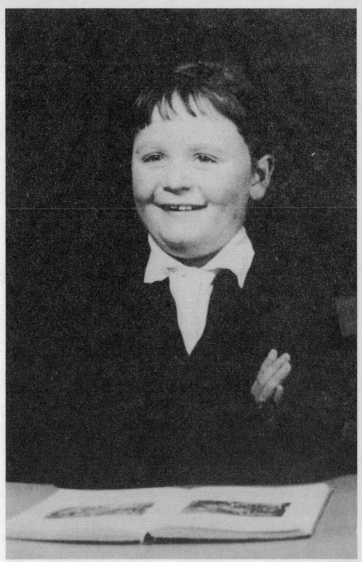

My public face; confident, not to say cocky, all uncertainties safely swathed in smiles and fat

pleasures of masturbation and orgasm, those marvellous gifts to myself, first bestowed accidentally by the four-year-old me and never thereafter relinquished.

Gifts, yes, but linked with loss. Quite literally, I kept my hands to – and for – myself. Ours was anyway not a physically demonstrative family but such offers of physical affection as there were I pushed away. And pushed them away outside the family, too. I was confusedly aware, at some level before or beyond language, that part of what I sometimes wanted when I touched other girls was not permitted. It would be, with boys, but that I didn't want. Better, therefore, not to touch at all. *Any*one. Ever.

Thirty years later I rarely touch other people with genuine spontaneity. My own strong sense of 'I'd better keep off' is, understandably, interpreted as 'Keep off!' by everyone else. Only the blessedly extrovert, so busy beaming out their own warmth that they've no time to be confused by my seeming coldness, break through, thereby enabling me to return the response I wish I could have offered first.

And I retreated by becoming a Watcher. Watching comes naturally to the powerless. To observe, note, record, compare is a necessary tool for survival: every beleaguered group knows that. In me the tendency was exacerbated: by those uncertainties surrounding sexuality; by household tensions; but, more particularly, by my position as a teacher's child.

The children of teachers are rarely 'real' pupils, not, at any rate, if they and their parents share a school. Teachers' children know too much, are too close to the source of power to make comfortable friends for fellow pupils. A certain wariness prevails in the playground. A sense of constraint pervades social intercourse. Teachers' children must prove themselves: prove themselves not to be sneaks, tale-bearers, presumers on privilege, possessors of illicit private information about an imprisoned father, an older unmarried sister's pregnancy, a regularly beaten-up mother, an incestuous family. (My mother was, in fact, remarkably discreet but by some osmosis I came to know of all those and other secrets. Punctiliously I kept my own counsel – a necessity drummed into me as into all teachers' children – but possessing forbidden and untransmittable knowledge added to the sense of apartness. As did arriving each morning in the lift-giving headmistress's car.)

So: easier not to get involved. Better to watch. By day I observed those who surrounded me. My role was, like that of most young children, passive, acted upon, responsive not initiatory. By night, roles were reversed. In fantasy and waking dreams I moved centre stage, became Director to their Supporting Players. Everyday adults underwent strange metamorphoses in an imagined serial which ran for at least three years in my night-time head. Waking dreams were set in a sinisterly rewritten Heaven where I was the Number One daughter of God (no less!), deeply misunderstood, much plotted against but, ultimately, re-admitted to the Divine, paternal favour. (In my moments of repeated triumph I never forgot to be unctuously forgiving to my downcast enemies.)

Real and recurring dreams happened in lesser-known concentration camps and the railway sidings where, often crippled and in a wheelchair, I awaited the cattle trucks. But, waking or sleeping, the dreams all had in common a masochistic vision of the world whereby the self is proved, redeemed – and ultimately victorious – only through suffering and humiliation.

Remnants of those dreams and the values enshrined in them remain. The implicit Jewish identification emerged more strongly in my very early teens when I invented for myself a secret German-Jewish persona, complete with changed name, parentage and family history (an adolescent experience, I later discovered, common to numerous other young lesbians at that time). Later still, it left me with an erotic pull towards a particular archetypal version of female Jewish beauty – embarrassing and a little frightening to admit to now when the very phrase, 'Jewish beauty', is open to charges of racism and inverted anti-semitism.

My grandparents were not the family's only urban exiles. My great-aunt Jinny and her husband, Alf, had settled in Middlesex early this century. There they became founder members of their local branch of the Labour Party and raised their family in the rented terraced house whose bookshelves held Dickens, Scott, nineteenth-century classics of economic and political theory and, that complete library for the self-educated working-class reader,

John Morley's Hundred Best Books. (Demanding reading after a hard day's work. They tackled it – with zest and enjoyment. Knowing that makes me prickle with fury and contempt when I hear patronising assumptions today about what working-class children can and can't, will and won't undertake.) In the 1920s they had a chance to buy the house: it was a mortgage or a car. Alf left the choice to Jinny. She chose the car because it gave her and the children a chance to get out of the house.

They were staunch trades unionists. Uncle Alf, an engine driver, was an ASLEF member (the 'gentleman's' union, unlike the more lowly NUR: family lore is clear on this point) and held union office. Even so he disobeyed a strike call in the twenties. He did it for a distraught and heavily pregnant woman, stranded on the platform with three toddlers clinging to her skirts. She knew no one in London, had no money for lodgings, had other children waiting for her at home and no means of getting a message to them. Uncle and his stoker took the train out for her.

His mates sent him to Coventry and kept him there for weeks. He cracked eventually under the strain and had a breakdown. (Later, in his seventies when he was becoming senile, he relived those weeks with a degree of vivid recall and distress which precipitated bouts of amnesia.) When explaining his action to his wife he said, 'I couldn't have left her there and called myself a man.' Properly suspicious though I am of those abstractions, Man and Woman, his explanation still seems to me one of the better ways of defining what it means to be male and human. And, twenty-five years after I first heard it, the story still seems a perfect example of the endless, terrible conflict between group loyalty and individual conscience encountered so many times over in the daily struggle to live our politics.

Mercifully I've never suffered anything to compare to his purgatory. But, at a much less elevated level, my seventh year provided perhaps a hint of it. One afternoon a policeman from the local station assembled the children of our street to conduct an informal interrogation into some petty vandalism and some far-from-pretty cruelty inflicted on domestic animals. What I knew on the latter count I told.

He left to act on Information Received. I remember still the uneasy but intransigent rejection of my peers as, one by one, they turned away in silence, then, loudly and unconvincingly casual, invited each other to go and play elsewhere. In angry and tearful confusion I wheeled my Triang scooter back up the hill, followed into exile only by the faithful Brenda.

The cat-torturer was a thoroughly unpleasant fifteen-year-old youth, the first person to teach me by his example that for some people physical cruelty and sexual pleasure are one and the same thing. There was no reason to feel shame or contrition for informing against him. But the sense of sinning against tribal loyalty was very great – and thoroughly reinforced by the lifetime-long three days of ostracism which followed.

Briefly searing for me but in no way comparable to what Uncle Alf endured. Much later, in the early 1980s, I too was to become embroiled in a six-month trades union battle, the one that surrounded the terrible death throes of *Gay News* which had been my life for six years. Like Uncle Alf, I came to hold union office. Unlike him I found no conflict of loyalties. But, with a mixture of amusement, surprise and raging fury, I discovered in myself an unsuspected passion about bad management and ripped-off workers.

'Bolshies', 'Reds', in fact 'socialists', were my mother's family – words I was accustomed to hear my father hurl at my grandfather in moments of high fury and defeat: the ultimate in insult and condemnation. No socialist, my tormented and choleric father. Six years my mother's senior he was just too young for the First World War, just in time to be one of the Second's oldest lance-corporals (Company nickname, 'Grandad' or 'Pop'). In him was a volatile amalgam of embattled elements: rank conservatism and astonishing anarchism perpetually locked in a war of attrition.

Theoretically he stood for Discipline. If it failed, Autocracy was not merely justified but obligatory: 'They need putting up against a brick wall and *shooting*!' Picketing strikers, demonstrating students, equivocating Cabinet Ministers, bishops in convocation, trade union leaders, the College of Cardinals: all who disgusted, perplexed or disturbed him drew from him this response. It rang out, a one-man choric refrain, punctuating every news bulletin for all my memory of him.

And yet this Tyrant (who abhorred physical violence in daily life and grieved if he trod accidentally on a spider) quietly subverted every value you'd expect him to hold. He loathed, for instance, the sexual Double Standard. (Although, being a good Victorian at heart, that meant he preferred men to be as virtuous as women rather than that women should be as licentious as men.) At twenty-eight, engaged to my mother and still a virgin, his restraint broke at last. He went to the West End, picked up a prostitute, did the deed, came home and sobbed for most of the night: for failing himself and for dishonouring *two* women, my mother and the prostitute. The incident arouses in me tangled emotions: anger and grief for him and that guilt-laden misery; respect and affection for his recognition that if his own moral imperatives demanded chastity, they demanded it for men quite as much as for women.

He was unfailingly gentle to adolescents embattled with their families, joined battle for them if parental expectations – at school, work, in courtship and marriage – were weighing heavily on young shoulders, feeding fears of inadequacy and failure. (Convinced that he was himself a failure, he couldn't bear to see anyone else labouring under the same burden, was enraged to see others imposing it.) His work as an insurance agent took him into hundreds of households each month. Some he visited for almost thirty years and he heard many confidences in that time. Often he intervened between a shocked and furious mother and her unmarried, pregnant daughter: he valued female 'purity' but he valued human mercy a great deal more.

He died before the word 'macho' had come into vogue but he wouldn't have been impressed by the values it conveys. He didn't think much of men who wouldn't – or couldn't – cry. In that respect, as in many others, he was an eighteenth-century man rather than a nineteenth-century one: for him the opposites of 'manly' were 'childish' and 'irresponsible', not 'effeminate' or 'unmanly'. A point nicely demonstrated, I think, by his later struggles in the 1970s to come to terms with Oscar Wilde (and, implicitly, with my lesbianism). 'I can't decide,' he confided to me one day, 'whether I think that Wilde was wrong or not.' Eventually he decided that Wilde was not wrong to take male lovers but was wrong to deceive his wife about them. Within his own moral framework (and the one that was supposed to be Wilde's) that seems to me a just and rather generous verdict.

Never quite knowing which side of any moral argument he'd finally come down on made life stimulating but exhausting. He was a past master at thinking on his feet. Voluble, excitable, eyes flashing, cheeks flushing, his very hair standing on end like an electric halo crackling with static as the words came pouring out, he was perfectly capable of changing his dialectical horses in mid-stream with scarcely a pause for breath and certainly not the slightest hint of a blush.

In sheer self-defence I learned to think fast, talk fast – and to keep going regardless of opposition. It was that or go under. (Although, unlike him, I try never to ride more than one horse at a time.) And it certainly proved invaluable training during all those later years of speaking engagements, debates and lobbying which I was to undertake for various gay campaigns.

Our fluency, persuasiveness and pugnacity came all of it from one source: the Blarney Stone, both literally (my father's father had kissed it) and metaphorically. For my father who, like me, had never set foot in Ireland in his life, was Irish, and so, my brother and I were firmly taught, were we. Being Irish provided us, in my father's eyes, with a temperamental blueprint: our greatest strengths, our greatest weaknesses were all attributed to it. Our verbal facility, mental agility, musical gifts, our sensitivity to language and colour, our power of mimicry, our fine oral memory, our championing of lost causes, our generosity to the underdog (and if this list sounds vainglorious, remember it was a father's pride which made it) – all these, it seemed, we owed to Grandfather Hennegan, that true son of Erin. And – more sombre gifts, these – from him and Ireland came our lack of staying power, our easy boredom, the temper which flared before the cause was clear and the surging melancholy which, unforeseen, unconquerable, would suddenly engulf us (and which finally did for my Aunt Kitty who 'went mad' in the 1960s and for her brother, my Uncle Bernard, who hanged himself at seventy-three, shortly after the death of his wife).

I believed in my Irishness utterly and was well into my twenties before I realised that this was a ludicrous and rather pernicious example of a false loyalty. Generations of Irish men and women went to form me, that's true enough. At a sentimental level I'm glad of it; at a deeper one, I'd like to know more about those unknown ancestors. Moreover, I can sympathise with my father's passionate desire for roots and, since he knew precious little of his English mother's early life, can understand why he decided to 'become' Irish. But he was not Irish any more than I am and it seems to me now that that curious rag-bag of touchingly cherished national stereotypes – many of them the product of nineteenth-century English imaginations – was in its way an unconscious insult to real Irish people living lives in real Ireland.

The ardent republicanism of New York Irish, who are as Irish as I am – which is not at all – seems equally insulting to me: a form of emotional colonialism which appropriates other people's experience and claims it as one's own. The same seems true of black women in North America and Britain who call themselves Third World. It seems true, too, of those American feminist literary historians who undertake to interpret nineteenth-century English women writers to English readers, apparently quite oblivious to the fact that we share a language but not a history.

But little of this is sayable in the current climate of feminist politics. So when Ireland or colonialism is the subject, usually – and uncharacteristically – I keep my head down and my mouth shut.

Grandfather Hennegan, the proxy progenitor of Ireland's blessings, was for me never more than a shadowy figure. Left on the steps of the Cork Foundling Hospital in the year of the Great Famine, or so said family legend (and the Wandsworth local paper in 1920 when he died), by some mysterious means he gained entrance to the Indian Civil Service. And to India he went, somewhere along the way meeting and marrying my grandmother by whom he had eight or nine (or ten or eleven) children. Numbers are uncertain because Consumption, that mighty giant, cut its incessant swathe through the family.

Of my father's mother I know little. I know she was a Yorkshire woman, that her surname was Redroof and that she must have had remarkably delicate hands and feet. Her tiny, tight fitting wedding ring I wear always on my right hand where it acts as a guard for my other grandmother's larger, looser engagement ring. I glance at them, touch them, often, liking to know that there, united on the one finger, are the rings which these two women, whom I never knew but who helped to make me, wore every day of their adult lives.

I value their part in creating the family line all the more because *I* shall not be perpetuating it. Lesbianism and motherhood are not mutually exclusive now (and probably never were in reality). Nevertheless I grew up in a world which said firmly that they were and I locked that away inside myself as a fact to be incorporated into my future and my sense of Me. If I seem obsessed with genealogies, descents and other people's pasts, it is in part because I shall not be leaving descendants to carry me into the future. (A fascination with the past, rooted firmly in the knowledge that, in that sense, there *is* no future, has, I believe, been a common experience for homosexual men and women over the centuries. I'd go so far as to claim that we owe Proust's *A la Recherche du Temps Perdu* almost entirely to it.)

Grandfather Hennegan was fastidious, 'gentlemanly' and elegant to the point of dandyism. Grandfather Watts was a Working Man, no masher and, fond though I was of the old devil, not even one of Nature's gentlemen. The two men never met but they fought their ancient class battle just the same in the endless border warfare waged between my oh-so-easily goaded father and my slow-moving, slow-spoken and canny, cunning old Grandfather Watts. Oh how skilfully he'd bait the trap and how helplessly my poor, out-manoeuvred father always took it!

Their incessant rows shook the house and would send me scuttling away up the stairs, into my bedroom, through the window out on to the flat roof of the bathroom and round under the lee of the chimney stack: a small, safe corner, invisible from the ground, unknown to the grown-ups. There I'd sit, knees to chin, huddling into the chimney's warmth, shaking, sobbing or trying not to. Doggedly I'd fix my mind on reassuring images, forcing it to create for me peace, order, harmony.

There seemed to me nothing strange about these moments of terror. They came too often to be extraordinary. But to my mother, coming upon me one summer evening when the row had been particularly violent and my distress proportionately great, they were clearly an appalling discovery.

The next day, a Saturday, she swept me off, with an unusually brisk and purposeful air, not to Leatherhead where she and I usually did the week's shopping, but four miles further on to Epsom. When I asked why, she said, uncharacteristically tight-mouthed, 'Because we're going to buy a house.' We did, too. Not actually then and there. But we saw in the estate agent's window one we thought would do and went home and told my father we were moving, without Grandad.

Mother had made her Declaration of Independence. Father, already wretchedly ashamed of the previous night's upheavals, conceded the territory with the minimum of protest and that, clearly, for form's sake only. (He never really took to the new house though, and throughout the next twenty years, at moments of domestic crisis, he'd accuse her all over again of her solitary act of insurgence.)

To me that Saturday was an astounding revelation. My mother had acted swiftly, uncompromisingly, unilaterally – and won. It was my first intimation that noise and bluster are not strengh and that my simple equation – Father leads, Mother follows – might be badly wrong.

Later, I *knew* it was. He was devoted to her, protective, quick to flare up on her behalf. Yet to me, watching, there was in his devotion always something of the anxious child's demand for reassurance, the embrace which recalled the clutch. He was, as the phrase goes, intensely sociable. But that's really only another way of saying that his need of other people was desperate. Without them he grew quickly apprehensive. Without *her* he was frightened.

I noticed, without fully realizing the implications at first, that he couldn't bear her to withdraw from him into her own private world – to read, really to *listen* to music, to concentrate on a radio play. He demanded the reassurance of constant response which he guaranteed by ceaseless interruption.

His own tensions set up complex reactions in me. In those early years I began to develop a coldness towards his emotional demands on me, a coldness which had become thickest ice by my teens. Yet I note in myself an anxious impulse to monitor the faces, tones, gestures of those whose love I seek or need. Even as I do it I recognise the reflection of that which, in him, so irritated and chilled me. And his constant demands upon my mother's attention have made me fearful of intimacy if intimacy must mean endless intrusions on privacy and solitude. This last is a dilemma I've barely begun to resolve.

The new house, just two miles away in a once-village called Ashtead, was very different from Woodbridge Grove. I was nine when we went there. It was solidly lower- and middle-class. Not much playing in the streets here: too many cars, although ours, an Austin 40, had had to go to help with the mortgage. Instead of the street there was the garden: a seemingly vast and fan-shaped third of an acre which my mother, an ardent gardener who'd been denied any real say in her father's narrow, fifty-foot-long plot, began to transform with the inspiration of pure passion.

For me the change confirmed the drift towards a not unpleasant isolation. I spent hours alone, reading up in my bedroom or downstairs playing the piano (at this time still the redoubtable 'Jacobean' upright which first came into my mother's life in 1917). She'd come back to her piano-less home for tea one afternoon and reported, 'May and Eva say we must be *really* poor if we haven't got a piano.' Grandfather said nothing but the piano, brand new, was delivered the next day. Family honour was satisfied. Eva, one of a trio of sisters surnamed Killingray and known locally as 'The Killingray Cats' because of their ferocious habits, became the wife for whom Uncle Bernard hanged himself some fifty years later.

Thus mother was 'put to the piano' and so, years later, were my brother and I. Piano lessons took me once a week into a different world. They involved 'going up the town', both literally and socially an up hill journey. Every Wednesday after school, clutching my chestnut-brown leather music case, cynosure of my schoolmates' mocking eyes and magnet for their casually loud and unflattering comments, I trudged the mile and a half to the Leatherhead School of Music.

There, in a pleasant mid-Victorian house, cool, fragrant, full of quietly beautiful furniture and mellow carpets, was a collection of truly magnificent pianos: amongst them a fine six-foot Broadwood grand and a dream of a Blüthner upright which, in my dreams, I lust after even yet. And, there, was the principal, Miss Fuller.

The only survivor of three sisters who'd founded the school in the late twenties, she was, indisputably, a Gentlewoman. Thin to the point of angularity and grey – in hair, complexion and cardigans worn twenties long – she resembled a French caricature of an English spinster. But there was nothing grey about her mind or her playing. Taught by Tobias Matthay (whose most famous pupil was Myra Hess), she reproduced faithfully at the piano those langorous, swooning, unabashedly erotic movements which he'd developed so carefully at the turn of the century: difficult to watch without embarrassment, difficult to hear without rapture.

My own teacher, a young unmarried woman, probably in her mid-twenties when I began my eleven years' pupillage with her, was very different. Tall – over six feet – she dressed always in beautifully hand-tailored clothes, all in the finest fabrics, all of them brand-new – and all of them at least thirty years out of date. This enigma – the mixture of care, obvious expense and seemingly unconscious eccentricity – I never solved (and, needless to say, I never dared to go to the source by asking her directly for an explanation).

She was one of the very few people I've ever met who truly merited the description 'androgynous'. She had thin, fine – but enormous – hands and feet, long legs, narrow hips, tiny breasts and closely cropped, glossy brown hair. And a face of quite remarkable beauty – the beauty of a shy but intelligent seventeen-year-old boy. She would, I realised later, have served as a perfect visual model for Stephen Gordon, the lesbian heroine of Radclyffe Hall's *The Well of Loneliness*.

Whether her sexuality was also that of Stephen Gordon, I never knew. But to me there was something deeply disturbing, compellingly attractive about the conflicting messages conveyed by that face and that body in those clothes. She was a pervasive influence and the archetype later for many an erotic fantasy. (Later still I wondered whether her seemingly flamboyant outmodedness

146

was in fact just another version of the disguise which I had sought in fat and quick-tongued attack – and for the same reason.)

Certainly the cataclysmic Friday Night Row precipitated our move to Ashtead. But I think it might eventually have happened anyway. Throughout my childhood, working away like yeast, unseen but transforming, was my mother's fierce determination that I should have my chance. I was already considered by my teachers to be 'very bright'. My brother was, too. But he, exercising that autonomous judgement which our parents prided themselves in allowing us, had chosen not to stop on at school and was already at this time apprenticed in the then thriving, soon to collapse aircraft industry. As it happens, his life has been a good and rich one. But when, at nineteen, he had the motorcycle accident which nearly killed him and left him with a permanently paralysed arm, his lack of paper qualifications in that certificate-worshipping period must have made his future seem perilous. I was ten at the time: life must be made safer for me.

Not that my mother regarded education as a meal ticket. Both my parents, but she in particular, reverenced learning for its own sake. The stages of their courtship were marked by the books they exchanged. Amongst them Marcus Aurelius, Augustine, Epictetus; the essays of Bacon, Emerson, Arnold, Thoreau, Robert Lynd and Alice Meynell; standard editions of the poets. I have many of them now: 'To Alice, from Boy'; 'For Boy, from Alice'.

'Things of the mind' was a phrase constantly and unselfconsciously on my father's lips. He deeply and sincerely admired intellectual women, was self-deprecating in their presence. My childhood was not so much overshadowed as warmly overhung by two of them whom I regard as my spiritual godmothers. The first: Miss Lacey, whom I never met, the headmistress who in 1922 looked at the thirteen-year-old Alice Watts, then destined to train as a hairdresser on a Trade Scholarship, and said, 'You don't *really* want to be a hairdresser, do you? Be a teacher instead.' So my mother became a teacher instead. Miss Lacey (my mother never knew her first name for sure, but thinks it might have been Helen), then middle aged but once a New Woman, was a feminist, and a friend of Shaw and Stewart Headlam (the clergyman who

147

befriended Wilde and was eventually unfrocked for his work amongst prostitutes). She was a gifted teacher, a fine headmistress and a power for good to the hundreds of girls who passed through her school. I revere her memory and thank her often.

The second warm, but usually unseen, influence was Dorothy Tarrant: a Wandsworth friend and neighbour of my parents' courting days. Daughter of a once famous Unitarian theologian and minister, she went as an undergraduate to Girton in 1904 and became eventually Regius Professor of Greek in the University of London. I met her only twice when she was in her eighties but heard her name mentioned constantly by my father with deepest respect.

Both 'Girton' and 'Greek' became words endowed for me with semi-magical meaning: each seemed in some way to be a key to mysterious, barely attainable riches. Somehow I meant to get those keys and turn them.

Quite early on I deduced that those tantalising riches came most often to women who didn't marry. Those women I most admired or who influenced me – Miss Fuller, my piano teacher, Miss Lacey, Miss Tarrant – were all spinsters. Moreover, they were all women of such dignity, such presence, that they became for me the definition of Spinsterhood. Very early on a word which was for others so often the cue for sniggering contempt signified for me female strength, independence and freedom.

In this I was confirmed by my parents, especially by my father. His own reverence for intellectual women engendered in him – or sprang from – a conviction that merely male husbands could only be an impediment. And, with his usual unpredictability, he saw no good reason why such women should pay for their independence with a lifetime's celibacy. They should, in his view, be free to live sexual lives as independent as their intellectual and professional ones.

I see, of course, that in feminist terms his position was hopelessly unsatisfactory, based as it implicitly is on the assumption that there are two kinds of women: 'real' ones, who do womanly things (marry, have children, remain faithful to their husbands); and other, less womanly, unchilded ones, who have minds and occasional lovers. Nevertheless, he got much more of the answer right than any of my friends' parents. Later I watched the dreary and disheartening procession of girls who left school before O levels or in the middle of A levels. Blinded by the dazzle of their engagement rings, they rushed to submerge themselves in marriages with men they'd outgrown half a decade later.

Today I watch any number of highly qualified, competent and more than competent women friends play eternal second fiddle to men with a fraction of their ability. One truth my father saw clearly: marriage takes from women the possibility of adult independence. I remain devoutly grateful that never, at any point in my childhood or adolescence, did my parents present marriage as a desirable goal, let alone as my inevitable destiny.

The move to Ashtead marked the beginning of a long and unplanned-for period of straitened means for my parents. It wasn't poverty. Poverty for my father meant the utter destitution he had witnessed in the 1920s during a brief spell as a County Court bailiff. In those days of gold-dust-rare jobs he gave that one up quickly. Money earned by harrying and evicting penniless families was money best gone without. Poverty to my mother meant those months in 1938 when she'd survived her first pregnancy sustained mainly by bread and jam and weak tea. My father, together with the other millions, was jobless.

No: our new state wasn't poverty. But it was, financially, a much closer shave than I ever realised at the time. Yet never in all that period did my parents grudge me money for books. For ten years my father went short to give me more pocket money than he could afford – stopped smoking to do it – so that I could buy books, and books and yet more books. He didn't always approve my choice. He read my copy of *Lady Chatterley's Lover*, loathed it and pointed out that it was clearly written by a man deeply fearful of women. With the smug certainty of thirteen, I told him he was wrong. Now, of course, I recognise that he was quite right. But, whether he liked or loathed the books, the money for them went on coming just the same.

In 1959 I passed the eleven-plus and went off to an Epsom grammar school – for girls only. Educationalists may now just be beginning to recognise that it isn't often girls who profit from secondary co-education. My parents knew it back in the 1950s. Ironically, at the time I rather favoured the mixed grammar at Dorking: mainly, I can now see, because of the gender confusion intensifying in me then and not to be resolved until my mid twenties. If I wasn't a *real* girl (and I wasn't: I was fat, a swot, a bookworm and *still* didn't menstruate at the great age of eleven) then I'd better go and join the other boys.

True to their principles, my parents didn't coerce. They suggested why I might be happier at the girls' school, then left me genuinely free to choose. I have never for an instant regretted my choice.

Thus was I launched upon my good, meritocratic career which was to end in an Open Scholarship to Girton in the days when it was still the women-only college envisioned by its feminist founders.

But Girton was still eight years off. Between lay my fortunate exposure to some quite outstanding teachers, Greek, the unconscious acquisition of my spuriously piss-elegant accent, the conscious recognition of my lesbianism and an adolescence in which I would replace my grandfather as my father's sparring partner.

Almost *too* full a decade, the sixties.

*I*T'S TAKEN my last seventeen years (ages nineteen to thirty-six) to recognise, disentangle and sometimes repair the web of true and false loyalties which I wove for myself in childhood and adolescence. There were so many things I was convinced I knew about myself: that I was not interested in politics, for example, and had no time, because I saw no need, for gay liberation and feminism. I made various stands of individual defiance – losing three stone, coming out as lesbian and going promptly into *fin de siècle* drag, for instance, as an undergraduate at Girton. But I saw no reason for, was indeed contemptuous of, corporate sexual political action.

Unsurprisingly, when I did begin to be involved with gay politics, it was via the safe, 'unpolitical' door of gay organisations which offered befriending and counselling. But that safe door opens, of course, on to a world of lobbying and campaigning:

arguing with newspaper groups who say their 'family' paper can't take advertisements for gay counselling; reasoning with Health Councils who say people in *their* district aren't *like* that; training sessions with psychiatrists who remain convinced that regular doses of ECT will sort out anyone's Little Problem (i.e., homosexuality).

My two years as National Organiser of FRIEND (a nationwide federation of gay self-help groups) taught me, shamefully late, that politics isn't just what happens in Parliament, government offices and town halls. It also taught me – a great shock, this – that many of my values and hopes were those traditionally associated with the left rather than the right. In adolescence I had chosen to identify with my father's early conservatism, not with the socialism of my mother's family. Why? Realising that there was a real question here and trying to find some part of the answer occupied much of my late twenties and early thirties. Gradually, and very unwillingly, I recognised that Father = Male = He Who Is Right (if sometimes terrifying); Mother = Female = She Who Is Lovable (but often muddled, poor dear, and quite likely to be wrong because, well, it's *like* that for women, isn't it?) Not a pleasing discovery and one that forced me to scrutinise other bits of dangerous lumber cluttering up my brain.

My first full-time job began in 1977 when I became literary editor and assistant features editor of the original *Gay News*. *Gay News* died a protracted and ugly death in April 1983. Its dying taught me and many of the staff a great deal about the politics of gender, ownership, management, company law, trade unions and the Press. (Anyone curious to know how and what we learnt should read *Title Fight: The Battle for Gay News*, written by my ex-colleagues Gill Hanscombe and Andrew Lumsden, and published by Brilliance Books.) Since *Gay News*'s demise I support myself, precariously, by journalism, and by freelance work for the feminist publishing house, The Women's Press.

Self-scrutiny, needless to say, continues, although friends frequently express astonishment – not to say furious incomprehension – at the bits of me I seem to think it's safe to keep. So, for example, whilst loathing many aspects of organised religion, I am a Christian in the sense that I cannot not believe in the divinity of Christ. (I did try very hard once, in a period when faith was even less intellectually respectable than usual, but I couldn't manage it.) Whilst longing ardently for the Disestablishment of Marriage as a state institution (long term), I remain a convinced monarchist (medium term) on the grounds that all those who actively seek power are, by definition, unfit to hold it and that with power-crazed loons like Hilda Margaret around we need to cling to every constitutional buffer we've got between her and us.

My sense of the past and of my place in it remains as strong as ever it was in my childhood. I am suspicious of the new, think the Luddites were almost certainly right and love my adopted home town, Cambridge, not only because its bricks and stones daily offer me tangible reminders of at least eight centuries but because I can, if need be, traverse the whole of it comfortably on foot. Of its traditions I am jealous, in both the conflicting senses of that word: jealous for them, anxious to preserve them; jealous of them when I am forced to recognise their hostility to women and exclusion of us. Living in Cambridge, as I have done since 1967, is a physical expression of that constant state of tension which necessarily exists for all women who are both formed by and in revolt against a particular vision of the world which variously ignores, co-opts and misrepresents us.

I'm perceived by half my friends as rather dangerously radical and seen by the others as a reactionary élitist. (My refusal to include that last word in my own vocabulary confirms the suspicions of the second group of friends but confuses the first.) Both groups are probably, on the whole, right about me. Clearly I find it no easier to achieve consistency than did my father.

Liz Heron

Dear Green Place

I was born in May 1947, when the whole of Britain was thawing out of a long, freezing winter made crueller by a fuel crisis.

A year too early to benefit from the National Health Service at this stage in my life, I arrived in a maternity home in Govan with the assistance of nursing sisters. Nuns, in a variety of roles, would populate odd corners of my later childhood.

My mother was thirty-eight, my father thirty-four. Both were born and grew up in the East End of Glasgow. Both left school at fourteen: my father to work as a butcher's messenger boy, my mother to learn machining in a shirt factory. She worked as a machinist until she married my father in 1946 and chose never to have a job again. They moved out of the city, to Lanarkshire, on its edges.

'You were a good baby,' my mother would tell me, 'good as gold.' She meant I didn't girn or make a fuss, and meant I should have stayed that way. In photographs I'm already scowling by the time I'm two: in an Argyle Street photographer's studio, clutching a rubber doll, dressed in a tailored coat with a velvet collar and an enormous bow in my hair; or paddling with my parents in the sea, somewhere off the coast of Ireland.

Ireland was everywhere around us, a protective blanket of second-hand memories and martyred history and bitter victimology. For it was Protestants who got better jobs, who skipped the queue for houses, who made my father work on Christmas day when the union voted against the optional holiday – to keep the Papes in their place. 'God Save Ireland' my mother would exclaim if there was news of world catastrophe on the wireless or the milk threatened to boil over. Ireland was already there with its litany of laments, not thinly preserved, like the cultural echo that accompanies some exiles and emigrés into a new country where time will absorb the native generation's traces of foreign identity and dispel them. It was late in the day and we were still waiting our turn; still wandering in search of the Promised Land.

All Saints was my first primary school. It was in Coatdyke, half-way between Coatbridge (Catholic) and Airdrie (Protestant). School and home were on opposite sides of the steep hill that was the main road joining the two. Trams went up and down it. We lived in the tenement block that ran its whole length, in a top-storey 'room and kitchen' with no bathroom and an outside toilet shared with several other families and reached by an open staircase. At night I slept in the big kitchen on the brown leatherette bed settee, and my parents slept in the box room.

This is a time of austerity, of playing with ration books, of knowing we are 'overcrowded', of squabbles between the women over doing the stairs and cleaning the toilet that are handed down to us children in the form of sectarian rivalries. 'I'd rather see you dead than turn your coat like her next door.' 'A mother's place is at home with her child' damns the mothers who aren't and answers my question about why I can't go to the nursery.

But out on the wide, untidy expanse behind the drying green and the wash houses the children must have forgotten, for we play tig and hide-and-seek in the long grass, running about in gangs of indiscriminate age and religion. And the girls have doll and pram races.

As an only child I was rare among my schoolmates; most Catholic

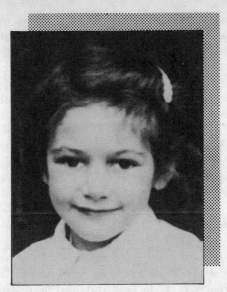

Me at five, or maybe six

families were more numerous, big brothers and wee sisters gave other children the advantage of additional, if vicarious, experience. My mother made novenas, but the longed-for infant who would share the burden of childhood with me never arrived. I am bowled over by my first day at school; there are scores of us sitting at long bench desks in a vast wooden hut. We play with plasticine, draw pictures and start learning to count; a white-haired lady with a navy blue costume and a bun presides. At three o'clock when I am collected to go home I can hardly wait to go back once I've had my tea.

The next three years at this school are the source of few and faint memories, but school relieved the loneliness of only-childhood.

If the benefits of large families were obvious in the Irish peasant society in which we had once had our roots, they had a certain value for us too; they scored vital points on the council housing list. In the early fifties Scotland's housing shortage was still severe. Larger families around us were being rehoused at a steady rate, but we were doomed to wait for ever. In 1954 savings were sunk in buying a 'room and kitchen with scullery'; it had no bathroom, but there was an inside toilet, and it was a better area. We moved to Uddingston.

The tenement building we moved from is now gone (as is the one we moved to), replaced by a row of council blocks of impressive ugliness, vintage early sixties.

I know those tenement-lined streets invite a nostalgic lament for the loss of community. But the nostalgia invokes the mythic existence of an interdependent and mutually supportive working class that was then broken up and scattered geographically, forfeiting its cohesion and everyday solidarity for the false promises of new amenities and material improvements, trading off its hopes of a truly better world for a bigger share in the spoils of the old one and the new fruits of the consumer society. This nostalgia for the Edenic community of poverty is not the nostalgia of working-class people but of others. Implicit in it is a belief in the nobility of the suffering victim and a judgement that sees the working class as inevitably corrupted by material things.

But to rely on the decline of pre-war forms of working-class life and the rise in consumerism as a political explanation for what has happened to working-class loyalties is the narrowest kind of mythic reconstruction. It appropriates the imagination of others.

For most people whose political and economic power is limited, history is something that is made every day, every week, in a way of living that might either accommodate to future possibilities or wrestle with them. For young people there is still room to invent them. That was particularly true for the generation I grew up in. Some people can go on inventing, of course, but with a different set of conditions attached to their lives.

Beyond 1945 and its immediate aftermath was the outline of a future permeated with hope. I find it hard to imagine what the end of the war must have meant. I look at a photograph of my father still in uniform, taken at Loch Lomond before he was demobbed, as he stands smiling between his younger brother and the English friend he had met in an Italian POW camp. In East Prussia only months before he had crossed fields strewn with corpses to reach the

156

American lines after the Russian advance had enveloped his prison camp. The details of his three years' captivity from the North African desert to the Eastern Front were not spoken of for more than another thirty, other than by occasional scant reference.

Once demobbed he planned to go to New Zealand and start a new life. Back in Glasgow he found his father seriously ill. The new life turned into marriage, my birth and an attempt to start a business with some of his demob money; he and his brother rented shop premises to sell painting and decorating materials. Neither had 'a head for figures' – the venture failed within months and my father found a job as a tradesman again. For years throughout my childhood he exchanged Christmas letters with another ex-POW in New Zealand. He had a daughter my age called Zoe and he sent me illustrated books of Australian flowers and bird-life.

Alcoholism is recognised as a major social problem in the west of Scotland. I don't know the figures for mental illness, but they must be of the same order, though better hidden. It can go on for years before families are forced to acknowledge the truth ...

On a taxi ride across the Clyde Valley – Hamilton, Motherwell, Wishaw ... going with my father to the psychiatric hospital where my mother had just been admitted, I was overwhelmed by the past, not just the place names that had filled my childhood when I'd lived in this part of Scotland over twenty years before, but another past to which I had even less access: a prelude to my own.

I have few clues that would let me construct a picture of my mother's childhood, that would explain her denial of mine as my own, and the rage that came with that denial. I only know there was a father who was both idolised and undoubtedly feared, a dogmatic and overbearing Catholic. He also had in him the wrathful patriarch of the Protestant religion, for he was the product of the two warring faiths, of an Irish Catholic mother and an Irish Presbyterian father, and of the Sunday ritual my mother would repeatedly describe as if narrating the auspicious early life of a saint. It was mother who sent the children to Mass, father who beat the daylights out of them when they got home; in the end mother won, father lost and, Protestant-educated, they grew up Catholics.

This grandfather of mine died in 1932, but his wife lived until I was sixteen. But long before her death my grandmother was a ghost to me, as if she was never really there, even though I visited her regularly as a child. She was a quiet, gentle soul, she had no malice in her, but I doubt whether she had the smallest capacity for taking care of other people. Maybe she had tried, but in her sixties she had slumped into forgetfulness. She lived alone in a block of old people's flats in the East End of Glasgow; around her, layers of dust coated the jumble of furniture and holy pictures and pious bric-a-brac, and the kitchen was filmed with grease.

At four I stay with her when my mother spends a week in hospital for a minor operation. I want her to talk to me, to tell me stories about her as a little girl, to play with me and look as I play, but she drifts off into herself. The flats face Carntyne dog track, and I gaze out of the window at the greyhounds as they sprint after the electric hare, then, late in the afternoon, transfer my attention to the road, in the hope of seeing my father appear again with sweeties, and notebooks for me to draw in. That week was an eternity of solitude and boredom.

Most Saturdays, too, had that time-stopped flavour, for then my mother would take me with her on her weekly visits. The only memories are of the long walk down from Parkhead Cross where we get off the bus we've taken along the Gallowgate from the centre of town. All the way past Parkhead Forge I drag my feet. I hate the heavy dirtiness of the area, the grit and dust in my eyes and mouth, the litter blowing along in the gutter of the deserted road before we turn under the railway bridge and into Todd Street. At my Granny's we hear the Parkhead roar all afternoon if Celtic is playing at home, and we take the train home from Carntyne station where a nauseatingly bad smell fills the air.

'What is it?' I remember asking.

'A piggery.'

'What's a piggery?'

'Where they melt down pig's fat.'

These were intimations of years to come when I, too, would be a sourly dutiful daughter. And years of Mass and Devotions, the Sacred Heart Messenger and a thousand shoddy pieties, of no make-up, of becoming 'a fine Catholic teacher', of enacting someone else's life as it might have been, as it would have been 'with my advantages'.

When I read Mary Gordon's *Final Payments* a few years ago I shuddered with relief at having broken the spell of what had been wished on me.

And then there is my other grandmother, Sarah, my father's mother. I was not given her name – that came from my mother and her mother – but I think I must have inherited her resilience, which my father has too. As a child I was kept at a distance from her, because of rifts in the family. I only got to know her a little as a teenager when I visited her on my own in the single-end where she lived in a Parkhead tenement, sleeping, washing and cooking in one room. Everything was scrubbed clean, as she was herself.

At eighty she sparkled with cheerfulness and good humour. She was well under five feet in height and her legs were terribly bowed because of rickets. She had had eight children, only four of whom survived, and had done hard physical work all her life because my grandfather had poor health. She was born in the reign of Queen Victoria, suffered malnutrition as a child and had brought up her own children in poverty. She died at eighty-four in an old people's home after having a stroke. I wish I had known her better.

This grandmother can be a heroine for me now, although it would have meant more to have been closer to her in life. I can only admire her courage. I can also acknowledge that there must have been many women like her, all over Glasgow; that there were then in the early 1900s when she was marrying and becoming a mother; that there were later. Many women whose courage has to be admired. Working-class women who endured hardship and self-sacrifice and survived with something of themselves still intact.

But there were also women whose courage failed them. Women who did not have the heart or the will to live up to what the moral and social order said they should be, but who lived by it nonetheless. Perhaps they could not be good wives and good mothers because they could not give what they had never had.

> The houses are Glasgow, not the people – these
> (Their character all shaded to suit their environment.

Life doesn't *take* there).
Are simply the food the houses live and grow on
Endlessly, drawing from them their vulgarity
And pettiness and darkness of spirit

wrote Hugh MacDiarmid in 'Glasgow' the same year I was born. For me as a child, Glasgow was its buildings; the city was physically oppressive in a way that is painfully memorable. How now to understand my passion for Glasgow that has grown over the years of absence from Scotland? My heart lurches when the train from Euston crosses the Clyde. Maybe it's the knowledge that my history isn't entirely mine alone. And now I'm seduced by the city's romance and generosity, its vitality and resilience. This is the 'dear green place' that its name may once have meant to the Celts.

My feelings about my childhood shift around all the time. My mother the past, my father the future. The line back to childhood memories is elastic. At seven it tightens and I feel a tug. It's just before my seventh birthday that we move. There's the excitement of birthday cards in a new house, and a new school where my classroom is again a hut with a wood stove.

At home there were often rows about spending money. But the year I was seven something gave. The world spread out for me in a new map of associations and sensations. We went to Paris to see one of my father's sisters. Both were nuns in the same religious order, one in the north of England, the other in France where she had been interned throughout the Occupation. This was my father's first visit to her since the war; what made it possible was the free travel concession he now had, working for British Railways as a painter and decorator.

In 1954 it was a long journey by rail from Glasgow to Paris, and it must have seemed longer to me. I remember the stale leathery smell of the trains, and sleeping curled up in station waiting rooms in the middle of the night. At the end of it is a Paris suburb, a bed with cool white linen and nuns fussing around me. A tall tree spreads its branches outside my bedroom window and everything is different from what I've known: to my ears, my nostrils and my taste buds.

New toys are found for me and I play in the courtyard of the high-walled convent or slide on the waxed floors, too shy to talk to anyone. I am spell-bound by the sound of French, infuriated when I can't read it in the books I am given. We are honoured guests; every meal is a feast, with spectacular displays of food on polished serving dishes: golden roasts and garnished vegetables, salads, new kinds of fruit and creamy custards, cutlery gleaming and glasses sparkling against the white napkins with their silvery rings, rings of crusty bread piled in a basket. Nothing is like at home. Here is a sweet-smelling haven of order and nourishment, peace and security. I decide to become a nun.

This aspiration reflected a craving for everyday structure that persisted over years. With a desperate envy I read adventure stories where childhood freedoms were supported by a hidden foundation of adult labour and organisation. These middle-class heroes and heroines returned from their exploits in the great outdoors of the Cotswolds or the Cornish Moors to the sound of the gong that summoned them to groaning tables. Hampers were laid on for picnics, parcels of treats supplied for midnight romps in Swiss Alpine dorms, and no child's insatiable hunger went unsatisfied. Only the orphan – until the final chapter, when even she would sit by a warm fire, rescued at last from a cruel world and adult depredations by the long-lost loving parent who waits at the end of every unhappy child's rainbow.

That common dream of children's literature, of independence from the power of adults, and a safe, warm place of their making, filled my fantasies. Often they were shared. At eight or nine I planned to run away with my friend Ann, to escape from the unjust punishments, the complaints of ingratitude, the wrongs I unwittingly committed. In our games we borrowed lives from the books we read or from the hardy and hard-done-by heroines of *Bunty*, *Girls' Crystal* or *School Friend*. We shared their dreams of escape and vindication.

There were other sources for our fantasies. On Sunday nights at home we listen to Dan Dare on Radio Luxembourg and that week's episode is replayed and embellished, with Ann and her brother, who also read it in the *Eagle*. Television at home came later; for now we watch it in the Italian café, where the price of a penny ice lolly opens the dusty chenille curtain and we can join the other children huddled in the darkness in front of the flickering screen in the corner. We sit on wooden boxes round the heavy tables with their curling iron legs, and because the lollies are set on sticks splintered from firewood you sometimes get a skelf in your mouth as you suck, intent on the Lone Ranger. Our admission charge rations us to one programme.

For a while television was a rare and special thing; not many people had it and they were well off. Then not having it rapidly became a sign of poverty. We got ours in 1956, and the filmed reports of the Hungarian uprising and of its refugees arriving in Britain gave me my first image of dramatic world events. This was of a different order from my imaginings about the Chinese communists, arch villains whose evil doings were retailed to us in the classroom with the same ferocious didacticism that accompanies the telling of a lurid fairy tale and enhances its horrifying fascination. The imaginary and timeless cruelties of the Chinese are relished as they frighten us, while the drama of the Hungarians is a disturbing intrusion of someone else's reality that, glimpsed on the television screen, is not entirely unlike our own: worried-looking men in square-shouldered, belted coats; forlorn children.

Television came in the wake of other consumer durables: a vacuum cleaner and a boiler for the washing – once used to cook a lobster my father has brought back from the Highlands where he's been on a spell of painting stations that will be closed by the Beeching plan a decade later. I remember squealing as we watch the black monster twitch its claws on the scullery floor.

In school this progressive acquisition of domestic technology was taken for granted, and we felt sorry for those children who lagged behind. These were the children some of the teachers looked down on because they came to school with unmended holes in their jumpers, or no proper shoes, only canvas sandshoes to see them through the winter. They were clearly destined for the junior secondary, with no hope of passing the 'qualie'. Most of us, children of tradesmen, miners and semi-skilled factory workers, were better off than that and had higher hopes, though there was a good scattering of nits and lice and dirty feet around the classroom when the nurse came to do her inspection. We'd been filled with school milk and cod-liver oil and orange juice, but only the few scheme-housing children had bathrooms.

In the 1950s the West of Scotland had no Catholic middle class to speak of. There was the odd professional, the occasional doctor or lawyer, but our closest link with another class, with an individual of social standing, was in the classroom. At primary school my teachers occupied the pedestal that should have been reserved for 'Our Lady' whom the catechism prescribed as *the* model of Catholic girlhood and womanhood. Our Ladylike behaviour was the touchstone for pious adult injunctions: 'Our Lady wouldn't whistle; Our Lady wouldn't go to Mass without gloves; Our Lady wouldn't show her knickers like that, be so selfish, so lazy, so cheeky.' A more benign and glamorous model was embodied in the young women teachers with their New Look skirts and wide-belted dresses. They were all in a state of becoming engaged or about to be married; nearly all virginal, but on the verge of something else.

By the time we reach primary seven, and I am ten, my class has become preoccupied with sex. We are mesmerised by the mystery of young women's bodies, trying to unlock their secrets with words that are whispered from desk to desk. 'What's *pregnant*?' 'What's *prostitute*?'

I looked them up in the big dictionary my father had bought for me by mail order at the beginning of the year. The same year I got a Pears Cyclopaedia from him at Christmas. In it I read and re-read the Greek myths and legends, consumed with a desire to understand the sexual exploits of the gods, capricious beings, sometimes part or wholly animal. Some of them I had already encountered in *Tanglewood Tales* I and II, which I'd read in the class library at a younger and less sexually conscious age, but the power of those stories also lay in what was only half-knowable.

The other kind of sex I learned about was the meaning of the four-letter words the boys chalked up on the playground wall, though the explanations were inadequate and puzzling, passed on by other children and received with incredulity. This kind of sex – 'how Teddy Boys said goodnight to their girlfriends' – was shocking and dirty, but couldn't be all there was to it. To love and romance and how babies were made. The mysteries remained.

Books were the key to making sense of the world around me, as well as the means of transcending its realities, and my reading was obsessive. I read my way through the children's section of Uddingston library: Rosemary Sutcliffe and G.A. Henty, travel books and career books, school stories and Enid Blyton's *Famous Five* and *Secret Seven* and 'Adventure' books. For Christmas and birthdays I asked for the red, hard-backed children's classics published by Dean and Co. and sold in Woolworth's: *Treasure Island*, *The Children of the New Forest*, *Alice in Wonderland*, *What Katy Did*, *A Tale of Two Cities*. And there were the prizes I'd accumulated through primary, books for Good Attendance or General Merit, in which I usually came top girl.

I read everything I could find about France (since France was my dream country, where I felt I'd been meant to be born and grow up ...) and developed a particular passion for the French Revolution, reading all the Scarlet Pimpernel books, the story of the first Madame Tussaud, forced to model the guillotined heads, and everything that I could find that would bring it all to life. I think I had the average child's thirst for blood and a more than average thirst for romance. I filled a notebook with names and stories about the Revolution and planned to write a book in which all my favourites would appear.

The only other fictional world I lived in with the same intensity was that of Louisa M. Alcott. I was not alone in the way I identified with the saga of the March family, nor was I alone in identifying with Jo (and presumably all readers do) in her hurts and disappointments, her longings for femininity that clashed with her dreams of independence and achievement; and in wishing for the ultimate fairness of all things as they were shaped by those nineteenth-century moral certainties. All mothers were good mothers, all wives were good wives. That was how I wanted it to be, but what made me ache was the knowledge that Jo couldn't have all she wanted: to be the writer of stories, whose stories were her children, but heart-breakingly not to have Laurie. I yearned for Laurie and raged at the injustice of Jo's making do with the elderly Professor Behr, unconvinced by the book's insistence that she was happy.

Books were solitary, but the stories and people in them were sometimes shared. So too were the made-up stories. With my friend

Ann, I go for walks across the hilly fields towards Viewpark or go playing on the coal byngs, and we make up stories, often vengeful episodes in which punishments are meted out to our enemies. Foremost among them are the Queen and the class bully. The Queen because she is rich and English, and the English are all our enemies because of Bruce and Bannockburn, and Bonnie Prince Charlie and Mary Queen of Scots.

We sometimes write down the stories and one summer with other children we put on a play we had adapted from a Russian folktale in *Folktales of Many Lands*. But we forget our lines when we see the audience, a rival group of girls to whom the only boy in our gang has defected. They jeer at our efforts and laugh at our makeshift costumes. But revenge is not to be allowed us, for when we turn up at their concert a phalanx of adults is there to make sure the audience behaves.

Ann's dad was a bookie. Her house had a bathroom, and a rose garden, and a grand piano in the front room. And at the back of the house were the wooden sheds that were our palaces, our temples, our ranches, our mansions. With her brother and others we pick brambles and wild strawberries along the disused railway line and gather gooseberries in the overgrown field next to the café. There are walks to Bothwell Castle where we picnic with tomato sandwiches and lemonade in the unkempt, wooded grounds or inside the ruins, always in a group of girls.

These are my childhood idylls, when summer holidays were always hot and sunny.

In the rough and tumble of my street there was less luxuriance. I had a sense of belonging, but I felt awkward with my body. Children of all ages played together, at kick-the-can and peever, hide-and-seek and steps and tig. I could never run fast enough and day-dreamed too much. The same went for all the climbing and jumping across the back court, over high walls and coal bunkers, that we did in the girls' gang. I could never keep up. I was small and thin for my age, had colds all winter long and was considered 'frail'. But we all went swimming on Tuesday nights at Hamilton baths, and I did better than some because my father had taught me to swim on holiday.

Everything changed in the late summer of 1958 when I went to 'the convent', Elmwood, my senior secondary school, and began to lose sight of all these children, now separated by age or by the hurdle of the 'qualie' that had kept some back and relegated them to the junior secondary where school ended at fifteen, divided girls from boys and clever from less clever. In my A stream class at 'the convent' I knew none of the other girls and rarely saw my former classmates.

In primary school the qualifying exam had been talked of for at least two years before the time came, yet I have no memory of when it did, only that our last term was punctuated with little exams and on two occasions we had something quite new to do: intelligence tests.

One day we sit up straight at our desks to be told who has passed and who has failed. 'Sorry, Jimmy,' the teacher clucks sympathetically at one unfortunate. 'You tried hard but you didn't make it.' The unfairness of this strikes me, since although we are all from families that vote Labour (no working-class Catholic would vote Unionist) Jimmy had been the only one in the class who'd known that Hugh Gaitskell was the leader of the Opposition in the general knowledge quiz.

I hadn't. But despite this gap in my knowledge, at the final prizegiving I pocketed the medal for Dux Girl, gold-plated and engraved and donated – two to each local school, regardless of religious denomination – by Mr Archie Tunnock of Tunnock's Caramel Wafers (Uddingston's only factory). My name was the first to go on the Dux board in the school hall of the brand-new, glass-walled building only just completed the year before.

The short brown gym tunic with its blue and gold woven girdle that I wore on my first day at Elmwood was a symbol of entry into a new world of lady-like refinement and academic élitism. At any rate it had been so in the past, when Elmwood had been a private school. The still-rarefied atmosphere received a heavy blast of different air as the school opened its gates to the bulging generation of girls born just after the war and a working class bound for higher educational achievements than it had ever had within its reach. My year was born in 1946 – I was younger than most of my new classmates.

Without the nuns the tone of the school would have been lower, but they maintained a discreet background presence and our spiritual as well as our academic guidance was delegated to a staff that were largely 'lay'. The women, the majority, were unmarried; the men, married. The men took more liberties and joked with us. The women's style was severe and more remote, protected by their teachers' armour – as if there was nothing more to their lives that could connect them with ours.

Discipline was rigid and we respected it, but resented it too, because of a particular juvenile arrogance that must have been founded on the knowledge that the world was changing a lot more than they realised, and it was for us that it was changing. There were hints that they too saw signs in our future; in second year our history teacher told us that things were easier now for Catholics than they had ever been, that we could have a place in the world, that there was even a chance that a Catholic would be President of the United States after the next election.

But the friendships, rivalries and enmities that were the daily humours of this densely female world were often underlaid by class differences, snobberies about who had what and who lived where – between the daughters of the traditional convent-school middle class and the rest of us. Yet with its residual gentility, its variegated forest of a garden where we had practical botany lessons, and the original Victorian mansion building with its labyrinth of pokey rooms and winding staircases, it must have seemed that the convent was an accidental inheritance, never really meant for us, and thereby reminding us that we had come into our own; we had *by right* something more than had once been intended for us.

Sprawling around the main house were the new wooden huts built to accommodate an increasing school population and almost encroaching on the distant row of classrooms that housed the still-private primary school. The whole school was closed down a few years ago. I went back to see it, first in a state of dereliction, then half-demolished to make way for a private housing-estate development.

I was a pupil at Elmwood for almost three years, until we moved house to Ayrshire in 1961. I continued to do well, but there was an increasing gap between my home life and my aspirations, as these became more like possibilities. It wasn't that these were definite; I just wanted life to be different, to be somewhere else. 'With education, the world is your oyster,' my father told me. But my mother's image of my future had to be challenged: I was not to marry; I would be her companion at all times in a perfect mother and daughter symbiosis; with my teacher's salary I would buy her a fridge and a washing machine and take care of her. This she had made me promise when I was nine and she continued to insist that my refusal to live my life her way was selfishness and rank ingratitude. I was ignoring the debt I owed her.

The debt was written off in a long, slow reckoning of my own, though by the time I reached my mid-teens I already had a certainty of the future waiting – a void to be filled as I chose, with nothing predetermined.

In a way that's the necessary, valuable mistake of youth at all times in history. Yet women of my generation were the first to have the chance to refuse burdens that just couldn't be borne, to understand that it was possible to refuse them without censure, to realise that if you still couldn't have everything, you could at least make some choices about what you could have.

I believed for many years that I could move towards the future and leave the past behind, that there was no need for me to return home. But the past too has to be claimed.

I WENT to Glasgow University from 1964 to 1967. In no sense did it correspond to the experience of student activism that so many of my generation were to go through elsewhere over the next few years. I left just a bit less naive than when I'd started, and a lot more confused; in the end I fitted neither with the industrious working-class student body (which was a large proportion) nor with the socially confident middle class who did less work but had better cultural camouflage to disguise their deficiencies. But the objective worth of my degree was far surpassed by its value as a stepping-stone to other places, other identities.

I didn't know about existentialism until I went to university, although at sixteen I had spent a lot of time agonising over whether God existed and what was Free Will, and had the frisson of reading Voltaire. In French literature lectures, Sartre became more than an academic discovery, though I understand only now why the idea that 'the person is nothing else but his freedom' and the revelations of *Nausea* had such enormous appeal for me. But I took on the idea of transcendence only at a personal level. Even though the politics were there to see, for me they had no context yet. There was the same gap between understanding and the possibility of action when I read Simone de Beauvoir's *The Second Sex* just before leaving university. I felt a lot of anger, but there was nothing I could do with it; then it faded, until I started making some connections with feminism at the beginning of the seventies.

I left Scotland at the end of 1968. There followed several years of working and travelling in Spain, France and Italy, punctuated by breaks of living and working in London. I've lived in London continuously since 1975. By that time I had some history of being involved in socialist politics, which helped make sense of the external world, and a dawning recognition that there was also an inner world to be explored and that the psyche couldn't just be dealt with by an effort of will. There's the same difficulty with achieving liberation on a collective scale. But while there's imagination, there's hope.

Ursula Huws

Hiraeth

For lack of anything better to do, one winter evening in 1980, I watched an old film on the television. Made in 1949, it was a mawkish production about the flooding of a Welsh village, with Richard Burton as the young male lead and Edith Evans as his poor-but-honest mother. The inhabitants of the village were presented much as the natives of a Mediterranean island might be, simple-minded, infinitely courteous and hospitable, much given to singing and dancing, bobbing their heads and saying *bore da* (Welsh for 'Good Morning') to the nice gentry. There were also a few nasty gentry, to keep the plot rolling and ensure that the village's tragedy could be explained as resulting from the actions of one individual psychopath, rather than any broader class or imperialist conflicts. My normal reaction to such stuff would have been amusement, detached analysis and eventual boredom. This time it was utterly different. I felt a smug little twinge of triumph when Edith Evans scored a point over the nasty gentry. I joined in with the singing. I wept as the dam opened and the valley flooded. It was as though the film made some direct connection with my tear ducts. I had occasionally been moved in the same way by huge crowds of people united in some common cause, or by a defiant brass band on a demonstration, but never as unexpectedly as this. I was astonished and intrigued and determined to understand its significance, so determined that at three in the morning I crossed Leeds like a burglar to fetch my typewriter from the office where I worked so that I could record my reactions to it.

Four years later, looking back over those notes, I find that *The Last Days of Dolwyn*, as the film was called, seemed to touch me so intimately because, at some subterranean level, it was my childhood. In grotesque caricature, it enacted many of the dreams which concerned me most centrally, parodying some of my deepest emotional responses, and highlighting contradictions which, to this day, are incompletely resolved. One of the most important of these contradictions concerns class.

The romantic interest of the film was a courtship between the poor young villager hero and the daughter of the lord of the manor (which also, of course, served the purpose of demonstrating that class conflict can be resolved by love). My father too was from a small Welsh village, apprenticed in his teens as a draftsman in a Birkenhead shipyard, of quite a different class from my mother, whose family's titles dated back to 1066, and who had been brought up in a houseful of servants in Hampstead, spending her holidays in rural stately homes. Part of his childhood had actually been spent living on the edge of an estate owned by some cousins of hers in Anglesey. Yet it would be a distortion to present their marriage as a Laurentian union between aristocrat and labourer. Her family was slipping downwards into the professional upper middle class, while his aspired upwards to the petty bourgeoisie (his father was the village schoolmaster). And they had met almost as social equals in the declassé Bohemia of Bloomsbury in 1930. However, there was no denying a gulf between them created by class difference, a gulf which made their children's social positions insecure and ambivalent, and which was further complicated by her Englishness and his Welshness, her Catholicism and his agnosticism, and by the eccentricity which was, perhaps, the only quality which they truly shared.

My tenuous grip on class identity was loosened still further by the

Me, aged about three, with my older sister Angharad. The picture was taken professionally so this must have been a special event, such as an agricultural fair.

fact that it did not remain static. As for so many others, the fifties were a time of social change. In our case, the decade was divided almost exactly into three by moves which coincided with changes in my father's job.

Until the autumn of 1953, when I was six, we lived in a tiny Anglesey village in a house which became more and more overcrowded as the family expanded. By the time my younger brother was born, in 1950, we numbered five children, with a gap of eighteen years between the two boys. My sisters, six and nine years older than me, and referred to as 'the girls', had to share a room with us two little ones, known as 'the children'. The whole village lacked electricity, gas and water mains. Our drinking water came from a well, and washing water from two large corrugated-iron tanks, erected by my father, which collected rainwater at the back of the house. The lavatory was an Elsan in a stone outhouse next to the goatshed at the top of the garden. Lighting came from tilley lamps which made a ferocious panting noise as they were pumped up, and, in our bedrooms, diminutive paraffin lamps known as 'moons'. My parents had lived there for fourteen years, and we were, or so it felt to me, an accepted part of the community, despite our oddities.

Where everyone was known to everyone else, and all, to some extent, shared the same material hardships; where nobody had a car, or a television or a washing machine, the differences which were most apparent were those of individual character and behaviour rather than class. Even my mother's otherness was not unique. The upheavals of the war had brought other foreign wives to the village. By the age of three I was happily integrated into the one-classroom village school, parroting alphabets and tables in Welsh and English and rewarded with approving smiles for my precocity. The carless lanes were a safe playground, giving on to other homes many of which were welcoming. There I learned a third language, the chanting Welsh-English of the village children, which had recently been augmented by some misapplied Liverpudlian phrases, snatched from evacuees.

During the war my father had worked in an aircraft factory in Beaumaris. The urgent need to design and produce new bombers created an atmosphere which he found exciting, cutting down bureaucratic procedures and shortening the chain of command, and enabling him to exercise his considerable mechanical inventiveness without restraint. They would, he said, always present him with a problem on Friday afternoon, knowing that by Monday he would have found a solution to it without any of the firm's time having been wasted. Paid as a draftsman, he was practising as an industrial designer. By 1950 production there had ground almost to a halt but he, infected by an optimistic sense that anything was possible in post-war classless Labour Britain, had taken himself off to London (leaving his family behind in Anglesey) to try to earn a living as a freelance designer.

I suppose we must have been poor during this period. My father could rarely afford to come home to visit us, and was desperately homesick. He used to stand in Euston station to watch the Welsh faces come off the trains. It was a tragedy when two fountain pens he had sent as presents for my sisters did not arrive. There was no way he could afford to replace them. I can remember too how one sister saved her pocket money for months on end to buy Mother a *blanket*. But some of the things that now seem evidence of poverty may well have been common experiences of post-war shortages and rationing. Mother saving every piece of paper with a picture on it, from old Christmas cards to *Picture Post* covers, to make scrapbooks for us. Clothes cut down from cast-offs which arrived in parcels from America, or lined with a brilliant yellow nylon known as parachute silk. Old ration books for drawing in.

Yet in some ways our lives must have seemed very luxurious to others in the village. My older brother and sisters went to boarding schools paid for by a sister of my mother's who was the only relation of hers we ever saw, apart from one great-aunt. And money must have been found somewhere for childminding, because I was looked after much of the time by an elderly neighbour, Elin Jones, my adored 'Doney', who sometimes seems, in retrospect, to have been the most important figure in my early life. Mother didn't go out to work, but then what work could she possibly have done in rural Wales? She wrote poetry, and reviews for the *Anglo Welsh Review*, and put a great deal of creative energy into stories and picturebooks for her children.

In 1950 my father's future in London must have seemed assured. He was commissioned to do some work for the 1951 Festival of Britain, including a spectacular moving fountain which tipped huge curving buckets of water in a random sequence, sounding, as he had intended, like waves on the shore, and attracting praise from critics and public. Yet by 1952 he was struggling. He explained it in class terms, though without any real analysis of class conflict. As he saw it, industry had been opened up to talent and democratised during the war; now, the public school twits were reclaiming it. He reserved particular bitterness for those businessmen who had sat the war out comfortably in Rhodesia or South Africa and were now using the wealth thus gained to take control of the engineering industry, which he regarded as the only market for his skills. The following year he accepted defeat, and returned to a job as a draftsman with his old employers; this time in the Isle of Wight, the Anglesey plant being by now shut down.

This meant abrupt and unsettling changes for me, aged six, and my three-year-old brother and to a lesser extent the rest of the family. We did not actually move to the terraced streets of East Cowes, clustered round the shipyard where my father now worked, but to posher West Cowes, to a semi in an endless row of others, lining a main road out of town. But our days were structured by the same hooter which blew three times in the morning, to get up, to leave home, and to start work, and again to mark the shift changes through the day. Life seemed at first more prosperous, but when the novelty of electric lights and flushing lavatories had worn off, I became aware that we were surrounded by people who owned things we did not, like cars and even yachts.

After her long Welsh exile, Mother began to make friends with women who, though socially below her childhood contemporaries, were well above most draftsmen's wives. The two I remember were married to doctors. It was my father who was now the foreigner, and he took it badly, especially in combination with the sense of having failed in his career. Class began to figure prominently in the rows between my parents, though inextricably tangled with questions of nationality. To him, the upper-class English were devoid of any real feeling. They mocked and humiliated other cultures and tried to destroy them. We children were being taught to despise our Welsh heritage and become facetious and dishonest. We were also being given ideas above our station which would bring us to grief. Our previous village life was recreated for us as an idyll of simplicity and pleasure, of respect for work and harmony with nature. Mother's views were transmitted less directly, but I suspect that from this period date many powerful ideas I must have received from her. Most important of these was a vision of a kind of drawing-room English culture which was infinitely knowledgeable and infinitely receptive, a world in which it would be possible to express the subtlest nuances of thought and be understood. It was a world of books and paintings but above all of talk – witty talk, serious talk and talk of the emotions. Beside it Welsh culture seemed limited and perhaps even a little crude. It was inconceivable that any language other than English could be the vehicle for such a broad linguistic sweep.

Yet, even the contemplation of this verbal paradise was fraught with guilt. For my father, to whom feelings were much too important to circumscribe with words and display for strangers to handle, my facility with the English language was a terrible betrayal. He became desperate that I should not forget my Welsh, scouring the bookshops, whenever he was in London, for Welsh children's books. Unfortunately those he could find confirmed all my worst prejudices. They were banal comicbooks, illustrated in a style that I had already learned from Mother to call vulgar. In English I was devouring *The Secret Garden*, *What Katy Did* and *The Would-be-Goods*. The nightly pleadings to speak Welsh and not to acquire an Isle of Wight accent became as great an ordeal as the equally unavailing appeals to stop sucking my thumb, and within two years I had developed a permanent block against speaking the language, although I still understood it perfectly well and, indeed, passed my Welsh O levels years later without difficulty.

In 1956, when I was nine, there came another sudden break. This time, the move not only took us back to Wales, but also pushed us firmly into the middle class. With the assistance of the same aunt who paid for our private education, my father got a job at Liverpool University, teaching design to first-year architecture students. During the week, in term time, he lived in a grubby bedsitter in Liverpool 8, coming home at weekends to Llanrwst, where he had established the rest of the family in a large, cold Victorian house overlooking the field in which the livestock auctions were held on fair days.

Llanrwst is claustrophobically sited in the Conway valley, which divides Snowdonia from the Denbigh moors and forms a funnel between the tourist resorts of the North Wales coast and those inland, like Bettws-y-Coed. Socially, it was a curious mix. Like most North Wales market towns it contained a small professional middle class – solicitors, estate agents and doctors, who were predominantly English-speaking, and teachers and clergy who mainly spoke Welsh. Then there was a large, Welsh-speaking farming population which relied on its schools and shops and, to serve them, a class of small shopkeepers who were also predominantly Welsh-speaking. However, there was also an English-speaking working class, dating from the days when nearby lead mines had been thriving concerns. Much of this labour had been drawn from outside Wales – Ireland, Poland, and even Malta, as well as England. Now, with the mines closed, there was little work for them: a factory down the valley in Llandudno Junction, work in a few expanding services like garages, or casual seasonal employment in cafés or hotels. For, creeping over this structure like ivy on a tree trunk, was another – the tourist industry.

It was this development, above all, which was disrupting the traditional hierarchies, raising new questions about what constituted richness and poverty, Englishness and Welshness. The tourists themselves, disparagingly known as 'trippers', were the newly affluent working classes of Lancashire and the Midlands, determined to have a good time at all costs. To the frugal, ascetic, often teetotal people of the North Wales mainland, their flashy clothes and conspicuous consumption were incomprehensible (the fifty weeks in the factory which underwrote the feverish fortnight in Rhyl or Colwyn Bay were, of course, invisible). On the whole, they left the noisy visitors alone, although some provided bed and breakfast in their homes in the summer months. It was other English people who best understood how to part the tourists from their cash, and many made substantial fortunes in the process, forming a new English middle class in the towns, with sharply discordant cultural values.

This analysis is, of course, retrospective. Making sense of it was a long and painful process. My first encounter with Llanrwst society was a traumatic one, the day I started at the local primary school. In the Isle of Wight I had been to a small and friendly convent school, where I had been something of a pet. The nuns there advanced children according to their progress rather than their age, so I had been pushed up two years ahead of most of my age-group. Had I remained there, I would have been in the top (eleven-plus) class. At Llanrwst I was placed with the other eight- to nine-year-olds, under a fierce and unpopular form teacher, known as 'Fanny Comp' for some reason I never fathomed. Right from the beginning she took against me. As the only new child in the class I was made to stand at the front and be cross-examined at the start of the school day. First, she mimicked my 'posh' accent. Then she made me repeat several times over the unfortunate name of my last school. 'Convent of Our Lady of the Sacred Heart?' she echoed in mock incredulity, '*Con*vent of Our *La*dy of the Sacred *Heart*? Well what do you make of that, then, class?' And she orchestrated them, grateful as they were that for once her sarcasm was not directed at them, into waves of laughter.

There was worse to come. I got all my sums right, in record time, but they were marked wrong because I had put a line under the total, a foreign practice which was frowned upon in her class. My writing was then judged incorrect because I had joined the letters up, an even greater crime, aping the style of senior classes where such things were legitimate. She hoped, I think, for a triumph when the time came for the language of the classroom to switch to Welsh and we were given a comprehension test to do. Unfortunately even here I was considerably better able to cope than some of the tongue-tied English children in the class, and she had to resort to more generalised forms of humiliation. My pride was considerable, and I think I might still have got through the day without tears had it not been for one more incident. During breaktime one of my plaits came undone, leaving me with an unruly bush of wiry brown hair on one side of my head, which prevented me from seeing properly. This was something which often happened, and was normally easily dealt with by simply approaching the nearest responsible adult and asking her to put the ribbon back in for me. It had never occured to me that this might be something I could learn to do myself.

I didn't quite dare to make a direct approach to Fanny Comp, but hung around in her vicinity waiting for the inevitable 'Well, and what's the matter with you, then?' When it came, there was not even a space to suggest that I was hoping she would help me. It was immediately followed by a hate-filled diatribe not only against me and my filthy slovenly ways but also those of all Catholics, particularly my mother. Her rage knocked me sideways. I was aware that Englishness might be a moral handicap, but this was the first time I had ever heard that Catholicism was shameful. I had no defence and collapsed, finally, into ignominious tearful incoherence.

Thus was my world turned upside down again. The qualities which had earned me praise in England were a source of public social disgrace here. (The handful of Catholics in the school, who were mostly also handicapped by being foreign, had to stand outside the hall during Assembly, and parade up to the front afterwards, to the audible jeers of other pupils.) The prevailing English cultural standards, which had been something to aspire towards, were here something against which both of my parents also united in disapproval. Neither her aesthetic snobbery nor his nationalism could abide the Butlins culture which was becoming increasingly equated with Englishness in the streets and playgrounds of Llanrwst.

In straightforward class terms, our position was, however, improving. We owned a large, if dilapidated house. My father's status as a lecturer earned him the nickname 'professor', locally. We began to acquire material possessions. A car (but no television), a hoover (but no fridge). Presents became more lavish. By the end of the decade I was the proud owner of a transistor radio, an alarm clock (not yet the watch I coveted), a hula hoop, and even a few new clothes (my first pair of jeans was purchased, against fierce opposition, out of saved-up pocket money). It is difficult to be sure to what extent this was the result of our own rise in the world and how much a product of the general surge in consumerism. However, it certainly left me with the feeling that I was lucky. I was constantly being reminded by my eldest sister that 'when I was your age we never had ...' and I believed in my own privilege at least as long as I remained at Llanrwst Primary, and during the year I spent at the grammar school.

In 1959, it was my turn to become the beneficiary of my aunt's generosity, and I was despatched to a boarding school on the coast, full of the daughters of minor diplomats posted overseas and Lancashire businessmen too snobbish to send their eleven-plus failures to a secondary modern. There, I was made aware yet again of how my family deviated from the bourgeois norm. My mother possessed neither a fur coat nor a pair of high-heeled shoes. Her hair

180

was long and unpermed. My father drove a second-hand Morris Traveller instead of a Jaguar and, most unforgiveable of all, sometimes wore a beret. When the other girls described their holidays it could have been life on another continent for all the relation it bore to my experience. There were the television programmes I had never watched, and expensive sports like horseriding or sailing. There was also a somewhat self-conscious suburban middle-class teenage lifestyle which seemed based on shared expectations and common values – tennis parties, tickets to Adam Faith concerts, 'dates' with boys in cinemas. Some of this aped American teenage culture, as embodied in the lyrics of songs by Connie Francis or the Everley Brothers and in films. What was astonishing about it, to me, was the extent to which it appeared to be connived at and encouraged by their parents who, unlike mine, seemed positively to want their daughters paired off as quickly as possible.

I was left, as a result of these experiences, with a strong sense of apartness and exclusion. There seemed to be no group I really belonged to, or understood the rules of. I could sometimes pass, for a while, as a member, but sooner or later my credentials would be examined and found wanting. To the Welsh, I would always be English; to the English, Welsh. To the poor, I would seem privileged; to the rich, an intruder in their private club. I developed a fear of situations where my ignorance of how to behave might be exposed – a working-class family gathering, for instance, or a dance – and took refuge in a deliberate, cultivated eccentricity.

This role was made considerably easier by the fact that I was already widely regarded as something of a freak thanks to a 'braininess' which, it appeared, might have been acceptable in a boy but was most peculiar in a girl. In retrospect, I suspect that I might have developed this quality, as my elder siblings had before me, as a way of resolving some of the differences in our parents' attitudes. There were few forms of behaviour which earned the approval of both, but doing well at school was undoubtedly one of them, even if this approval was often accompanied by visible contempt for the schoolteacher. Outside the family, however, it caused quite as many problems as it solved. With the exception of Fanny Comp from

Llanrwst Primary (for whom I now feel a sneaking sympathy) I was generally a success with teachers. I quickly learned how to please them, producing sentimental verses, humorous essays or detached analysis, as their individual personalities seemed to invite. Needless to say, this did not assist my popularity with classmates. I was rarely in with the in-crowd at school, though bought off outright opposition by offering myself as a resource, often doing the homework of five or six girls at a time. I had no close friendships with boys who, however, generally kept their distance and didn't tease me as they did some others. There was one boy who entered into a fierce academic competition for a while, defending his position at the top of the class which had been unchallenged until my arrival. Eventually he retired, vanquished. Years later, now a mechanic in a local garage, he picked me up when I was hitch-hiking, and I was humbled by his lack of any trace of resentment.

From an early age I must have been aware that this qualilty of cleverness placed me outside any possibility of conforming to normal feminine stereotypes. At the age of three, when asked what I wanted to be when I grew up I would reply 'a witch', presumably the only literary model I could find which seemed remotely likely to fit me. This identification persisted for years, and I was still playing the same part in the Llanrwst schoolyard game of 'fairies and witches', where nobody else in the girls' playground was prepared to take it on. I can vividly remember the poignant combination of loneliness and exhilaration I experienced when a gaggle of giggling fairies scattered at my approach. It must have been a little like being a man.

As puberty loomed, there was less tolerance of my deviance and even teachers withdrew their approval. At the convent, we were often told 'You're here to learn to be young ladies', and textbooks in the appropriate skills were circulated. I remember one, called *The Book of Charm*, full of tips on table manners and make-up and how to get gracefully into a sports car without showing your knickers. Like the women's magazines, it encouraged the reader to categorise herself by an elaborate sequence of typologies. Your hair was dry, normal or greasy; your face, round, square or triangular; your style, romantic, classic or contemporary; your tastes simple, sophisticated or sporty. Nowhere was there advice for an intellectual. Even the nun who taught us Latin, whom I had regarded as a secret ally, let me down when she snapped suddenly one day, in front of the entire class, 'God help the man who gets you, Ursula Huws.' It wasn't until the sixties that I developed a style which led to some measure of social acceptability, at least among men. This was a 'sexiness' which successfully concealed the existence of any mental activity whatsoever. (At a party when I was twenty I accidentally let slip a mathematical term to the man I was dancing with, whom I had known for several years. There was genuine shock and some indignation in his voice when he commented, 'I had no idea you were *clever*.' Clearly he felt cheated. He had accepted in good faith what he believed to be a real woman, and here I was revealed to be counterfeit. We never saw each other again.)

Looking back over these years, I feel that many of the contradictions have been, if not resolved, at least understood. Through conversations and consciousness-raising sessions with other women I have learned how intelligence can comfortably inhabit a woman's body, and how common is the experience of incommunicable isolation. The very features which I felt separated me from other girls at school have become the basis of closeness with other women in adulthood.

Although I have never met anyone with precisely the same class and religious mix in their background, these issues too have been talked through with others who share elements of the same experience. And just as feminism has given me a framework for thinking about gender, so Marxism has provided a set of analytical tools for making some sense of it, and a language for communicating that sense.

It is when I come to consider Welshness and Englishness and what they meant for my growing up that I find I have no easy analysis. When I excavate memories for the insights they can give, I encounter forgotten pains and facts which surprise me. By living in England and speaking English, I have cut myself off from any sharing of these experiences, and thus from the consciousness-raising process which produces understanding. It must have been this fact, more than anything, which was responsible for the sudden raw gush of emotion in response to *The Last Days of Dolwyn*.

The scene which produced this response at its most intense was the film's climax, one of those moments where literal reality and symbol are collapsed seamlessly together in a single image. It was the moment when a huge dam was opened, flooding the valley of Dolwyn for good. Sheep were shown being washed away and drowned while a huge choir sang laments in many-part harmony.

For anyone brought up in North Wales in the fifties, the literal force of this image should not be underestimated. Real valleys with rich farming land and flourishing, ancient, village communities were being flooded to provide water for England and nuclear power stations. In a land of barren mountains, this was simultaneously an outrageous act of physical vandalism, and a blow to the traditional culture. It threatened not just the self-sufficiency and prosperity of the people, but also the environment which allowed their language and music to survive.

The flooding of the valley was not the only destructive force at work on the landscape. Inland, the Forestry Commission ravaged huge areas with their marching rows of conifers, draining the water from surrounding farmland, eroding the hillsides and irrevocably upsetting the ecological balance. Ironically enough, the wood they eventually produced turned out to be almost unsaleable. In equally geometric formation, long lines of caravans disfigured much of the coastline.

Simultaneously, the language was invaded. Hard new English words entered Welsh as the commodities which they named crept into our lives. Television; aeroplane; electricity; snack bar; three-piece suite; juke box; jeans; lipstick; nylon. They had, of course, become necessary, and were welcomed as much as they were resented.

Remembering this destruction, I am filled with a shock of rage, as after a physical assault, which astonishes me with its force. Yet this was only half of the surprise produced in me by that scene in the film. The other half consisted of an equally intense and shocking recognition that I found the music incredibly beautiful. Mingled with the pain and outrage was a seductive sweetness, the contemplation of which unlocked another set of memories, of pure and private pleasures. Of seeing the safe blue peaks of Snowdonia hovering on the horizon behind the friendly gorse-studded Anglesey fields. Of climbing the side of the valley to a high field behind our house in Llanrwst for the joy of singing alone at the top of my voice. Of standing, waist-high, in a crowd of hundreds improvising harmonies at the annual mass hymn-singing, the *Cymanfa Canu*, which rounds off the National *Eisteddfod*.

These pleasures very quickly assumed for me the character of vices, to be indulged guiltily and in secret. They were associated with something which seemed to be inevitably doomed, and to enjoy them would simply be to prolong the death agony. Besides, the only people with whom I could share them had, I believed, rejected me. So I developed a detached and rationalistic pose and immersed myself in the second-hand pleasures of books.

I am not sure how I came to relegate Welshness to the past. Perhaps it was merely a way of ducking yet another set of conflicts. In reality, even in the fifties, the culture showed a remarkable resilience, of which I must have been aware. Several members of my family were active in nationalist politics, and involved in the resistance to the floodings. This took the form not just of vociferous campaigning but also the planting of the occasional bomb. However, the predominant impression of nationalism was a gentler one, of rambling rhetoric and singsongs, and much looking backwards. Twenty years later, when young Welsh Language Society activists had taken to setting fire to the English-owned second homes which had such a destructive effect on Welsh village life, my father, typically, condemned the action, not because he disagreed with its motives, not because he deplored the damage to property, but because it was inauthentic. The Welsh, he thought, didn't do that sort of thing, it was 'imitating the Irish' (this was not a condemnation of the IRA, whose right to develop their own forms of action he fully supported).

It was the nostalgia which I found most suffocating, despite a strong attraction to it. I saw people whose whole lives seemed immersed in the pleasurable contemplation of past culture, and envied them, even though the enjoyment was so closely mingled with melancholy. Yet every instinct of survival told me that this was a dangerous swamp. The way forward lay in developing a wider knowledge, and communicating with a larger world. English was, in many ways, inadequate. It couldn't even find a translation for the Welsh *hiraeth* (my dictionary gives 'longing, nostalgia, grief', but it is all of these and more, encompassing homesickness and impossible yearnings of many kinds). So the very quality it was hardest and most necessary to leave behind couldn't even be acknowledged.

But English was the language which unlocked history, science, thought, my own possibility of development and autonomy. It was English, too, which enabled me to learn that there were other cultures which had been assaulted and colonised, to begin to understand the processes by which this took place, and to communicate with others who were asking similar questions.

It was a painful process of rejection and synthesis which enabled me to assemble a coherent adult identity from the ill-fitting and contradictory components I was issued with, but Englishness is now indisputably a part of that self, whatever the regrets.

*I*N 1963 I left both home and boarding school to go to a day school in Oxford, where I lived in lodgings. After an interlude working in Greece, I went on to London University and graduated in 1970 with a degree in art history.

It is nearly a quarter of a century since the fifties ended. During that period I have tried on a number of identities: hippy, sexpot, bright young media person, trade union activist, bureaucrat, victim, sophisticate, naive idealist, earnest researcher. The most enduring common denominators, steadily strengthening and becoming more central as the years went by, particularly since the death of my most constant human supporter, have been a commitment to socialism and to a feminism which I find richer and more intellectually nourishing the deeper I explore it. I now live reasonably happily in a rented flat in North London with my daughter, supported somewhat precariously by freelance earnings from research, writing, lecturing, consultancy or whatever else turns up. I have reclaimed the motto which I first inscribed on a school exercise book in 1960: 'There's no security like no security.'

Sheila Rowbotham

Revolt in Roundhay

At seventeen I liked Nescafe, sausages, cooking apples and Camus. I fancied myself as an incipient existentialist. I wore black stockings, tight skirts from Leeds C & A cheaper separates, the largest black sweater I could find and black high heels. I put eye-liner round my eyes and green eyeshadow on my lids. I made my face and lips as white as I could. I aimed to get long straight hair – but it was really bouffant growing out. Some social pressures were impossible to resist. Indeed, getting kitted up like a beatnik represented a self-help endeavour, of which, if he could have made an imaginative leap, Samuel Smiles himself would have been proud. It was me against the known world.

Nothing like it was seen in Roundhay in 1959. 'You an art student?' people said on the shopping parade. 'No,' I'd say with a mysterious air. If you knew the place in 1959 you'd realise that lectures on Camus and Sartre would have fallen completely flat. Roundhay wasn't exactly the Left Bank. I hadn't been there from the age of seven without learning what went down in Roundhay. An enigma was all I could hope for. Barmy was the more likely response. But this was the thing with being an outsider – even in my

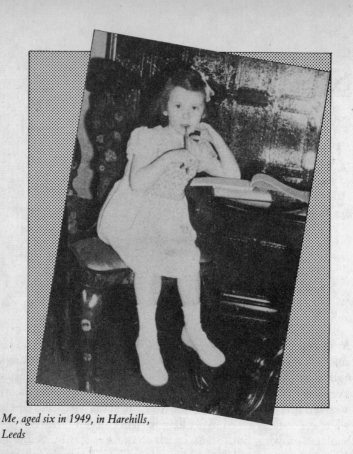

*Me, aged six in 1949, in Harehills,
Leeds*

small way. Look at Colin Wilson. Really you needed a sleeping bag, didn't he sleep out in Hampstead Heath? I'd never been there but there would have been a terrible fuss if I'd taken off to Roundhay Park or Woodhouse Moor or somewhere.

My father growled and my mother giggled. You were only young once she said.

I can't remember much of what I wore when I arrived from Harehills in 1950. There was a green taffeta party dress, white socks in summer and in the winter long grey socks with garters at the knee. Every night my mother curled my hair with rags and my face was covered in freckles.

We had arrived from Harehills on the up and up with the booming coal industry. My father was a salesman for an engineering firm selling pit motors. First the old Morris I liked had been exchanged for a Jowett Javelin. And now this new posh house with its cream urns outside.

When you are small the world you are born into simply *is*. The forces which made your parents as they are, the making of what is assumed can take a whole lifetime to unravel. But at first it is just what surrounds you.

The change from Harehills to Roundhay was in a sense part of the given. People moved – it was taken for granted. Yet the shift in surroundings was also an indication of hidden meanings. Why did some people move and others stay? And it was not only the walls and paint and curtains which differed, or that the garden was larger now; there were the people too.

Slowly, as I grew older, I began to move backwards, searching to place everyone. I learned of my father's childhood, one of a family of fourteen on a South Yorkshire farm, his scholarship to grammar school and engineering classes at night. He met my mother when he was in his early thirties and she must have been in her teens. They ran away to India in the 1920s, and there he worked as a colliery engineer. When they returned to Britain it was the Depression. He could not get work and eventually went back to being an electrician in a colliery. Even in the fifties my mother was still so relieved they were not poor anymore that she found spending money reassuring.

The move to Harehills in the 1940s and buying a Morris was a new-found stability which came to them only in middle age. But to me, who had grown up without knowing want, the prosperity which accrued around them through the fifties and early sixties was of little account.

Years later I could observe their lives not just as the chance affairs of a family. Our clump of existence was related to the fortunes of others after all and to the more remote circumstances of industries, coal, engineering, clothing, printing. Even the economy beyond Leeds and Yorkshire pulled my parents and their friends and acquaintances, small to medium middle class. They schemed and dreamed busily of mortgages and mistresses and new cars and carpets and posh hotels and the South of France. There was the glance over the shoulder now and again to make sure they kept some distance between them and the white proletariat which erupted in new housing estates, bringing property values down. The new black immigrants at the bottom of the pile were hardly mentioned. They threatened only the privileges of the poor.

The most passionate prejudice was reserved for the Jews. Resentment of their success in the Leeds business world acted to explain anyone else's failure, without questioning individual acumen or the inherent virtue of capitalism. My parents' steadfast refusal to countenance the anti-semitism common among many of the people they knew was my first lesson as a young child against accepting hearsay rather than the evidence of your own experience.

I still cannot hold that tension between the immediacy of the world of my childhood, the towering hugeness of my mother and father and my grown-up brother, back from Germany and the RAF with his rifle and a suntan, and the interconnecting pattern of the economy, their class and politics. Even as I try to follow the interweaving, the world of childhood reasserts itself and Leeds and Yorkshire become again the centre of existence. It is as if the years in between were inhabited by fragile observations, mere scratches and traces on the skin. The stuff of it, how it came to be, how it was shaped and turned and moved, still evades me. No such self-consciousness at seven.

I grinned out of photos with confidence. I had been a gang leader in Harehills – first administering the lives of younger children, then by brass, bossiness and imagination extending judgement even over older boys. It was partly an implicit class authority. In Harehills I belonged to the upper crust of the lower middle classes who were getting out as fast as they could. Physical ferocity and an eye for human responses – the latter fostered by my mother – did the rest.

True, I'd had the occasional setback, like proposing to Tony Kessler when I was four. He was sorry, he said, but he wasn't allowed to marry me because I wasn't a Jew.

I recovered. Three years is after all a long time. We were just friends. But there was big ginger George next door. He was nine at least. I think he was interested in watching once when I was peeing.

There was this mystery around taking your knickers down. Once he congratulated me on my gang. Such honour.

Roundhay was different. I was somehow not right. Being tough got me nowhere. The kids wouldn't even fight. They just bawled. As little girls returned covered in dust and mud a parental boycott developed. I was 'common' they said. 'What's common?' I asked my mother. 'It's when you scream and play rough games and get dirty.' I tried not to shout so loud. But Anne next door was a bit tame. She just wheeled her dolls around and played on her swing.

I learned to be alone. I was in effect an only child – my brother was seventeen when I was born. I was a mistake.

Years later I learned that my friend from Harehills, Jane, had walked to Roundhay and been turned away by my father. I still feel a pang at the thought of her all pink and blonde and sticky and snotty nosed.

Next thing *Dandy* and *Beano* were banned. I was learning bad language.

This 'common' lodged inside me – the lost good times. Cut adrift from nearly everything I'd known before seven, I turned inward and invented story games to play alone.

Three years went past. In the summers I rode for hours on a white pedal car with a hooter and real spark plugs. I went to feed the ducks at Roundhay Park, greeted the bluebells, presented bouquets to visiting dignitaries at my prep school, fought my enemy Nola Mote, had my front tooth knocked out by two large Bradshaw sisters. Girls will be girls as they say. I wore shorts, read about Queen Margaret of Scotland and a missionary heroine in *Girl*, listened to Dan Dare on Radio Luxemburg.

In the winter I constructed a bustling social existence of teddy bears, led by a ruling family of bears called the Cubbinses. Complicated personal feuds, broken romances and diplomatic intrigue kept me and the bears pretty busy. We extended into municipal services. Me and the Cubbinses opened a library and my school friends came to borrow books.

It would be too extreme to say I was unhappy. Extremes of any kind would have been unfitting in Roundhay. But certainly some ebullience in me was checked, held in and turned inwards.

There were two continuities with before. One was my fox terrier dog Simon, whom I loved passionately in my loneliness and shamefully deserted and neglected in my adolescence. He had a lovely grin. Simon and I were always in trouble because of the garden. The garden was my father's pride and joy, the real expression of his creativity, perhaps some echo of his boyhood on a South Yorkshire farm. The trouble came because it was also the place where Simon liked to pee – and on the newest plants from the market garden in Boston Spa. 'That dog'll have to go,' roared my father. My mother shielded me and Simon as much as she was able. So did a succession of home helps who were also the source of strange tales and occasional adventures. One old lady from Wiltshire told me if the Germans had come they'd have killed off old people like her. What a relief we'd won the war. My favourite was Ivy who was blonde, buxom and fun and took me – oh what delight – to see Roy Rogers in *Son of a Pale Face*.

The other link with Harehills was an elderly couple called Fred and Ethel Thompson who had looked after me when I was little. I was not only a late mistake but my mother had just had her breast removed because she had had cancer before I was born. I lived quite a lot of my early childhood at the Thompsons' house behind a shop on Harehills Parade. They had been country people and I was taken off to visit relatives and friends in Shepley and Harewood, sucking mintoes as a treat.

There were two worlds co-existing. In this one you got Yorkshire pudding first and Uncle Fred ate his gravy with a knife and no one frowned upon it. You had to eat your sausage skins: 'Some children would be glad of them.' There was a lovely mongrel dog Judy, a yard where the washing was laboriously done with much boiling, squidging and squelching, an oven lit by the fire, outings and picnics and dominoes with Uncle Fred in the park with his old cronies. I became a demon domino player. And once when I was very little I sat with him on his horse-drawn dray at the station with him in his bowler hat.

But after Roundhay the connection was more remote. I did not visit so often.

Eventually I made a new friend around the corner. Her mother didn't bother about screaming. Indeed normal conversation in their house was of such pitch and volume that a scream would hardly have been heard. Here I was a veritable mouse.

Janina's father was a Polish Jew who had come over to Britain to fight in the war. Her mother was from a Leeds Jewish family and her Granny lived with them. Her father was only at home for short times; he owned a button factory in India. He wasn't very talkative, but he was an imposing man. My mother said he had 'fluence'. It was mainly the two women's voices, cascading with emotions which erupted with a startling suddenness and burst explosively into the surface of life. Extraordinary in Yorkshire, where the most profound emotion slowly worked up and out, tightly wrapped into the cold air, channelled through flat vowels, into a word or at most a single sentence, while all the rest was conveyed only with the slightest movement of the body. I was at once alarmed and relieved amidst the noise and the dark bright colours Janina's mother wore. I took to Rakusen's matzos and chopped liver. It was my first taste and glimpse of a world beyond potted meat from Perkins on Roundhay Parade and primula cheese and sardines and salmon for a treat and those fifties pastel colours.

For Janina's family Leeds was accidental. Leeds, Manchester, New York, Vienna, even India and Poland were network extensions. It was not so difficult to leave Roundhay. You could come and go in the world.

My mother's stories also led me away from home. I used to listen for hours about her girlhood in Sheffield: smoking out of the window; the young soldier she visited in hospital in the First World War, who gave her his rosary and went off and was killed; of her suitors; the fuss surrounding her affair with my father, who was much older than her (and already married, though this she never told me). She described again and again how they went to India in the early 1920s and returned in the Depression, his work as an electrician in the mines, poverty, living in digs with the old soldier who polished the shoes and got my brother to put the finishing kaybosh on them. Then came the war, the Home Guard and the black market, and anti-Jewish feeling which she thought stupid. 'Mr Kessler was very kind to me when Lance had his stroke.' The war was somehow left behind in Harehills with the browns and greens and the Home Guard helmet on the cellar door. But India came with us. The spoils of Empire, elephants, buddhas, screens and incense jars, sat in the lounge. My mother had more stories of India than the war: my mother dancing with young men at the club, the cobra she saw on the veranda, the retired doctor in the Indian army who sent her his travelling rug before he died.

Everything exciting seemed to have happened before I was born. I cursed my luck and began to invent adventures.

Diamond thieves used old shoes in the woods in North Lane to pass on the goods. I told my friend Bridget it was up to us to keep watch. They left messages in a hollow tree on Seacroft estate. I led a desperate expedition. We got lost, returning home at ten, trembling with terror at our own inventions. I was banned from playing with Bridget. I was over-excitable.

'Imaginative. Shows promise', said my school reports. I liked history and writing and reading. I wrote a play and directed it on our garden lawn.

I had become a skinny, sickly, snuffly bronchial child. I missed a lot of school.

A doctor told my parents of a children's holiday scheme in Switzerland. He thought it would do me good. I went for a month when I was ten. The other children were from the south, all older than me and posher. They imitated my voice. I didn't realise I had a Yorkshire accent.

At first I was completely alone, reading or wandering around. Then I became friendly with two boys, one eleven and the other twelve, and bashed my way to equality. They stuck up for my right to walk as far up mountains as the older children.

The woman who organised the holiday lived in London. She was a socialist. When she corrected my accent one evening she said, 'It's all right for other people to have regional accents but not for oneself.' I puzzled over this. I could make no sense of it.

Separate from my parents in another country, I came to a new knowledge of me as a self apart. I was conscious of a kind of pause between beginnings and endings. There I was in my shorts and T shirts, my hair straight, gripped back, the curling rags long abandoned. I could swim and run and walk and fight.

But in the pause there was an expectancy. Why did all the grown-ups giggle so much when Richard (the younger of the two boys) and I went to the fancy dress party as Adam and Eve? And there were those funny pouches in my swimsuit which flapped over my chest – 'Until I grow busts' I told people, and they all laughed that laugh again. I became very conscious that I must cover my chest. I felt a painful modesty.

As for outside events, in these three years or so there was a cluster of royal funerals, weddings and the Coronation – which I watched on Janina's new television. I tired, even in the novelty of TV, of the interminable species of soldiers and what-not filing past. I heard of Korea and the Festival of Britain, the A bomb and the H bomb.

I read through my brother's *Reader's Digest*, where I learned that Stalin was a bad name. I learned about St George and King Arthur. Good men. I read *Our Island Story*, *The Famous Five* books and *Swallows and Amazons*. *Little Women* and *Anne of Green Gables* represented the far left of my reading. But I got hold of *All Quiet on the Western Front* from my brother's bookshelves. And then, most startling, a book called *War, Wine and Women* from which I learned of the existence of prostitutes and lice. I was amazed.

Then at eleven off I went, trunk packed, inventory in order, labels on, to a Methodist boarding school in East Yorkshire, close to the sea. 'Healthy air,' my father said. 'Good for the chest, bracing.'

There I was until I was seventeen, to emerge improbably as an existentialist.

For the first few years I romped to cover up the new loneliness. This time I missed my mother. But there was a lot going on at school. You could play commandos in the grounds, learn tracking in the Guides, keep a garden, eat sticky buns and suet puddings and sweets. There were complex power struggles of a desperate kind, for there were no grown-ups to appeal to. There were intrigues and ambushes. I fought but was never good at diplomacy.

One attack shook me. It was not proper fighting but something more frightening. One evening a girl jumped on me when I was lying on my bed in my cubicle. Scratching at my eyes, she began to rub her cunt on top of me. I fought her off, shaking and bewildered.

But then such a fuss about who was wearing a bra, had slip-on shoes, heels, roll-ons. I became an expert at putting my rollers on in the dark and listening to the Top Twenty under the sheets.

Thoroughly braced, desperately consuming carbohydrates against the howling winds of the North Sea, I changed shape. No longer skinny, I became awkwardly chubby in the wrong places.

Home in the holidays, wretched at thirteen in my school coat. Oh for a sling-back coat and high heels. I gazed at Teds and my friend Pam's cousin Malcolm who had a Tony Curtis and a bootlace tie.

While I was still listening to 'The Surrey with the Fringe on Top' and 'Some Enchanted Evening', rock and roll burst about my ears. The first record I ever bought was 'Love and Marriage', the second was Lonnie Donegan 'Diggin' My Potatoes'. It was a sign of the times. 1956. Elvis's 'All Shook Up', 'Any Way You Want Me', 'Love Me Tender', 'Heartbreak Hotel' and 'Teddy Bear' followed. But Elvis was too scary. My heart was given to Tommy Steele, 'Rock with the Cavemen' and 'Elevator Rock'. When I won an essay competition in 1957 on 'Why I was proud to be a citizen of Leeds', organised by the Variety Club of Great Britain and the local evening paper, the big event in my London visit was not Buckingham Palace, nor having Norman Wisdom put his arm round me, but gazing at a skiffle group which had played in the 2 I's coffee bar with Tommy Steele. The place had a sacred significance.

I fell in love with a boy with a crew cut who came to mend our roof, with the window cleaner who grinned at me in my rollers and the boy in Vallance's record shop with a spotty face.

The commando chief Rosemary lost interest in leading desperate missions. Instead she read us letters from a boy she had met in the holidays. Such sloppy letters. I teetered between awe and scorn.

Then we discovered pen friends. Pen friends were encouraged for learning French, but in *English Digest* there were advertisements from Burma and Mauritius and from servicemen. The replies were extraordinarily amorous. We started a lively correspondence with about five pen friends each, scribbling away under the desk in lessons. It was very time consuming.

One English lesson I got detention. Our punishment was to listen to the teacher read Keats's 'Lamia' aloud. Bored, sullen, resigned, I listened. Then suddenly the words wove within me, transporting me through another's imagination. It was a delight more magical than the panto and the circus had held when I was little.

When I went to Roundhay first I could still see fairies. If I pressed my eyes tight shut they came, gold and black and red and silver. Once I even thought I saw one with my eyes open. But I never was quite sure. And then they had faded. Words could open these strange worlds again. Radiant, I walked out of detention and listened avidly in English lessons afterwards to Keats, Byron, Wordsworth and Shelley, then Milton and Shakespeare and Marlowe.

I discovered Rupert Brooke's poems in the school library. Containing the headmistress's books in large numbers, it was weighted heavily with books from the inter-war years. I thought he was very handsome, tragic and iconoclastic. An angel coming to Mary – what a thought.

We all read *True Romances*, *True Confessions*. I hoped my mother would be shocked into recognising my maturity by these. In fact she didn't bat an eyelid. They were expected of me. Then I came across Rousseau's *Confessions*, which took a bit of reading but was more interesting than the love mags. I found the *Social Contract* in the school library and was bewildered. No one had told me there was a thing called political theory. I read it doggedly in the hope that it would be some kind of follow-up. How could two such different books come out of one person?

I bought a cheap biography of William Godwin and learned about Mary Wollstonecraft, who became my heroine. Byron was my hero and they've been slogging it out ever since.

Reading a lot made me a little odd but no one bothered much what I read. I borrowed *The Saint* from my father and historical novels like *Katherine* from my mother at home. At school I read Jane Austen, the Brontes, Thackeray and George Eliot, along with Russell Braddon, Douglas Bader, Winston Churchill and the life of John Wesley. Books were a jumble and I had no notion of discriminating between them.

Religion was the first vehicle for general thoughts about existence. I was brought up in oblivious paganism, but school introduced two services a day, Scripture several times a week and Bible class with theological criticism and the occasional lecture on *Pilgrim's Progress* as a special treat.

I read the Bible over and over, then theological commentaries and historical background, books about heretics, books about enthusiasts. I knelt on the wooden floor in the East Yorkshire winter praying, 'Dear God if you exist let me be warmed.'

Nothing happened. The minister explained that this kind of frontal approach was the wrong way to go about it with God. You were not to challenge God. It was arrogant and his ways were mysterious. Indeed, goodness itself was not enough. Spiritual pride was a trap. We had to receive grace.

I pondered all these things. In Bible class we discussed whether the bread was indeed his body. Surely remembrance was more probable. Didn't the Anglicans try and have it both ways? Either it was or it wasn't. I decided I wanted to be received as a Methodist. I went to chapel in the holidays and to the youth club.

Suddenly an enormous row blew up. My father said I could not be received. I was to be confirmed. This made no sense. He had never taken me to an Anglican church, he never read the Bible. Yet chapel was banned; worse, my theological learning disregarded.

The religious fracas shook the house, our sleepy old house where no one debated principles. I had already come into conflict over race and patriotism. My father said Eden should have kept the troops in Suez and only the British had moral integrity. My history teacher, who was a liberal, joked about such attitudes and I followed her cue. But this time it exploded into violence. He bashed me over the head and took out a knife to threaten me. My mother got me out of the room. Hysterically light with fear, I ran sobbing to my room.

Somehow a negotiated settlement was reached. I could go to chapel if I agreed to be confirmed when I was older. But I felt towards my father, with the clarity and ruthlessness of adolescence, not merely hostility, but contempt.

His sudden rush of Anglican devotion remained unexplained and incomprehensible. My mother said that in his South Yorkshire village Methodists had been looked down upon. On another level, perhaps he was fighting a wayward spirit he could not control. It was open battle from then on. 'Time is on your side,' my mother would say wearily, looking outwards, as if towards a hidden wall beyond immediate seeing.

She was unconcerned herself with my scholastic interest in theology. I was indignant when one of her friends told me my mother had believed my Methodist conviction was because I had a crush on the minister. In fact I did not. But he was the first grown-up person who assumed I could discuss ideas. He had been a railway worker and was called to the ministry. Perhaps he felt sympathy towards someone struggling to hook ideas together.

My mother did not tackle the world through the intellect. Neither politics nor organised religion affected her. Yet without fuss she dwelt obstinately on the meaning behind surface meaning. An inner reserve of spiritual strength was always there. It was not spoken of but drawn upon when it was needful. And I grew up respectful of the strength of her inner soul, superior in my school learning but knowing here was something beyond knowledge.

Where it came from goodness only knows, but it survived illness, unhappiness and the humdrum of Roundhay. Her laughter and her stories teased the stuffy old pompous world of matter. She mocked the lessons of her copybook. 'The daily round, the common task is really all we need to ask.' There must be a world of delight beyond Roundhay, where Victor Sylvester always plays and all the men are gentlemanly and such wonderful dancers and my mother spinturns for ever in their arms or elegantly allows them to light her cigarette. Fred Astaire still twirls Ginger Rogers and Donald Peers croons 'Give me the moonlight, give me the girl and leave the rest to me.' 'If you were the only girl in the world and I was the only boy, nothing else would matter in the whole wide world,' my mother would sing inappropriately.

She liked Eartha Kitt and Marilyn Monroe. 'Diamonds are a girl's best friend,' she'd tell me. 'And every cloud has a silver lining.' There were men that 'passed like ships in the night' – the good ones and men like 'your father' who snored in the night and roared in the day who it was best to put a pillow between. 'Oh slave live for ever.' She'd play even with her own destiny, smiling approvingly at Mitzi Gaynor in *South Pacific*. 'I'm going to wash that man right out of my hair.'

Yet somehow delight and freedom could be found. My mother's mischief and spiritual fortitude spun out into the fabric of the unknown. Braver and deeper than the evangelical adventure the minister promised to the Christian.

The sticking point in faith for me was abnegation. Was it stubborn pride or reason which defied surrender? Unresolved, I clung to the nub of 'I', perhaps sensing that I needed 'I' if I was ever to hurtle to freedom. I wanted to get out without any conception of where I was going.

Janina's father told me he had no faith in God. He was not simply indifferent to religion. He denied it. I wondered at this.

Copying Janina's parents, I started to read the *Sunday Times* instead of the *Sunday Express*. It gave cultural shape to a world outside school and home. Somewhere there was a great concourse of the high-minded who, in between the *Sunday Times* each week, spent their days pondering weighty ideas, discussing plays and foreign films. I read a review of a biography of Havelock Ellis which described his mystical union with nature. I found Olive Schreiner's *Story of an African Farm*.

I tried to become one with nature on the gamesfield, which made me unpopular with the enthusiastic cricketers. At night when storms lashed from the North Sea I gazed in awe at the hill where the Hunmanby Dane had built his wooden castle and yearned to enter the past.

As I tussled with Christianity and to order the world in my head, I became conscious of an oscillation of temperament. I was drawn to contrary poles. I yearned towards the mystical earnestness which saw through the outer facing of existence in a oneness and blinding intensity which went direct to some essence of being. But I could appreciate a countervailing vision of tolerant scepticism in which the surface texture of life was a source of amiability and pleasure. Here reasoned choice between lesser evils was the course which brought the least ill on humanity.

They seemed to be wherever you turned, these two sources of enlightenment. In Donne and Ben Jonson, Shelley and Jane Austen, in Methodism, in Protestantism, in the Reformation and Renaissance. Even among my two favourite teachers. Our English teacher was a Northern Irish mystical Protestant who breathed Milton and explained the imagery of Dylan Thomas. The history teacher was a Methodist from an East Yorkshire farming family who liked Baroque architecture, appreciated eighteenth-century reason and read *Vogue* and *Nova*.

Despite these dashes of earnest high-mindedness, I had the outer appearance of normality. Under our summer dresses we wore full petticoats with hoops and white high heels. At fifteen I had a smart brown jersey skirt and a light green jersey dress and a Leslie Caron 'Gigi' hair-do.

Thoughts buzzed around in my head and I might pursue the world of the spirit, but dressing up was equally important. So was a labyrinthine knowledge of pop music, remnants of which have survived the years.

And there were boys.

In a sense it was true they had always been there. You fought them, dared them, had adventures and special likings, thought they were daft or dirty minded. But they appeared to vanish altogether

Aged fifteen on holiday in Switzerland, 1958

for several years to return mysteriously, to look, to whistle and back chat. I was tongue-tied and shy. The proud fighter who took every challenge, was overcome with fear that they could mock me with their chat, but delighted to be noticed. The worst of fates was to be a wallflower passed over and rejected. A terrible song from a concert at Blackpool echoed back from when I was a tiny girl: 'I don't want her you can have her she's too fat for me.' The humiliation made me shudder. I hid on bus seats, pressed myself into corners – anything to evade the danger of being noticed and found wanting.

Pride made me disguise this. I was above such things.

When the wolf whistles came though, I decided I wasn't after all. There was an exhilaration in this strange new power. They didn't even need to be shown how high you could climb, how bravely you could wrestle. All you had to do was walk past in high heels and a tight skirt with your popper beads hanging down your button-up cardigan and a bra which shaped your breasts into sharply protruding cones and they exploded into admiring noises, gave you the eye, even followed you home.

But how did you ever meet them?

Janina's family, Methodism and history turned out to be the answers. They were to be not only the routes to culture and the intellect but the means to romance and sort of sex. Sort of sex because I was a bit slow on the uptake by modern standards. Also information was exceedingly patchy and opportunity sparse.

Practical inexperience and rare encounters did not stop us talking about boys. A school friend Joanna had lived in Trinidad and was American, worldly-wise about dating and 'how far to go'. At thirteen she had an extensive collection of Esther Williams photos in glamorous swimsuits and the most advanced information available about what to do with boys. If 'they' tried to kiss you with your mouth open you must keep your teeth tight shut. (Well who could want such sloppy kisses anyway thought I.) And if you lay full length with them on the beach it was a 'sign' you would go all the way. Joanna's moral purpose blurred at the edges. Were you to fend them off or drive them crazy? I ascertained that the aim was to achieve some ideal unity of the two. I couldn't imagine quite how.

And anyway the problem was academic. The strict controls over our life at school, our terrible school uniform and the climate of East Yorkshire conspired against either of these sexual eventualities, which had apparently been the common run of existence in Trinidad. And as for Leeds, the only boys I met were at teenage dances. They twirled you around in the Gay Gordons at Ilkley with clammy hands. They showed no propensity towards sloppy kisses. And there were no beaches in sight.

It was two years before I tested Joanna's theory in practice. Janina's family took me to Switzerland for a holiday. We went dancing in discos and an Italian boy, Giacomo, kissed me at the end of a dance. On Joanna's instructions I set my teeth resolutely. When I sat down I told Janina's mother, expecting her to tutut approvingly at my astute virtue. Instead she threw back her head in laughter and said, 'Next time he tries, open your mouth.' It was exceedingly confusing. Everyone seemed to have different ideas of what you should do. But this was evidently the sophisticated thing.

I danced rigidly with Giacomo, kicking his shins and treading on his toes. But I did open my teeth and the strange sloppy kiss was done. Did he like doing this I wondered? He certainly seemed very intent on it all. My brain wandered off, surveying the amorous absurdity of it. Yorkshire me snorted inwardly, all this soppy stuff to look sophisticated. But Janina was rather impressed at my catch.

Earnest me anyway slightly hankered after another Italian boy, Joseph, who had invited me out for a walk. Some walk! It went on and on. Joseph must have been a country boy. He took mountains in his stride. Up and up we went and when I could walk no longer he lay me down and covered me with kisses and love bites. Joanna had missed out on love bites. But my father had taught me how to make them on my arm, fox-bites. So I thought they were all part of a jokey game. But there was some funny feeling. Joseph seemed to be curiously affected by the game.

I was convinced it was not a romantic passion. I had rather formal notions of desire. Boys fancied you when your make-up was just right and your freckles didn't show and your hair was tidy. I was all scuffled and pink.

Then Joseph proposed. I was alarmed. I was alone on a mountain with an unpredictable and completely un-Yorkshire person who appeared to have been touched by the sun. I declined. I didn't know him well enough, I mumbled. I hoped it wouldn't hurt his feelings.

Undeterred he burst into song, serenading me in a loud baritone with Italian pop songs. At this point Yorkshire won out. Such a display of emotions was horrifying. I stared at the path. Oh if only the ground would proverbially open and swallow me. If anyone should hear him. Immolation rather than anyone hearing. All those gushy words.

Yet also in some way I knew he was sincere. Part of me was moved by his tribute. Joseph was ridiculed for being serious. Giacomo was okay because he was not.

This puzzled the earnest Protestant me. Surely sincerity was better?

The orderly American 'dating' we saw in films or heard about in pop songs never happened in my adolescence. Instead there was simply a series of holiday encounters of a strange kind – nearly all of them away from Roundhay.

At a Methodist sixth formers course at Eastbourne in the winter holidays when I was fifteen I met David. True romance this time. When I came home and told my mother she sighed, 'People write poems about this.' I scampered off and wrote an obscurely pretentious verse.

David's family were Welsh but he was brought up in London. He and his friend Keith took the mickey out of the rich. They were working-class grammar school boys and they were going to university. They said outright what I could not find words for.

I won the competition for being the girl with the dreamiest eyes. Better than the knobbly knees one at any rate. I came home pretty chuffed and in love. We wrote for a term.

Arousal the following summer entwined with religious questing. I went this time on a Methodist missionary course in Canterbury. Well how else to get out of Roundhay? A boy began talking with me. He was from Sheffield and worked as a clerk, and was in a fundamentalist evangelical crusade. They sang Jesus songs to a guitar and sought converts. Conversion was overwhelming. Physical transport and the release of emotion were integrated in worship.

Intense feeling erupted about everything.

He was angry about class, hypocrisy and the establishment. He read John Osborne and Alan Sillitoe. He liked wandering around as I did, exploring old churches and ruins.

After a witnessing session in which everyone opened their hearts and emerged exalted we walked out into the night and began to neck. The exaltation brought a strange energy which slipped easily into desire. 'Lust' as Lindsey would have said if she'd been there. He drew back, saying it had nearly happened with another girl but she was a Catholic. I was not certain whether it was Christian principle or a more cautious understanding of contraception than I had. Nor was I sure whether I was relieved or disappointed, respected or rejected.

I suppose there are dilemmas at such moments in any decade. But they seemed particularly so in the late fifties. Where lay true morality? Not in conventional respectability I decided fiercely.

Contradictory values surrounded us. Freedom and smirks. Honesty or making yourself cheap. It felt painfully difficult to hew out another course. Yet all my friends wanted to find another way of being. We wanted reason and mischief, danger and trust, love and freedom. We were all woefully ignorant of contraception. For the next two years fear of getting pregnant was constantly producing panic, misery and confusion. I had no idea what having a baby would mean, only that it would make escape from Roundhay impossible.

My friend Lindsey said I was consumed with earthy desires and unable to reach the higher planes.

My friend Bar, though, was an East Yorkshire farmer's daughter, and while she was cautious about my intellectual defiance of convention she had a country practical acceptance of the body and physical desire. At root you went for what was good for you – why deny it? She had a sensual certainty about her, though she experienced as many philosophical doubts and emotional woes as the rest of us. If our culture was hard-won, the stalwart conservatism of her background made Roundhay a den of Bohemian anarchists in comparison.

Years later she reminded me of a forgotten and to me everyday kind of question. When we first became friends in our early teens I'd asked her if she fancied one of the young men in the village. She said with a shock that she realised she had grown up among the men on her father's farm without seeing them as people you could conceivably fancy. They were in some differing order of human being, for she was gentry. Though the word was hardly used, the distinction was immutably there.

I had grown up with class but it was a shifting, unstable, changing force and you fancied across it regardless, for the world was open. Even my father repeated 'It's not what a man has but what he's going to make.'

My close women friends, like me, were all straining beyond our backgrounds. Art school, university, we were going out of Yorkshire and nothing could stop us. Life was what you made it.

Our teachers were the nearest guides because they had travelled these routes before us (though of course we wouldn't *teach*). Their attitudes to literature, art, fashion, politics were seized upon, devoured, turned over, re-sited. Ideas and culture were a way of life and education was never just about learning subjects for exams. Socially mobile within the middle class we were going not so much up but sideways, heading towards sub-cultures, which as yet did not exist, and which we could envisage only hazily. There were too many of us to be Bohemians. We assumed we were going to change the world. How, we were unclear. Socialism was remote. Though I tried to read Marx I couldn't connect what he said to the world I knew. The anger of the outsider made purer sense. Were we to live this permanent estrangement till the end of our days? Or was the world to wake up renewed? And what was it to be like? Meanwhile, how was I to turn into Juliette Greco and Brigitte Bardot and Simone de Beauvoir all rolled into one? Leeds C & A cheaper separates just did not stretch far enough.

Oh to get away so I could exhaust myself with intense experiences, where everyone spoke of intense subjects and *never* said 'pass the bread and butter'.

It took several years to acknowledge that all this higher searching was based on my father's money. And several more to note any similarity in pattern between the Yorkshire self-made businessman and myself. Though the connections were obvious to relations on my father's side. 'She takes after our Lance,' declared Rowbotham aunts and cousins, and I would scowl his scowl and confirm their verdict.

I preferred to resemble my mother, who had in my eyes, grace, wit, allure and dignity.

But she also concurred in the view that I was like my father. 'You take after your father, liking sex,' she'd say in the regretful tone you might use for a hereditary disease.

I think most fundamentally she transmitted her inner core of pride and I acquired from him both doggedness of purpose and the confidence to decide what was just and unjust in the world as I met it. Such qualities have their disadvantages but on the whole I'm thankful.

But beyond this it is unclear. It is still hard to say I am like him, like her, unlike her, unlike him, in this or that way.

Are your parents always rather too close for comfort?

Then they went. Bar and Lindsey to university. My friend Pam stayed in Halifax and became a secretary, but one of her boyfriends worked in advertising and went to London. He left her his Champion Jack Dupree records. But Pam had done with her radical phase. Her new boyfriend was a young businessman and drove a Sprite and Pam thought he was a good catch.

One night he drank a lot of whisky and told me I was 'one off'. He said that was what you called cars which had the wrong parts.

'Huh,' I thought. 'Pam can have him.'

As I walked to get the bus in Leeds, stiletto heels clicking, the town night enclosing me, I mused on the pavement. Walt Whitman would have merged with a kerb like that. The kerb remained intact and external. And this sex, perhaps individuality was a mistake. Perhaps really it should be anonymous merging, at random, with all comers as you walked in the night. But this was surely fantasy. If I met Pam's bloke coming down Briggate I'd give him a wide berth.

How to be an existentialist intact and a Whitmanite continuously merging. I was stumped and seventeen.

A young man in a black leather jacket jumped up at the bus window. He was gesticulating wildly.

209

'Who are you and where are you from?' I asked, all *sang froid*, for the bus was anyway about to leave.

'I'm a psychopath and I come from Bradford,' he announced, matter-of-fact.

I grinned a welcome. At least there were a few discerning spirits in Yorkshire.

It was 1960.

I DID make my escape from Roundhay — by a route taken by many of my contemporaries: higher education.

I went to Oxford in 1961 with my beatnik uniform, sandals and black sweater. I became a socialist there because while I did not agree with everything said by the Marxists I met and with whom I became friendly, they gave me a language for understanding the painful separations of class. I also had excellent advice from one of my history tutors: 'Don't read people on Marx; read Marx.' I did — with admiration, though I never assumed he was to be taken without criticism.

When I left university in 1964 I went to live in Hackney in North East London. I was doing a thesis on working-class education in the late nineteenth century at Chelsea College. The bus journey alone is eloquent of class inequality. I joined the Labour Party Young Socialists and received a basic Trotskyist education. My knowledge of history and myself made me ask awkward questions. The real learning came from the people in the group more than the talks.

I was involved in opposing the Vietnam War, began to write for a left newspaper, *Black Dwarf*, and became part of the beginnings of the women's liberation movement. I earned my living mainly from teaching. Writing began out of the tremendous need to understand why those of us who formed the early groups were suddenly seeing our lives and the history we had learned through new eyes.

Women Resistance and Revolution, *Women's Consciousness Man's World*, *Hidden from History* and *A new World for Women* all came out of this preoccupation.

I also wanted to understand socialism and class in the light of the political indications of women's liberation. The lessons of one political movement are vital to relate to many others. *Dutiful Daughters* with Jean McCrindle, *Socialism and the New Life* with Jeff Weeks and *Beyond the Fragments* with Lynne Segal and Hilary Wainwright came from this concern.

The clarity of vision in those early years of women's liberation has gone. It seemed possible then to order the past through the focus of feminism. It is less one-dimensional for me now. Feminism is a given – but I want more than the political outline. I want a culture which you can tug and shape with complexity.

Perhaps it is this point of political reassessment; perhaps it is because I am mid-way through my life – the time when the past stretches widespread enough to contemplate, and the future is no longer infinite – which makes me want to catch memories. Catch-as-catch can, for what is done has gone – and yet when you re-enter memory it seems as if time is the dream.

Gail Lewis

From Deepest Kilburn

I was born on the 19 July 1951 in a 'Mother and Baby Home' – the euphemism for an unmarried mothers' home. And, like Billie Holiday, when Mum and Dad got married I was three. I was sent to my (maternal) grandmother for that occasion, so I missed the whole thing, which I'm sure was a real shame, since all of the parties my parents and their friends had – and there seemed to be one nearly every weekend – were fun for us kids too, with endless supplies of bun, crisps, R Whites and ginger beer (home-made of course).

That was also when I was first exposed to what I now know as the 'contradiction between race and gender', but then it was just the trouble between Mum and Dad.

The first home I remember was a basement flat at number 61 Granville Road, Kilburn. We lived there until 1960 and so my memories of the 1950s are split between that house and that of my Mum's mum who lived in Harrow on a late-twenties council estate. It was one of those new estates which was part of the spate of house-building in the inter-war period which was to provide a lot of working-class people in the north-west London suburbs with their first decent housing.

My Nan's house was on the back of the main rail line that ran from Euston up to the north of England and Scotland, and the suburban line from Euston to Watford and Elephant and Castle to Watford. Compared to the flat in Granville Road Nan's house was luxury. It had an inside toilet, a separate bathroom, two down and three up, a fairly big garden in the front and an even bigger one out back which ran down to the railway bank. I remember that when I was very small I used to run away terrified when the big trains came by – they were so big and there was so much soot. The soot in fact was a real problem for all the women on that side of the street, since all their nice clean whites which went up like clockwork Monday mornings would get speckled with the stuff. There was an audible sigh of relief when diesel engines became the norm. But while the women may have welcomed the arrival of the cleaner engine, we train-spotters mourned the grandeur of the old steam engines on trains like the Royal Scot which passed every day at about 4.10 p.m.

With rehabilitation and modernisation those houses would still be some of the best family housing publicly provided. But like many such houses they were to suffer the fate of housing department rationalisation and planners' dreams and were demolished in the mid-seventies. For my grandmother this was a very traumatic event since she had lived in the street for all of her married life, most of it in that very house.

The Granville Road flat was completely different. The whole house, a big late-Victorian terrace, was let as a tenement, in a combination of bedsits and two-room flats, to black people, mostly Jamaicans. The house itself was owned by a Polish man who lived with his wife and two sons in Clapham. My Dad had lived there since his arrival in this country in 1950. How he came to find it I'm not sure, but since he arrived on his own I assume it was through network contacts that operated both here and back in JA. It was, of course, a lonely and tremendously brave thing to do, just to 'dig up' (as they say in JA) and try your chances in the 'mother country', especially for a young man of eighteen with no knowledge of what to expect. It was an act based on complete trust in the propaganda being dished out by the British government and by various British firms and public corporations, and on the need to find employment

Me, aged six, in Kilburn

and a better career than underdeveloped Jamaica could offer. Among other things, he was already qualified in aspects of catering, electrics and carpentry, but it wasn't until the seventies that he became a fully qualified electrician. In some respects I suppose you could say that the decision to uproot paid off – he has a house and a skilled job and lives relatively comfortably. But it's not been without its costs: the obstacles to racially mixed marriages, the continual adjustment to the effects of racism on black people's lives and the disappointment that has been woven into the lives of many black people of that generation. They came looking for the rainbow and got abuse, subjugation and disillusionment instead.

My Mum was the only white person who lived in the whole house, a point not unnoticed by me since I often asked her how come she lived there with us when everyone else was black – or brown as I would have said then. As she would later remind me, children can say very painful things.

We had two rooms and a kitchen, with our own outside toilet at the end of the air-raid shelter. We had no bathroom at all in the whole house but there were public baths and a laundry at the end of the road so we would have our weekly bath there, and in the week have a full wash-down in the sink. We children were always told to emphasise the 'full' of the wash lest people think we were dirty, and given that most white people thought all black people were dirty it was a counter to any racialist-type thoughts that people might be harbouring. This may seem pretty elaborate when you consider that this was the situation for most people in the street and that the white working class had a tradition of 'proving' their cleanliness too. But it's illustrative of the way in which 'race' and prejudice serve to fracture the working class and make for an inability to share common experiences. In this case there was a kind of cleanliness chart, and we black people and Mum were aiming to be at the top. Dad had an advantage in this because he could get a bath every day at his work. He worked alternate night and day shifts then, in a Godfrey Davis tyre-remoulding factory somewhere off the North Circular Road. All the workers were entitled to a shower because they used to stink of the rubber so much. Even so I can remember Dad's clothes smelling of rubber all the time, despite the fact that all of our clothes and bed linen was sent weekly to the White Knight Laundry across the road.

The entire house was infested with mice which meant that everybody was in constant battle against their droppings and their smell. Needless to say the mice won in the long run, especially in terms of their smell, and even now just thinking about mice I can smell them. Still, overall we thought ourselves lucky because a lot of other houses in the street had rats as well as mice, which was much worse because at least mice don't bite or nibble at human feet! Even so I was determined not to let any slipaway rat or too-big-for-its-boots mouse come and try my feet for dinner, which meant that going to sleep was difficult; I always had to ensure that my feet were at least ten inches inside the very firmly tucked-in sheets and blankets. Despite these precautions I was always convinced that one day I'd find a mouse in my bed and that added to my perpetual fear of night-time. I remember once seeing a mouse run down the disused but open fireplace into the front room and I immediately went into that slow-motion vision that comes with a combination of disbelief, fear and loathing. I slept in the front room on the studio-couch, which meant I felt even more vulnerable, but sometimes I got lucky and was able to sleep with Mum in her and Dad's room.

Apart from our outside toilet there was another indoor one which was to be shared by everybody else. This was on the first-floor landing and opened on to the shared first-floor kitchen. The kitchen itself was just a part of the landing; there was a sink, a cold tap and a cooker. I can only remember the name of one adult on that floor – Uncle Lester – but I know that he and his wife lived in one room and someone else lived in the other room on that floor.

On the second floor lived Pearl and Clarence and their children. The eldest was Jimmy, who was one of my best friends. They had two rooms in which the five of them lived. One of the rooms served as their kitchen-cum-overspill bedroom; the other was living room and bedroom. But despite the overcrowding I liked it up in that part of the house because it was always sunny and bright.

At the very top lived Aunt May May and Uncle Stickey. They were absolutely my favourites and Stickey was a great hit with the white kids in the street. Looking back I realise that it was that peculiar kind of liking which white children sometimes display for black adults: patronising, superior and chauvinistic – the kind of liking that a six-year-old Shirley Temple would have for the black 'boy' or nanny in whose care she was.

Miss May May was a gentle, kind woman, who combed my hair beautifully without hurting a bit. So it was to her I'd rather go when I was sent upstairs to get my hair combed and oiled and plaited – that is, if I didn't manage to get away with not having it done at all. Hair was to prove a major problem in my life until 1970 when I ceremoniously and proudly went and had my hair cut to a short natural 'afro', never to have another hot comb or relaxer in it again. At this age, however, my 'problem' with it centred on my fear of having it combed; the fact that my Mum was too easily persuaded to let me off was in the long run the worst thing she could have done. The fact is, I believe, that only black (African)

217

women really know how to keep black children's hair well and impose the discipline on the child to make sure it's kept combed and plaited regularly. My Mum knew it too; that's why she liked me to have May May do it.

May May was also a devout spiritualist, believed strongly in Obeah and frequently went into religious frenzies. Her eyes would roll, and she behaved as if in a fit – it was all a bit frightening, but somehow because it was her I could never feel really frightened because I knew she would never hurt anyone, let alone me.

There was also a variety of other people who lived in the house, for shorter or longer periods. Often it was relatives or friends of us permanents, who used it as a temporary place to stay on arrival until they found their own bedsits or whatever. When they moved they would stay in the Kilburn area or they'd move to the Grove, and some even went to other cities. This was especially true of women who'd train to be nurses or men who were shoemakers or cobblers. I remember a friend of Dad's, who was a cobbler and who moved up to Leicester or Nottingham where he thought he'd get work in the shoe-making industry based in that part of the country. This was a great shame for me since I liked to pop into the shoe-repairing shop he had just round the corner from us, on my way home from school. The machinery fascinated me but most of all I loved the smell of the leather and the rubber. Even now I can't resist putting my nose into a new pair of shoes and inhaling the smell (though its not like it was in the old days).

For most people though it was into the factories and warehouses along the North Circular, Western Avenue and beyond, or into the National Health Service or London Transport. I can remember at least five people – mostly cousins of mine or Jimmy's – who did this. One was my aunt Verna who came around 1956 to train as a nurse. She was very young when she came, probably eighteen; she came in the winter and the cold was just too unbearable for her. So much so that for a while she thought she wouldn't be able to stay. She did, of course, and eventually got her Nursing Certificate which she took home with her and was able to put to good use back in JA. She endured and survived incredible racism during her course, as she made her contribution to the super-exploited pool of overseas nurses who helped Britain supply 'the best public health service in the world'.

Granville Road was a long street running between Kilburn Park at one end and Queens Park at the other. On our side of the road it began with a pub at the corner, then the laundry and the baths which took up a good stretch. There were also some warehouses behind the laundry, the place where many of us girls received some initiation into the secrets of sexual play. For me such 'experimentation' was often quite a frightening event because the big boys were the same ones who were always calling me 'nigger' or 'sambo' or 'junglebunny'. My 'going with them' was out of both fear (they threatened us with all sorts of things if we didn't) and, in a funny sort of way, an attempt to fit in, to become one of the gang and get them to stop calling me names. It was only when I was in my twenties that it struck me that this was simply a continuation of the centuries-long relationship between white men/boys and black women/girls.

These sexual forays were not all so horrible. In particular I remember one time when I and another little black girl did some experimentation with each other, and that was highly enjoyable. But I do remember that afterwards I was terrified that our parents might find out and blame me. I was the older, and somehow I knew this was even more unacceptable than what we did with the boys. It was an incident that was to haunt me for years as an adult. While I was struggling to 'come out' (a process that lasted literally years) I kept remembering it and would cite it as evidence of my genetic abnormality. Even after I 'came out' I couldn't tell anyone – I still harboured secret fears that it meant I was 'born' a lesbian. I only overcame it when I learned of more and more women, heterosexual and lesbian, who had similar experiences as children.

After the baths came the long terrace of houses which went along as far as a playground which had a huge wire fence and an iron gateway. Then there were a few more houses and, as the road bent round, a small row of shops.

Among then was a Home and Colonial (now International) Store with its marble tops and rows of big tins with loose biscuits in.

There was also a tiny sweetshop run by a tiny old woman who lived in the rooms at the back and from which she always emerged bringing with her that slightly nauseating smell of greens and gravy. It was thought a good shop because you could get tiger nuts, 'Spanish wood' (a kind of chewing stick) and huge humbugs, two for a penny.

There were only a few houses on the other side of the street. A small terrace opposite the laundry baths ended at a road junction, with a few more houses at the other end. In between were two primary schools, one Catholic girls, one mixed Church of England, with the White Knight Laundry between them. Further up there was a big dump which was cut off from the road by wooden gates which were securely padlocked. It was against these that we used to play cricket, stoney and a host of other games.

The whole street was a patchwork of no-go and go areas for me. I was not allowed to go into the playground because that's where a lot of the young Teds hung out; I couldn't go too far to the other end, nor was I supposed to play back and forth across the road, though I did. I was only allowed to cross the road to go to school, get things from the shops two streets away for Mum, and to go to the White Knight. I could go to the Rec, but I wasn't to hang around in those parts of the street where people from the house couldn't see me and where the Teds hung out. Mum and Dad were frightened that racialist adults or children would abuse me or even physically harm me, particularly because I was a girl. From this I was to be protected as much as it was possible to be, without pampering or spoiling me.

I negotiated this chequerboard of on-off bounds easily and didn't really experience it as hardship. The only thing to avoid was the gangs and individuals who were at great pains to keep 'their territory' free of 'blacks'. In fact another bit of the road, which we called 'Little Granville', was full of kids with this aim in mind.

But most of these kids were members of that post-war generation who cared little for authority in one sense, but who were ardently and vociferously patriotic and deeply racialist. For many, MacMillan's 1959 slogan 'You've never had it so good' had little meaning in experience. Many sought refuge in the armed forces, even after conscription ended in 1958. It was access to a trade, and wasn't the British army the best in the world, and wasn't there still a call to duty in the Middle East, in Africa? Of course this had no meaning for us children at the time, but it was still taking its toll on us. And most of our interactions embodied the tension that results from white people's belief that black people, whether struggling for independence or living in Britain, were not yet ready to function properly in a 'democratic' society, and from black people's refusal to let this interfere with their everyday lives.

As it happens I can't actually remember any particular incident that demonstrated the need for observing the no-go divisions in the street. Which isn't to say that the fears of the adults existed only in their paranoic minds. Our house was in fact firebombed during the 1958 Notting Hill riots, fortunately with no particularly harmful material results. One of those old paraffin-filled red warning lights used to cordon off road works was thrown through the basement window into our front room, but luckily there were people at home and they put out the fire right away. But it did serve to make everyone acutely aware of the potential danger we were in. We children were kept under lock and key and I was sent up to my Nan's for a few days until it cooled down a bit. The incident certainly gave meaning to the chequerboard, because it operated to keep my playing area carefully demarcated from the houses and hang-outs of any youths suspected of being sympathetic to the racists, or even those who looked like Teddy boys.

I did, however, have one other source of protection. That was my babysitter friend, Sheila. Sheila was a young girl who lived down the road from us; her family was very poor and because they liked us and needed the money they let Sheila be my babysitter. But because Sheila and her family had lived in the street for years and were white, I got a kind of extra protection because she knew me. Anyway, she could fight and threatened to beat up anybody who did anything to me. Sheila was my friend as well and it was she who would take me and collect me from Brownies on a Friday night, which is how I got to go in the first place.

Everything seemed to be brown in those days. The shops, the insides of houses, the atmosphere. It was as though the world were sepia-tinted – black and white photographs were just pretend. Occasionally there would be a break in the brownness; the marble tops of Sainsbury's and Home and Colonial, the orange of the United Dairies milk float, the green of the fish and chip shop. But this only served to accentuate the brown of everything else.

Home and Colonial was one of my favourite shops (one of the smaller ironies) simply because of the marble and because they sold Blue Mountain coffee and I loved the smell. My Dad had told me all about the Blue Mountains and how beautiful they were. He obviously associated these with home and had a wallet with an outline of them embossed on the front. Whenever I smelled the coffee I always imagined I was there in those wonderful high slopes, shrouded in the blue mist. Funnily enough, he never actually drank any coffee – he didn't like tea either. This only made sense to me when I grew up and thought about the reasons for Dad's tastes. While a lot of 'tropical' produce was already becoming part of working-class consumption here, it was still completely beyond the reach of working people in the producer countries.

But then the other kids didn't have the delights of chocolate tea, or cane or bun. This was the best thing about people arriving from the Caribbean – they would carry with them some delight or other which was either completely unavailable or far too expensive here. And even mangoes were pretty well unheard of then – though I suppose you got them at shops like Fortnum and Mason's. The best things were the short pieces of cane that took so long to chew but released the sweet, refreshing juice; and the round ball of hard, bitter chocolate was absolutely wonderful since it meant real chocolate tea instead of just Cadbury's or cocoa. It took a long time to make the real thing: grating the chocolate, mixing it with milk and water (often condensed milk), grinding the nutmeg and maybe a little mace, then adding a bay leaf and leaving it to boil. As it was cooking the aroma of the nutmeg would fill the house. When I rediscovered chocolate tea it was from the smell. I immediately remembered it, and it was the first time I'd had chocolate tea in years.

This chocolate drink was very different from the kind we used to get at the nursery every morning. This was always nice but very mild and sickly compared to what we had at home, and there was always a faint taste of plastic that you get when you drink out of those early pre-space age plastic cups.

The difference between the Jamaican and English aspects of my life at that time often revolved around food. Saturdays really exemplified it. Saturday-morning breakfast would usually be fried dumpling and egg or saltfish fritters, sometimes sardine. If it was at my Nan's it would be cornflakes or porridge, the Scottish way, with salt – my Grandad was from Edinburgh. Then for Saturday dinnertime (lunch) my Mum would let me go and have pie, mash and liquor at the pie and mash shop. She would give me a shilling and I would go off and eat this very English working-class food sitting on a wooden bench at a marble table. I was the only black person in the shop. Now when I pass one of the few pie and mash shops still left in London and see that green, slimy-looking liquor I really wonder how I ever came to eat it, but it still serves to remind me of my roots. Dinner in the evening would be either saltfish and ackee (still one of my favourite meals); home-made oxtail or pea soup, or maybe pigs' trotters and rice.

This stark difference would be replayed throughout the week, with English dinner at nursery or school and something more Jamaican in the evening. At my Nan's, of course, it was English all the time (although there may have been Scottish variations of which I was unaware). In particular I remember the high tea on Sundays – bread, celery, tomatoes, ham, prawns, perhaps some mussels or cockles, eggs, and of course salad cream. Occasionally Nan would cut up an avocado pear that my Dad might have given her if he'd managed to get some down at the Shepherd's Bush market. Another thing that reminds me of the 'old days' is horse-drawn carts. That's because the milkman would do his round with a horse-drawn carriage; he and his weekend helper would sit at the front. The milkman's horse was called Ginger and it was a huge great orange-coloured horse that would take lumps of sugar from you if you were brave enough to offer them. I was always too frightened to do that but I did eventually pluck up enough courage to stroke him, taking great care not to go too close to his back legs – I'd been told that if you do, horses have a tendency to kick you. Being very much a city girl I had no idea whether this was true or not, but I sure as hell wasn't going to risk finding out the hard way. But it was really nice on weekend days to lie in bed and hear the clip-clop of Ginger's hooves on the cobbled street. On Sundays he would have to compete with the brass band of the Salvation Army that came to save our souls.

Apart from the delicious milk that we used to get from the milkman (milk is still one of my favourite drinks, only now I'm always told how bad it is for me while then we were always told how good it was for us – a dreadful burden for those kids who hated it but were forced to drink their third of a pint every weekday morning), we also got wonderful little bottles of orange squash. Saturdays and Sundays we had these delivered for the kids in the house, which was a great treat. Jimmy and I used to play at putting our lips inside the wide tops to see who could get furthest down the neck of the bottle. One day the inevitable happened and I got my lips stuck in the bottle. I was scared, my Mum was scared, everybody was scared, but people were also laughing at this spectacle of me walking around with a bottle hanging from my mouth. It was awful and I was getting madder and madder that people could find my misfortune so hilarious. After a little while the bottle slipped off of its own accord to leave one swollen-lipped petulant little girl to sulk in the corner.

The most wonderful orange we got was the NHS concentrated type that came in medicine bottles. I was given a spoonful of this each morning along with my cod-liver oil, which was never as bad in my eyes as everyone else seemed to think. It was in asking how there was such a difference between the kinds of orange juice that I learned that a really ripe orange could be green, or at least greeny-orange, and not the bright orange of the kind we got here. I couldn't imagine a green orange – a contradiction in terms – but then there was lots I couldn't imagine about JA. So I just used it as a way to trump the other kids at school in a geography lesson or something.

As the Chicago Art Ensemble would say, I like 'great Black music' – that is, black music in any form so long as it pulsates with

224

the experiences of my people; so long as it helps to find the link between the present and history, and the continuous and discontinuous. From Fats Waller to the high falsetto of Eddie Kendrics; from Pukumania to heavy dub, from Aretha to Carmen McCrae; from scat to ska; from melody to the revelation of structure that the transformation of content reveals in dub or 'new wave'. And this, I think, lies in the fact that music was a central feature of my life at Granville Road. There were the regular parties at which all sorts of black music was played; there was the jump up and clap of Pukumania from May May in particular and there was the calypso, 'blues' and other Caribbean music which came predominantly, but not exclusively, from Clarence's sound system. He was a part-time DJ who wished he could do it full time. So he would 'play out' in the hope that he could earn a good living like this (much as many a black teenager does today) and when it wasn't enough he would have to get some form of waged employment. Much to Pearl's annoyance, this wasn't always enough.

Jazz was what my Mum and Dad played most – everyone: Lester Young, Bud Powell, Sarah Vaughan, Lena Horne, Ella Fitzgerald, Lionel Hampton, Charlie Parker, Billie Holiday, Miles Davis, John Coltrane, MJQ, Paul Desmond, Stan Getz, Dave Brubeck, Eydie Gorme, Nat King Cole, Ben Webster, June Holloway and a whole lot more I can't remember. Eydie Gormé's 'Our Love is Here to Stay' and Nat King Cole's 'When I Fall in Love' were my favourites, with the Cole number being the first song I learned to sing all the way through. But generally I just loved the sound of music and the way it made you feel. I liked the way it made the adults change their behaviour so much, with all reservation gone (even if they weren't high). Like when Mum and some other relatives and their friends would tape themselves taking it in turn to follow Ella with their own renditions of scat.

In many senses these were great times, but more importantly they were for me times when I internalised powerful images of my people's capacity for laughter, enjoyment, good times and above all the love of self and the generosity that goes with it, despite terrible housing conditions, huge disappointment, long and dangerous hours of work and the continual threat of racism. What I learned is that contrary to many white people's conceptions, racism is a conditioning, not a determining feature influencing the quality of our lives. Its potential for destroying does not inevitably destroy. Rather, in the face of and often despite its destructive potential, black people's creativity has been unleashed. The music embodied this and conveyed to me a lesson I am still learning. I can love myself, have dignity and hate racism but without succumbing to the force of bitterness.

Of course in my case most of the family or household events were racially mixed occasions. The kind of 1960s integrationist dream, where we can all dance together, all eat 'ethnic', be beatifically patronising (as only the English know how) and become the 'experts' on black people. Nevertheless, they were important and happy times and served to distinguish between those white relatives who would have nothing to do with us and those in whose houses we were welcomed. That division still exists today.

School was a dismal affair until I was about ten years old. Apart from nursery school, which I loved and which I attended free after my parents had (on appeal) passed a means test, my very first infants' school was in Harrow. This was because of my mother's concern that I get as 'good' an education as possible and be free from the harrassment of bullies. At least these were the reasons she gave, but I can't help feeling that there was at least a hint of suburban working-class snobbery against London working-class culture. Anyway, because of this I went to live at Nan's for about a year and started school there. There are only four things I can remember about that school: playing the violin; doing English country dancing; being in the remedial reading class and constantly being asked why I was 'brown' and did it come off.

I can't remember a single thing about the process of my being classified remedial for reading purposes, but no doubt there was some more or less arbitrary system of identifying me as 'a slow learner' or below my 'reading age'. I do know reading *was* hard. I also know that the books we learned from weren't much inspiration. *Janet and John* was full of blonde kids and Janet was about the biggest sissy I'd ever come across: definitely not much of a model – she neither looked like me nor acted like me! None of this was helped by the fact that at my first primary school I remember what seemed like hours and hours of being read *Uncle Tom's Cabin*, which only made me retreat from the written word even more, because if black people on paper were pathetic, miserable, powerless and infantile 'creatures', worthy only of white paternalism and moral vindication, then I'd stick to the black people I knew. And anyway, being able to read well didn't protect me from racialist insults from the other kids, so I concentrated on the things which would – sports and being able to fight: the latter because if push came to shove at least you'd have a chance, and if you got a reputation for being hard then you got fewer threats; and sport because you could compete against the white kids and win *and* still get some recognition from the school. It fed every stereotype we were being dished up, but this didn't occur to me, nor did I care because stereotypes didn't alter the glory.

I eventually learned to read at the age of ten on my grandmother's back doorstep, thanks to her tireless efforts and the skill and patience of one particular teacher in my second primary school. I remain convinced that it was because he was Welsh, with English as his second language, that he became the first teacher with whom I had any empathy. He taught me that if these words we were reading didn't speak to us, then being able to decipher them was the key to finding words that did. It is of course a search that still continues.

I eventually had to leave my infants' school because my mother's brother, who still lived at home, objected to me being there. I remember this as a simple question of prejudice on his part – what about his friends who came to the house, what about his girlfriends, what would they *think*? While this may be the distortion which comes from childhood memory, race definitely had something to do with it, because my Mum had to come up to Harrow to 'discuss' the issue with the family. Inevitably my uncle got his way, with only Nan objecting.

It was a foggy November evening (they definitely don't have those like they used to) when my Mum came to collect me and take me home. The whole event had happened very quickly so it was the middle of term when I abruptly left this school. Mum came from work and we had some tea and then set off for the Bakerloo line (the one which ran at the bottom of the garden) back to Kilburn. My Nan came out into the street with us and she and Mum spoke about it all for a while. It was one of those moments that seems forever to occupy a huge space in the mind. I think that's why I can remember it so clearly. It was also the first real incidence that I can remember of racialism within my family, directed at us; or rather, it was the first that I was aware of as a racial incident.

In the street, I remember my Mum saying: 'It's all right Mum, I know Alec will always get his way over me but I don't blame you', and my poor Nan feeling helpless and crying and no doubt somewhere inside her resenting the fact that as the 'woman of the house' she ultimately had no say over how this little situation was resolved. Her husband and her son had decided the matter. It was, then, also my first remembered lesson in the power of men over women.

For my Mum it was just another painful incident in a long chain of rejections by her family because of her relationships with black people. Her father was always at the fore of these incidents and for her this must have seemed like a replaying of his refusal to allow her to come home when she was pregnant with me, even though she was quite literally homeless.

I was sad not because of school, or my uncle, or my Grandad, since I didn't really like any of them. But I was very, very sad because my Mum was, and also because I was leaving my Nan, whom I loved (and love) as much as my Mum.

Despite this we had a nice ride home, with Mum all the way trying 'to make it up to me' as though what had happened was her fault. She promised me that the new school wouldn't be too bad; that I'd make new friends, and I'd see her every day (hooray!). Of course I'd still be able to see Nan, which I used to do often both because my Mum would go to the garden to sunbathe and because I'd get on the train myself when I got a bit older and go and see her myself. It's a sign of how quite well off we were that both houses had phones, so I'd ring Nan first and she'd meet me at the station.

When we got home there was a big mug of chocolate or Horlicks and lots of reassurance and love. Next day Mum arranged for me to go to the local infants' school, which I would attend for two and a half terms. Two days later I started the new school – Carlton Vale Infants. Mum took me there that day, going into work late for the second time in a week, for which she could easily have lost her job.

We started out at about 8.45 since the school was only about five minutes away. The first things to greet us as we rounded the corner into Carlton Vale were shouts of 'nigger' and 'nigger lover' from two adolescent boys. Mum gripped my hand tight and shouted something back, and I remember feeling the anger and anguish she was feeling. No doubt one thing that crossed her mind was the thought that her brother was implicated in all this. Who could blame her?

I hated Carlton Vale Infants (now the Carlton Centre) and my sole memory of the place is my standing in the corner of the playground at breaktime and crying, feeling wretched and sorry for myself. I left two terms later to go to Kilburn Park Primary, the school of the endless *Uncle Tom's Cabin* and sports.

As a result of Grandad's refusal to 'forgive' my mother for 'going with blacks' he had never adjusted to my existence, so we never really got to know each other. Ironically, by the time my sister was born, ten years after me, Grandad had got used to the idea, and he and my sister were very close until he died when she was about two.

I had never particularly liked him; for one thing, I didn't like the smell of Brylcream that always followed him about, and I was a bit afraid of him. Occasionally he used to get drunk and then he'd get all weepy about me and try and get to me, ostensibly to give me a cuddle. Seeing that I was frightened, Nan would fight him off, an act for which I was always grateful. Gradually I became indifferent to him and his racialism, so that by the time he died we had a kind of aloof but amicable relationship. However, the images of him both ignoring me and trying to hold me are still very strong.

But my Grandad did have a fundamental influence on me in one respect. That is in relation to politics. It was he and my Nan who first taught me that class is real and that it matters, and that the working class is in a struggle with the ruling class and with bosses of all descriptions.

They had both been strong anti-fascists in the pre-war years, more because of the threat to all workers than because of anti-semitism.

229

They had also both been committed trade unionists and Labour Party members for years, although for my Nan, who her whole life worked as a 'char lady' (cleaning middle-class ladies' homes for them), being a member of a trade union was out of the question, as was any full-time active participation in political activity. She did, however, canvass for Labour at election times, support local strikes when they occurred and generally imbue us all with a sense of working-class struggle. Grandad on the other hand had seen periods of quite active participation in local Labour Party politics, even serving for a short time as a local councillor in a Wealdstone ward, in ultra-Tory Harrow.

Their working-class politics were, however, trapped in the ties of Labourism. They truly believed that the victory of the working class lay in the degree to which it could, through its organisations, the trade unions and the Labour Party, elect a government and reform capital in a way that would enable workers to participate in the running of the economy and government. Socialism was the Welfare State and the implementation of clause 4, part 4. Politics was about securing that. As they saw it, by the 1950s at least some of the battle was already won with the Welfare State and all, and all that needed to be achieved now was a returned Labour government which, along with the trade unions in industry, would complete the process. Internationally Britain would show that it was still great by 'granting' independence when the colonies were 'ready', and this too would demonstrate how Labour were better than the Tories, since weren't they about living with each other as equal human beings? My Grandad died believing that; that's why he felt no contradiction between his espousal of the international unity and dignity of 'mankind' and his profoundly racialist and chauvinistic views. My Nan has, however, lived to see a different age and has moved on to a much more truly socialist politics. Grandad's son, on the other hand, has followed in his father's footsteps.

It was the product of my mother's own racialism that she couldn't know (in a deeply unquestioning sense) that black people, as a people, refuse 'to diminish themselves as human beings by succumbing to racism' (as Alice Walker says in 'The black writer and the Southern Experience' in *In Search of Our Mothers' Gardens*).

It was also a product of her racialism that she tended to deride those aspects of transplanted and changing Jamaican culture that she did not like. She was therefore typical of many white people in mixed relationships in that she selected from the black package she knew those aspects that suited her, while attempting to distance herself from the rest. Fairly untypically however, she liked and had a deep respect for black *women*. And in the last seven years of her life she slowly but steadily began a reassessment of her view of black culture. This was inevitably a painful experience since it involved a re-evaluation of her understanding of the dynamics of her life with Dad. It also meant that she came into conflict with her daughters who in many respects had forced the re-evaluation upon her. It was a process carried out in loneliness and often with bitterness, and it is a tribute to her strength that she even embarked upon it.

On the other hand, it was a product of my Dad's sexism that he truly believed women were there just to serve their men, and when not out at work to wait at home for the man, and when out together to enhance the man's image by the appropriate behaviour. He believed, at that time, that the man could tell the woman what to do with regard to dress, smoking and behaviour. And if she didn't take notice then it was right and understandable that he would 'give her some licks', hit her that is. I don't believe he has undergone a reassessment of his views, unlike Mum. At the same time, he has clearly changed. It was then as a result of these two tensions that the most difficult thing for me at the time was precisely the relationship between Mum and Dad. The most common or garden variety of arguments would be riddled with race/sex tensions, which at worst broke out into those awful scenes of him hitting her. For me this was a nightmare, and although I can't remember it occurring all that often, when it did I have yet more slow-motion images of me either tugging at him or running upstairs to get Lester or Clarence, and always feeling helpless. The last time he ever hit Mum in my presence was when I was about sixteen and they had already split up, but on that occasion I avenged all those times of helplessness by attacking him with a carving knife and a baseball bat. I didn't get him but he stopped hitting Mum, and knew he'd never try it again.

Anyway, it wasn't even the violence itself, so much as the threat of it and the incredible tension that sometimes existed. It's a kind of tension that I believe is unique to inter-racial domestic situations – and one which it's difficult to see how to resolve. It's also difficult to describe for those who do not know it, but the race/sex thing would get played out by the two of them entering into competitions for superiority or domination. Him calling on his maleness, she on her whiteness. And there *was* a kind of excitement in it so long as it wasn't violent or demeaning.

Most of all, of course, the battleground was just the normal everyday kind of thing, like dinner not being cooked on time, or the shirt not ironed 'properly', or him not being 'man' enough or inadequate in other ways. One of the main things, though, was my Dad's refusal to 'allow' my Mum to smoke. She did, of course, but not in his presence and secretly. I remember I used to go and get her cigarettes and she'd hide them from him. This always had a slight sense of adventure for me because of the act of conspiracy between me and my Mum. It did, however, also cause me concern since I knew it was a potentially dangerous situation. Another thing was my Mum's contempt for my Dad because of his humble demeanour in the face of white authority. Throughout their marriage it was agreed that Mum would deal with any authorities that had to be faced. If we tried to get new housing, Mum would go; if we had to go to the school, Mum would go; if they had to go to the local authority or LCC, Mum would go. And since they both believed that by 'rights' the man should do this kind of stuff, then it only served to reinforce their shared belief in my Dad's inadequacy. Which led to him having to 'prove' himself by reasserting his dominance over her as a man. It was a situation that was fed by racism *and* their attempt at overcoming it. It was also a situation that couldn't exist in an all-black relationship.

My Mum was in fact quite independent since she always worked full time and kept her own money to herself. She worked in shops as a counter assistant, mostly in chemists but occasionally in some of the big London department stores. Selfridge's was one of them and she told me about how during the fifties they wouldn't hire black counter assistants. She went back to work there briefly in the early sixties and by then they had started to hire some black people (mostly women) on the counters – but always only the most light-skinned. She always used to comment on that when she shopped there, right up until she died.

Work gave her some of her closest friends, especially women who were also involved in relationships with black men. It was also a source of her identity, and the independence was something which she cherished not least because it meant that she could provide for me, alone if necessary – though to some extent the reason for her marrying and staying with Dad for so long was 'to give me a name and a father'. The irony was that after she had her second child she only stayed with him for five more years. It was, however, Dad who caused the final break-up, by getting involved with and having a child by a woman, Louise, from Jamaica. It made my Mum quite bitter, but it was later to serve as a starting point for my discussions with her about 'race', racism and mixed relationships.

Despite the problems with their relationship, Mum and Dad were important models for me, both in their own way giving me the foundations of a perspective that informs my politics today.

By June 1960 Granville Road had been declared a slum and put into the council's housing programme. We were all offered alternative housing, mostly in the high-rise flats that are at the junction of Cambridge Road and Kilburn High Street. Mum refused to go and live in one of these and used it as her chance to get us to move away from the area, back to Harrow, only further up at Harrow Weald. We moved to a purpose-built block of two-bedroom flats, and so for the first time I had my own bedroom, and we had a bathroom and hot and cold water. It was absolute luxury, but it had its costs. We could only afford the rent if both Mum and Dad were working, but it also meant that Dad and I were in an almost completely white area. There were a few black GI's and their families who also rented flats in the block, but overall it was white. It took its toll on Dad, and on their relationship, so that in the end Dad was hardly ever in. It was during this time that he met Louise, his second wife. Mum became pregnant soon after and as well as being left alone for much of the time had also to face the worrying prospect of paying for the place alone. Dad lost his job because the factory moved to

Liverpool, and though he soon got another one the whole business served to embitter my Mum.

As for me, it was at this time that I learned that Dad was not my 'real' Dad, in the biological sense, though he was in every other way. It was also the beginning of my losing touch with my blackness in any cultural sense and I was to await the surge of the Black Power era to put me back on that path again, ten years later. But I had had a good grounding and still had a mother who was committed, despite her contradictions, to seeing her daughters become independent women – black and proud and free and strong.

THE SIXTIES proved to be a decade of mixed blessings. Better, more expensive housing at the same time as my Mum had to stop working made us poor, and being isolated from a black community served to increase the pressures on my parents' relationship. This situation really deteriorated after the birth of my sister. Overall, my Dad proved to be a real bastard as far as my Mum was concerned, and he was usually never at home for more than two or three nights a week.

Financially we were really poor, so that often by Wednesday we literally didn't have anything to eat. In these situations my Nan would come to the rescue either by bringing us food or coming to my playground to give me money so I could take food home from school. By Thursday the situation got better again because it was Family Allowance day.

School got much better, in fact I positively liked it, but still I didn't exactly excel academically. I didn't pass the eleven-plus and can't even remember taking it, and I feel sure that not all of us did take it. We had been pre-selected to sit the examination on the basis of our work over the year.

Our poverty was relatively well hidden at school – Provident cheques saved us there. There was, however, one exception: shoes. I often had to wait for a new pair of shoes, and in the meantime I'd stuff carefully folded pieces of newspaper into them in order to protect my soles from the holes. Mum did always try to keep me in a new pair of plimsolls so at least they would look all right, but generally she didn't want me to wear them in the street because, being very dress-conscious, she thought they looked scruffy.

Things got better again when in the mid-sixties we moved to my Nan's house. The idea was that Mum and Dad would save to buy a house of their own. That never happened and in 1966 they split up. Anyway, the whole process of negotiating with the relevant bodies – estate agents, vendors, the LCC, and so on – only served to exacerbate the tensions in their relationship.

Following a sudden spurt of academic progress in the third year at secondary mod, I left school at sixteen with two low-grade O levels and went to a further education college for one year, where I got two more. Given my previous academic record this was seen as a great success. After that I went to work in a variety of clerical/telephonist jobs and also got heavily into drugs. It was, after all, the decade of 'speed' and I was one of its greatest advocates. I was into drugs for about nine years (starting at fourteen), but as I began to get interested in Black Power and consciousness I gradually cut down on the drug-taking and eventually gave it up altogether.

As I became an avid book reader I also began to have fantasies of going to college. All those accounts of black political prisoners in the USA who 'discovered' their 'brains' gave me a model to dream about, but it did still seem so out of reach for me. As a form of vicarious satisfaction in this field I got a job at University College London Library (to my Mum's absolute delight – she was temporarily living in the USA at the time) and from there my life began to change.

I got married to one of the students, did the obligatory middle-class hippy hitching trip round Europe and the Middle East, went to live in Sri Lanka for almost a year, and while there resolved to 'come out' as a lesbian and do A levels to go to university. All of which I did, and I did very well in academic terms. Having got a degree in social anthropology at the London School of Economics, I went on, after a year working in a Housing Advice Centre, to do an M.Phil in Third World development at the Institute of Development Studies at Sussex. I got involved with the Angela Davis Defence Campaign and this led to increasing involvement in anti-racist, anti-imperialist and black feminist politics. And that's where I am now.

Denise Riley

Waiting

I was born in 1948 in Carlisle, the daughter of an unmarried working mother and a father whose name I do not know. I was brought up by adoptive parents as an only child. They lived in Gloucester. Both had left school at fourteen. My adoptive mother came from Tyneside. She had done clerical work before she married, at which point her widowed mother came to live with her. My adoptive father was the son of a South Shields shipyard worker; he had managed to get a job as an office boy. He taught himself to become a local government accountant through night schools and correspondence courses.

I have no way of writing fluently about this past. When I say 'I' and add the past-tense verb, I am at once in the realm of untruth. 'I' was never a child. I use this as the voice of synthesising adulthood, oiling the disjointed, making an easy tolerability out of the unbearable, making a lubricated narrative out of what has no characters. There was no order of events, and there were no events. All that counted was the detail.

I am the same. I have not changed. I cannot describe anything, any more than you can ever describe or wish to describe a loved person, because that love strips them of possessing characteristics. I don't understand anything. What I remember vibrates in a permanent present.

You had bitter aloes painted onto your fingernails to stop you biting them.

You sit in silence through the crashing external noises like a snail in its shell. You nestle, are hunched inside your own skin and clothes. You pursue inwardness more and more forcefully. When you look outwards, you must also look upwards to see people.

To hide in the raspberry canes. To go crazy with emotion, studying eye-level ants. To be jealous of the dog. To think that your name was She until you were about four. Or not. Your grandmother had violet cachous, fox collars with bead eyes, paste jewellery; her sister was lost in the Boer War. Your grandfather had been a Poor Law Guardian and sharpened his razor on a leather strap that was also for giving beltings. That was what you needed. You gave out emanations of virtue and vice at once, at school and at home respectively; you were therefore a deceiver, and so were bad in truth. You were the murderer, and the little Princes in the Tower. I have only just understood that this logic was so.

Nothing happened in the 1950s.
I was not my parents' child, but I did not know that then.
Time did not pass. I was held still in it.
The little decorations of social history are thin traces laid over a surface.

In 1952 I was sent to a local convent school until I was eleven, although my adoptive parents were Protestants. Later it was closed down. I was always described as the heretic at school, a designation which was theologically accurate enough and didn't particularly disturb me; it seemed a not unkind acknowledgement of whatever distances I carried with me.

Art trained the eyes, that was what it was for. We drew pencil ellipses; we copied the arcs made by the tops of flower vases. On

238

Saint Theresa's day I had to paint a frieze of watercolour rose petals to run the length of the classroom walls. We had a statue of Saint Theresa, creamy-faced and brown-robed, transfixed in her shower of sweet carmine roses. The painting of the Sacred Heart. Christ in the corridor under the snaky thorns with a grave and tender gaze. The Blessed Virgin as Stella Maris, the star of the sea, deepest indigo blue, sparkling. My patron saint was Saint Jude, the patron of lost causes.

I studied the lists of heresies at the back of my catechism.

In 1953 it was the Coronation. The school had to go to the park with stiff paper flags. Then I had to write a composition about the Royal Visit. 'The Queen waved and smiled. She wore a blue dress.' I smudged the ink in my copybook; I did crossings-out and smudged them again. So I got caned on the palms of my hands. I didn't much care; it was only the clumsiness of my fingers around the dip-in pen which was at fault, and nothing more intimate.

The quietness of daily outward life.

The first gold star in the exercise book came in 1953 too, when I was five. I had written what was judged the best essay on the topic of the Mortification of the Flesh: 'Why do we mortify our flesh in Lent? ...' But this account of achieving grace by the easy means of a self-chosen deprivation did nothing to mitigate the deeper shame; some original wrong had been done and at home this was known. All the gold stars of school could not prevail against it.

We learned a copperplate at my convent, with elaborate curlicues of capitals I have not seen in any other calligraphy. I can still write it fluently. We did transcription, copied out set passages in this arching, long-looped hand. I wrote out, over and over, with a calm satisfaction: 'I should like to live among the leaves and heather like the birds, to wear a dress of feathers, and to eat berries.' This sentence seemed to me to possess an utter and invulnerable completeness.

The soul was accessible to the gaze of your guardian angel. He could see, by looking behind your eyeballs, into the back of your eyes where the quiet incandescent space of the soul hung; he might see it spotted with sins like trampled snow. The Blessed Virgin was immaculate and that meant unspotted. 'Womb' was an intimate and horrifying word although you heard it as the incarnation of the Virgin.

On the classroom wall was a coloured print illustrating a Brothers Grimm story. The wolf was about to descend on the little pigs. Later the wolf would be cut open while she was asleep, filled up with heavy stones once the little pigs had scrabbled out of her, stitched up again by the woodcutter; and then she would be driven by thirst to the river, would topple in and drown with the weight of the stones.

The Sacred Heart pointed mournfully to his breast; the crown of thorns radiated from his head.
The King of the Golden River. The Water Babies.

Your grandmother would not have any demurring at meals. The caterpillar you had found boiled was a part of your cabbage. It was not, you went on thinking, knowing vaguely about butterflies, a future barred to the wrinkled and whiteish corpses on your plate, tinged with green as if out of obedience to your grandmother's convictions they had surrendered their essences to the cabbage.

Your father read the *Daily Express*. Then your mother and grandmother read its scandals aloud to each other in the kitchen, with a monotonous note of sustained outrage that was never sated. Their voices rose on this note from the kitchen to saturate the bedroom above where on summer evenings you lay rigid with wakefulness.

You tried to make patterns out of the flowers and ribbons on the wallpaper. Having brought them into being with your eyes, you tried to force them back in again before they writhed and proliferated everywhere. Years of my life may have passed in this enforced study of wallpaper.

You would go to the women's prison. You had heard that there was one, Holloway, and that was for you. Some wickedness you would

Aged six, 1954

perhaps unknowingly perpetrate would see you in there, or some gesture towards a justice which no one else subscribed to. Your cell was already waiting for you. How could you endure the time? You rehearsed word games in preparation for your confinement. The best of these was changing the punctuation in a sentence in your head, seeing how you might shift its meaning by putting a comma in different places. In the 1950s people were killed in prison. A woman was hanged. There were agonising nights and mornings. You will sit alone in your prison cell. It will go on waiting for you until the day you enter it.

A headband of pale pink cloth roses and almond-green leaves on wire stems, cotton and velveteen, for parties. Boys who controlled a dreadful game; they'd blindfold girls and thrust dismembered parts of human bodies into their hands: there's your brain! your eyeball! your liver! These were jelly or peach halves filched from the party table, but knowing that did not help you, and you hid.

Red tap shoes. A drawer of hair ribbons. A liberty bodice; the smooth intimacy of its neat rubber buttons and tabs. Slaps. Privacy.

Illness. M&B the first antibiotic which you thought was one word, emmonbee. Walking the floor to prove to yourself it was not rising to crush your bed as the walls slowly gathered in towards you and the ceiling lowered itself steadily downwards until it was an inch above your face. The wolf came to your door in human dress at night. You barricaded your door against its tall figure. The door was gradually forced open against the weight of your body clinging to hold it shut. The light was snapped on. You woke up to the figure in the dress with the head of the wolf.

Where did you get the words for happiness and unhappiness? Was it from children's books in which families smiled? No, that was not enough of an explanation.

Maxims fell all around you, insistently repeated: Ask no questions and you'll hear no lies. Speak roughly to your little boy, And beat him when he sneezes, He only does it to annoy, Because he knows it teases. Honour thy father and thy mother. Eavesdroppers hear no good of themselves. There'll be no discussion of sex, religion or

242

politics in *my* house. Children should be seen and not heard. As you make your bed, so you must lie on it. Spare the rod, spoil the child. Labour tries to level everyone down instead of levelling up. A child has to have its spirit broken. Obey without question.

The long brilliant, shocking lines hidden under your mattress to read in the endless summer nights: a copy of Palgrave's *Golden Treasury*. Poor Ruth, thou hast been worse than dead. Or let my Lamp at midnight hour Be seen in some high lonely Tower Where I may oft outwatch the Bear. The tufted crow-toe and pale jessamine, The white pink and the pansy freaked with jet, The glowing violet. He hangs in shades the orange bright Like golden lamps in a green night. Where thou perhaps under the whelming tide Visit'st the bottom of the monstrous world.

In the quiet of the new suburbs, regrets for the past: 'There'd always be some life about. We were always in and out of each other's houses.' A used car came in 1959, a television and a telephone some years later. But life was over; it had been left irretrievably behind before the war, and with it an animation which could never be resurrected, if it had been at all.

It was an existence conducted as if in poverty, but my adoptive parents could not actually have been poor; still, it was ruled by insistences on not wasting, on eating everything up, on being grateful, on saving light and water. There were recalls of the Jarrow marchers, as if a volcanic lava that was the death of security had devastated the country and with it peace of mind had gone for ever. The house was closed; there were almost no visits.

Once you saw the word 'prostitution' in a church magazine and asked what it meant, and once 'rape' in the newspaper. These were questions you should not have asked, and you were not answered; but you heard that men were animals, and could not control themselves. Later in your life you would spend many years attempting to disprove this thesis.

A test of faith at school when I was seven; an aerial photograph of mountain tops under heavy snow. What could we discern in those folds of black on white? We passed the picture gingerly around the class. It had been taken by a pilot who was shocked out of his atheism and into the Church by what was revealed to him in his darkroom. Not snow fallen on peaks alone, but the image of Christ as on Saint Veronica's cloth, the dark eyes and the crown of thorns scorched and scarred on its folds and pleats. Until this was pointed out to me, though, I could not see it.

I had failed a test of faith; faith was a gift of God, yet a gift you must have to live. But how could a waverer be censored if God had elected to withhold this gift? It might at any moment be lifted away from me utterly and I would be left exposed.

The catastrophic and arbitrary loss of love that you had not earned in the first place.
The suspect struggle for innocence.

And where did the idea of 'love' come from, or 'justice'? Perhaps from religious instruction, I don't know. In times of danger you said rapidly under your breath, Hail Mary full of grace – with a great leaning breath onto the H – Holy Mary Mother of God Pray for us sinners Now and at the hour of our death Amen. This was a great comfort because it guaranteed you a guardian, a communality, and an end.

Every Tuesday morning you forgot your thimble, every Tuesday afternoon you held out your palm for the cut of the cane. Each caning made you forget more thoroughly. We did hemming, sheets and pillowcases; we did embroidery, tea cosies and gym bags and table napkins with loop stitch, knot stitch, lazy daisies, satin stitch, herringbone. When we were four and five we had to sleep in the afternoons on long mats made of shiny grass that left ribbing marks on our skin.

'The doctor says she needs a good beating if she won't eat properly.' You tried to say you couldn't stomach the welling blood the brains the private thinking tissues of the dead animal the pipes rivulets channels conduits and gulleys with their muscular veinous edges, tripe, brains and tongue. There were iron pails of sheep's heads in the kitchen for boiling into broth. There were monthly pails of bloody white rags soaking. You had to eat everything that was put before you, to sit there alone into the afternoon while the winter dusk drew in and what was on your long cold plate had thickened until you had eaten it all. By the time you were four and old enough to go to school you were practised at enticing the dogs in to be fed, undetected.

Concealment. Privacy. But nothing unique. I am writing about a monstrous ordinariness. What have you hidden? What have you got there? Perhaps, in the light of day, nothing.
Why can't you forget these ordinary things?
It is from the dread of misremembering.

Black Babies were there for the saving. Our classroom had a chart; on it an apricot glow marked the apotheosis of a vast flight of yellowed marble stairs. Here God waited flanked by all the races of the earth, the whitest and pinkest thronged next to him, calmly gowned; below, the heathen in descending shades from deep ivory to buff to coffee. Bordered by these figures, the towering expanses of the stairs were bare save for the toiling brown dots of the Babies inching up to the divine presence. You each had a Black Baby and the donation of a penny a week out of your pocket money meant that the Sister could move your small paper cut-out one step higher to God. I do not remember if the Babies descended, were re-named, and started their laborious struggle to the light over again; I can only trace them in their perpetual slow motion upward.

There were daily chances of grace. Roads were hazardous practical examinations in virtue. Your challenge was to encounter a dying man or child, the victim of an accident, and to have the presence of mind to rescue his soul, in a terrible elevation to sacred power, by the formula of baptism. In such a way a child's promptness might save a soul from the long blankness of Limbo, or a child's inattention or failure of nerve condemn it to years of the deadliest waiting until the day of Judgement, held still in the amber of the centuries.

When they turned seven, the boys had to go away to boys' schools. Seven was the age of reason. But although I was not sent away, I still did not have a sex. My body was all of a piece, it did not have any seams.

We swung on the school gates with our panamas trailing. In summer we wore candy-striped dresses with Peter Pan collars.

'To make a Liberty Belle: white ballet skirt with a layer of blue net dotted with silver stars. Back and front panels of red and white striped cotton. Tie bandolier of white stuff over one shoulder and under opposite write word LIBERTY in Indian ink. Cut headdress from gold or painted paper. Coronet of same with screw of orangey-red paper inside to represent the Flame.' Instructions I copied out from a girls' annual for 1954. Annuals, cigarette cards, scrapbooks, cut-outs, scraps with gummed backs.

Sister Superior, from the waxed scented and echoing chambers of the convent where we usually never set foot, sent for me to remind me of the Parable of the Talents. These to her were not biblical coins but natural capacities bestowed as a gift. The recipient had an obligation to use these talents to help others; and since I was a heretic, my duties in this respect were all the more pressing. No possibilities here to warm to any feeling of myself as 'clever'; the aching question instead was why the divine hand had seen fit to bestow these talents on me and not on the next child. The Magdalen herself had dried Christ's feet with her long tangled perfumed hair; wavy hair beyond doubt of the ripest corn-yellow. Everywhere the capricious darting hand of Grace had lighted on the fallen, the ordinary, and they had been briefly lit up and magnified in that illumination.

Russian tanks were in Hungary in 1956 and we prayed at school for the dying, who were not Russian. But it was Cromwell who remained the arch repository of true evil in the world, Cromwell who had persecuted Ireland so greatly as to overshadow even Queen Elizabeth who, vilifying Mary Stuart, had put her to a martyr's death.

As well as history, we studied the natural sciences. The theory of evolution was a modern heresy, we learned; for God, in this instance not without a taint of mortal sadism, had created the world perfectly finished as it is now, in an instant's flash of concentration. But he had made it complete with fossils and dinosaur skeletons buried under the earth; red herrings put there to expose those of little faith. These apparent pointers to evolution only demonstrated the folly of those who accepted them, thus vindicating the superiority of God's plan.

There could be an industry of broken memories of convent childhoods. Still, something was expected and hoped of me there; I was credited with a future, and I called some fondness into being, even though this was because they did not know what lay under my surface.

The daily crossing of the easy boundaries between badness and goodness, from home to school and back again. Intense drabness with a secret scarlet heart. In all this my life was not novel, except that it had no witnesses, because I was an only child.

You were grateful not to have been born a boy, for that meant the probability of dying in war. All men fought; all men in England had been to India for the duration of the last war, leaving behind them a country of women. Your father had gone. Had he killed anyone? He would not talk about it, and you knew not to ask more, but you realised that it must have been the time in his life when he most resembled himself.

A surge of silent tenderness surrounded the name of India, as nowhere else.

It seemed a hideous unthinkable accident to be born a man, so you would have to become a soldier. He said once at the time of Suez with a charge of bitterness, 'Those Egyptians are rats.' Again you knew not to ask.

The sickening feel of woollen gloves being pulled onto your hands and hitting and blunting your fingertips so touch was lost. Ribboned panamas. Could you kill yourself by putting your fingers into the electric socket? Your fingernails were cut too short.

You live in a frozen universe in which emotion resonates without any chronology. There is no story because there is no past tense.

No ameliorating reconstruction is possible.
There is cruelty which cannot be dissolved into history or sympathetic sociology. To claim 'understanding' would be a kindly

fiction. I understand nothing, and refuse to.

In the autumn of 1959 I was eleven, and I went to the girls' grammar school down the road.

I FIND MYSELF caught in the toils of having to give a personal explanation for why I can't write a personal explanation for the formation of my adult beliefs. I could tell a story about political tendencies, children, employment, poetry, unemployment, history; I could say, for instance:

'My life was formed only by means of the public library which provided me with my only uncensored access to books. When I was fifteen or sixteen I found a confirmation of my interest in what it is to take on your own past in some of Sartre's work. I read *The Second Sex* and *A Room of One's Own* at the same age, and thought of myself as a feminist, although this had to remain a privately held conviction for several years more. In this spirit I joined the Abortion Law Reform Association while still at school; this was just before the passage of the 1967 Abortion Act. The political developments of 1968 and the first national conference of the Women's Liberation Movement spanned my time as a student and rapidly thereafter as a mother. As for many, the Vietnam demonstrations of 1967 were my first.'

But this would only be a story, and would not ring true. Besides, I want to protect the remains of my privacy; I don't want to appear cold-hearted or stubborn; but I know that when I try to make my life give me its answers to how I have come to my current concerns, I can't do it without feeling that I am on the edge of a dangerous fiction of self-description.

The bare facts are these: in 1966 I got an open scholarship to do English at Oxford. I left after a year and went to Cambridge in órder to read Philosophy and Art History, which was my first degree.

I have two children and I live in London. I have mostly worked as a researcher, writer or teacher. I am the author of *War in the Nursery* (Virago, 1983), have contributed to several books and journals, and have published collections of poetry, the most recent of which is *Dry Air* (Virago, 1985).